51

Printed in the United States.

DEAR MCSWEENEY'S,

Last week I spent two nights in a motel straight up out of *Jesus' Son*. There was a closet without a door and one of those sad wire shelving units that an old man might keep in his basement or garage or workshop. The room smelled like cigarettes and take-out food. I didn't want to have sex in this room and I didn't want to sit in bed and watch TV, because I was certain the bed had bedbugs, so I wasn't sure what to do with myself or my girlfriend. This was in Salt Lake City, Utah.

I have been meaning to write to you for a few weeks, but I fell in love recently, and time got away from me. Sorry about that. Right now I'm in Sheridan, Wyoming, at a Hampton Inn off the interstate. This Hampton Inn sits grandly on top of a hill like a castle. In the lobby of this chain hotel is a counter with a built-in garbage receptacle, three carafes of coffee and one of hot water, a few packets of hot

chocolate, and a pyramid of Cof-fee-mate creamers. My girlfriend is the only person I know who drinks the hot chocolate. This is her recipe: with a plastic straw stir hot chocolate powder plus half the hot water you'd nor-mally use plus five Coffee-mate creamers. She asks me if I want a hot chocolate. I say no.

Behind the front desk there is a mural of two black-and-white cows. I tell my girlfriend that I think cows are cute. She disagrees. She saw a cow drink-ing its own shit-water at a dairy farm in Pennsylvania. Basically, the cow was standing in some water, then it shit, then it drank the water. Also, she said, the cow had flies in its eyes. You see, I had always thought cows were cute, but now I don't, and I blame Sarah Gerard. I suppose this could be considered a form of loss. My therapist said my entire life has been informed by loss: adoption, death, suicide, a horrible breakup, et cetera. She said I have withstood the most horrifying of horrors and, therefore, whatever comes next will be relatively minor in comparison. I'm so glad I pay this therapist thirty-five dollars a session.

Lately, I've felt my life slipping away from me, and I don't recognize what it has become since I met Sarah in March and she changed everything in my life. The other night, Sarah and I did mushrooms in Sedona. We were sitting by the hotel pool underneath the night sky. What we thought was a hummingbird skimmed the surface of the dirty pool. Maybe it was a bat. There was a cockroach near the hot tub. I told Sarah I made a diorama in third grade for the science fair. I used cotton balls as snow, and blue plastic wrap as a river. My mother was a volunteer at the natural history museum, and she brought home some small plastic animals. My diorama was the best diorama in the history of dioramas. Our assignment was to come up

with a question related to the diorama that could be answered through an experiment. My question was "Why do animals hibernate?" Unfortunately, I got a C+ because this was a research question, and I answered it by reading a section on hibernation in an encyclopedia. It seems that my entire life, I have been asking the wrong questions.

Sarah and I have spent the last two weeks together in a car, driving from Los Angeles to Wyoming. There are real cowboys in Wyoming. We met a man named Bill who was trying to sell his vintage army ambulance for six thousand dollars. We asked him the mileage and he said he had no idea. There was no odometer. He was reading a book by Sherman Alexie. We agreed he was the coolest person in Sheridan, Wyoming. Sarah wanted to buy this ambulance, but she lives in Brooklyn. I told her it would be hard to find parking. The army ambulance is huge, and could transport a class-room of children. It has trouble making turns, and it can't go above 60 miles per hour. The good thing about this ambu-lance is that it is a vehicle, and if you want to be someplace else, not very far away, possibly it could take you there.

We are ending our road trip in Wyoming because Sarah will be at Ucross for three weeks so she can write her second novel. It's about love, but I'm not a character in it. She says she doesn't want to reduce me. She says I am sacred and precious to her. "So it's a matter of tone, then," I said. At first I was upset. Am I not worthy of being a character in a novel? I am perfect material for a novel! I am paranoid and anxious. Also, I am very good at sex. But I've come to understand she's purging her past, the way some acne medications bring all of the bacteria to the skin's surface, causing more acne, making things worse before

they get better. I think it's like that. No one has asked me what I plan on doing with myself while she's at Ucross, but I'll answer that anyway. I will go back to Brooklyn. I will water her plants and take care of her cat. I will sleep underneath an orange blanket. I will call my parents after a few weeks of avoiding their calls. I will feel so lonely at times; hopefully, I will be the object of someone else's sympathy. If I deserve even that.

Best,
PATTY YUMI COTTRELL
NEW YORK, NY

DEAR MCSWEENEY'S,
I was at the Jewish Commu-nity Center gift shop today, looking at mezuzahs. All the ones I like, I can't afford. And the ones within my price range all look like vape pens: smooth cylinders of brushed steel in an array of candy colors. Too futur-istic and sleek, incongruous

containers for a scroll inscribed with Torah verse.

The other problem with a mezuzah that resembles a vape pen is the possibility of theft by a young traveling person. My home is close to Haight Street, which, although the Summer of Love ended fifty years ago, is often populated by folks selling bad art, requesting cold beer, putting costumes on their dogs to attract the interest and generosity of tourists, et cetera. This is fine with me; they were certainly here before I was. Someone did pee on my door once, but that was easy enough to clean up.

People use the recessed entryway to my home as a seat and occasionally as a place to sleep. Because of this, it feels more like a public place than other doorways. For example: I grew up in an apartment building; our front door was indoors. No one but the other residents of the sixth floor, their guests, and people delivering food had the chance to notice our mezuzah.

The real problem with a mezuzah, which I've been avoiding so far, is, of course, Nazis.

Something that bothers me is that I don't remember wanting a mezuzah for my home until the recent resurgence of white supremacist violence in our country. Is my desire reactionary? Is that a bad thing? Do I recognize the beauty, power, longevity, and uniqueness of Jewish cultural traditions more now that they're threatened?

Do I want to mark myself as Jewish now that people are openly threatening violence against Jews? Do I want to resist passing (although you don't quite need to put triple parentheses around a name like Berkowitz)? Was I a coward before?

Is my desire for a mezuzah empty of real meaning? I never thought about my parents' mezuzah. I guess I was glad we had it, because I understood something vague about the value of being able to freely express Jewish identity.

Is my desire just a desire to provoke? Do I want—and this is a question I keep coming back to—do I want to draw attention to my home as the home of a Jew? As a survivor of sexual violence, I especially value the safety of my home.

According to mezuzahstore. com, "Halacha (Jewish law) rules that if you live in a place where it is dangerous to put a Mezuzah outside your door [due] to anti-Semitism and the like, you can put it up on the inside." (What, I wonder, is "and the like"?)

Not long after the inauguration, my partner went to DC for the Association of Writers & Writing Programs conference. He brought me back a pile of books as well as a fake identification card from the Holocaust Memorial Museum. I opened it and read the girl's story; she was from Hungary and she survived the Holocaust. "You're supposed to take one randomly," explained my partner, "but I picked up a few before I found a survivor for you."

A friend points out that we live in San Francisco, probably the most liberal city in the United States.

A friend points out that there's a Patriot Prayer rally this weekend at Crissy Field.

On Facebook, a friend of a friend named Dan Fishback says: "I am concerned about the potential for white Jews to be so consumed with terror that we might disrespect people of color by not acknowledging that we fear the POSSIBILITY of what is ALREADY HAPPENING AND HAS ALWAYS BEEN HAPPENING to them."

I'm concerned, too. I feel conflicted about taking up space with this letter, because I'm aware of the difference between violence against Jews and violence against people of color. While the rise of anti-Semitism in the United States is relatively recent and tied to white supremacist hate groups, violence against people of color, queer and trans people, and disabled people is ongoing, state-sanctioned, and so mainstream that anyone not targeted by it is likely complicit in it.

Still undecided about the mezuzah,

AMY BERKOWITZ
SAN FRANCISCO, CA

DEAR MCSWEENEY'S,
I was in my last year of high school when I loved Therese. We called her Aunt Therese: a sweet, burned-out waitress from the Denny's in my hometown. She was probably thirty-five and wore a blond bun on top of her head. There wasn't much to do where I grew up, so all the hippies, punks, and heavy-metal kids gathered at Denny's at night to chain-smoke, drink coffee, and eat french fries. I

waitressed for fifteen years and I know I would have shot myself if I'd had to wait on us night after night. Cheap, chain-smoking teenagers demanding endless free coffee refills. Therese never shot herself when we were her customers. In fact, sometimes, mid-shift, she'd slide into the booth with us, smoke a cigarette, and tell us how she and her boyfriend were trying to quit cocaine again. Remember when Planet Earth was still good and you could chain-smoke in restaurants with your heroes?

In high school, writing was my lifeline for my many, many feelings. I was gay but trying not to know it. I would dig my pen so hard into the pages when I wrote that these journals were practically three-dimensional pieces by the time I was done. I'd been arrested for drinking and having LSD in my swim-team locker and when the administration came to talk to me about it I was drunk and smoking in the hall outside my English class. A low-speed footrace through the halls of my high school landed me in the nurse's office surrounded by police and administrators. When they went through my backpack it was filled with poems and razor blades; everything but a bell jar. I was a cliché. Off I went to the county mental hospital on a seventy-two-hour hold. Handcuffed inside the police car, I kicked the window for effect as we pulled out of the school parking lot. On the freeway, I looked out the back window and my neighbor was driving behind us, a girl who used to babysit for me and my brother. I saw her see me and mouth the word *Ali?* I found it so comforting that the chaos of my inner life finally matched the chaos on the outside.

The mental hospital was as sad as you can imagine. Throngs of Thorazined people drooling on themselves. I gave my watch to a schizophrenic woman with a rose tattooed on her wrist. I know you won't believe me, but patients were issued foam slippers with happy faces embossed on the toes. The irony wasn't lost on me at seventeen.

After I got out, I was allowed to go nowhere except home and school. I had a typewriter in my room, so I sat in there and typed, pretending my writing was schoolwork. I clicked off some bad poems and then started a short story called "The Potato God Revolution (Tribute to a Denny's Waitress)." It was about a Denny's waitress named Aunt Therese who gets sent to a mental hospital because instead of the regular black waitress shoes and shoelaces, she wears carrot tops as laces and the townspeople think she is the devil. In the hospital she is threatened with a lobotomy because she'd beat up a girl named Hominy Winters in the ninth grade. The only way out of the mental hospital is to eat the mental-hospital food from the compartmentalized tray in the right order. Mashed potatoes, hominy, chocolate milk, orange Jell-O. Aunt Therese knows she doesn't have good odds so she just eats her dinner alone in a room while the psychiatrist and staff watch with anticipation from behind a two-way mirror. Aunt Therese accidentally cracks the code. The psychiatrist can't believe it and everyone becomes afraid of Aunt Therese's special powers. She's released without a lobotomy and promoted to manager at Denny's. The End.

If it's true that writers basically rework the same story their whole lives, then I'm still reworking this one. Waitresses, mental illness, class, ostracism. I've been working with the same components forever.

I thought it would be a great idea to bring a typed copy of "The Potato God Revolution (Tribute to a Denny's Waitress)" to the real Aunt Therese at Denny's. Don't ask me what's wrong with me. In my defense, all I can say is I didn't know better. I'm pretty sure you could get arrested for something like this today. But I was dying for connection with someone.

I still know exactly what the light looked like when I walked through the Denny's front door with the paper in my hand. It was a slow morning. A few waitresses were clustered behind the counter. Nuclear-colored desserts glowed in a glass cupboard above their heads. I approached with my story in hand and asked if Therese was working. She wasn't. She worked later that night. "Can you give this to her?" I asked, handing the strangers my story. I don't think they knew what they were taking. One of the women looked at me slightly confused and then the small group of waitresses began to read my story, right there and then. My body slowly filled with shame as I drifted out of the restaurant. I can't remember if Aunt Therese ever read my story. I really hope not.

Love,
ALI LIEBEGOTT
LOS ANGELES, CA

DEAR MCSWEENEY'S,
I've just come home from my fourth lifetime outing as an ad hoc, highly unorthodox wedding rabbi. (Previously, I was the "rabbi" at the "wedding" of Art Spiegelman and Françoise Mouly—actually, it was Spiegelman's fiftieth birthday and when Françoise asked him what he wanted by way of a gift, he said what he was really pining for was a real wedding, since their actual marriage, twenty-five years earlier, had been at City Hall only for anarchistic green-card purposes, so she recruited me as the rabbi and R. Crumb headed up the party band! More recently I'd officiated the marriage between two guys in Houston, the Art Guys, and a tree, nuptials that went tragicomically bad, and which you can read about by googling a little piece of mine called "Dogged by Trees.")

Anyway, this time was for the wedding of my dear artist friends Trevor Oakes (one of the "perspective twins") and his longtime on-and-off-and-on-and-off-and-finally-on-again ladylove, the ex-architect painter Gerri Davis. Gerri had hit upon the idea of staging the ceremony a few hours from her parents' place near Asheville, North Carolina, in the lee of the Great Smoky Mountains, in the tiny creekside hamlet of Topton, along the very spine of that recent transcontinental total eclipse, on the day of the eclipse itself. "Come for the eclipse," went the invite, "and stay for the wedding!"

And believe me, the total eclipse itself (between 2:38 p.m. and 2:40 p.m. on a blessedly cloudless afternoon) was all that and more: don't even get me started.

About twenty minutes afterward, though, with the sun peeking well past the now fast-receding moon shadow, a makeshift band of instrumentalist friends (amateur oboist, trumpeter, ukuleleist, keyboard player, and guitarist: the Eclipse Philharmonic, as I'd taken to calling them) launched into a surprise flash-moblet rendition of "Here Comes the Sun," herding the scattered, still-awesmacked congregants Pied Piper–like over two little bridges and onto a leafy, breezy little island in the middle of the lazy rapids, where chairs and flowers and candles and a podium had been set up. Once everyone was seated, I led the mother of the bride and Trevor's father led the groom over the bridges to their respective places (a few moments earlier I'd ducked away to don my rabbinical gear, beige suit and tie, draped over with a black-stripped white

tallit shawl, all capped by a red yarmulke), and then on the far side of the bridges the trumpeter (Gerri's father) launched into a buoyant New Orleans–style solo medley, culminating in "Here Comes the Bride," his radiant daughter clinging to his side as he now led her over the bridges to the podium, where Trevor and I stood, awaiting her splendid arrival, awesmacked all over again.

The congregants *ooh*ed and *aah*ed and finally grew silent, whereupon I approached the mic to begin my homily. (Do Jews even do homilies? Beats me.) "About four months ago," I pronounced solemnly, "I got this pesky little splinter on my pointer finger, which thereupon began to bleed continually, so I called Gerri here in North Carolina, asking her to ask her mother about it, because I knew her dear mother was some sort of hand therapist. I told her it seemed like I was suffering from a stigmata sent down upon me by a singularly incompetent god, which Gerri repeated to her mother, whereupon in the background I could hear her mother's confused retort, 'But Gerri, he's Jewish, isn't he, and Jews don't *get* stigmatas, do they?' 'Precisely,' I responded. 'Like I said, we're dealing here with a singularly incompetent god! Guy doesn't even know whom to smite, let alone where.'"

And then I continued to recount to the congregation how just a few days ago, our mutual friend Bill had asked me what I was doing for the coming weekend, and how I'd told him I was headed down to North Carolina to serve as the rabbi at Trevor and Gerri's wedding, at which point he'd asked, hesitantly, "But neither Gerri nor Trevor is Jewish, are they?" To which I'd responded, and now told the congregation, "No, but then I'm not really a rabbi, either." Whereupon, reaching into the depths of the podium, I pulled out a full-on sort of

Hasidic-style headpiece (actually a pleated cardboard approximation) and placed it upon my head. For greater authenticity, I hoped, somewhat haplessly.

Anyway, I thereupon launched into the meat of my rabbinical discourse. Because hadn't that eclipse been something, or what? Everyone whooped in concurrence (always good to get the congregation on your side at the outset is what I believe and try to practice). And yet, I went on, it's worth pausing for a moment to ponder the near infinite, indeed precisely *astronomical*, odds against such an occurrence even transpiring at all. Because for total eclipses to happen, on any planet anywhere, the sun and the moon in question have to occupy precisely the same acreage, as it were, of celestial real estate. Which, in the case of our own planetary system, happens only because the sun is precisely four hundred times the size of the moon, and the moon just happens to be precisely four hundred times closer to Earth: hence the perfect, veritably lid-like fit. And what are the odds against that sort of alignment? In science-fiction films, one regularly sees total eclipses happening on other planets, but it's not bloody likely that such an uncanny congruence occurs elsewhere, certainly not in our own solar system, likely not anywhere else in our galaxy. Top that near-inconceivable coincidence off with the fact that it should occur on the very planet upon which life has evolved that's intelligent enough to appreciate and marvel at it—what an infinitely further unlikelihood. And not only that, but it's even more unlikely that such intelligence coincided with the relatively tiny temporal window in which such perfect eclipses have been occurring on this planet—for the moon's orbit is gradually receding from Earth: several million years ago it was too close, and several million years hence it will be too far, the required conditions thus pertaining for only a relatively minute fraction of the planet's entire existence—*what are the odds of that?!*

"Makes you wonder," I pronounced, portentously.

"And yet all of that is as nothing," I said, rounding the corner on my extended analogy, "is as nothing," I repeated, "as all of us here gathered (their endlessly put-upon friends) certainly realize, compared to the odds against *these two*, our beloved Sun Lady and Moon Man, ever getting their act together enough to finally marry, for god's sake!"

And so forth: it was a fun ceremony. Great after-feast, fantastic honky-tonk dancing into the star-dusted night.

But the reason I'm writing *you kids* about all this is that in the days since, I've been thinking, and I no longer think it was all mere coincidence, or at any rate sheer random happenstance, that intelligent life

15

arose here, on what may well
be the sole planet anywhere
whose moon and sun were thus
arrayed, and indeed during the
relatively tight interval, geolog-
ically speaking, when they were
thus arrayed.

Isn't it perhaps rather the
case that it was the occasional
occurrence of such total eclipses
(granted, very occasional, only a
couple hundred times a century,
spread all about the globe's surface, such that the chances of any
individual tribe of protohumans
ever seeing one were themselves
virtually infinitesimal) that in
turn (because, really, the sudden
unexpected occurrence of such
a celestial event *is* utterly aston-
ishing, terrifying, unnerving,
enthralling, certainly profoundly
memorable, and unlike anything
else that the primitive creatures
would have ever witnessed)
might itself have jump-started,
as it were, an ensuing cascade
toward the kind of abstract
intelligence we humans all now
(granted, to varying degrees)

seem to evince and take for
granted?

I say "primitive," but as
Jared Diamond and Yuval
Noah Harari and their like keep
reminding us, it's a complete
misprision to imagine our distant forebears as knuckle-drag-
ging morons of any sort. If anything, they were all, every single
one of them, much more intelligent than any of us are today
(stupefied as we have become
by all our labor-saving conve-
niences)—they had to be (little
naked near-defenseless runts that
they were) just to get through
the day, to evade predators and
secure food, shelter, clothing,
fire, and so forth for the night.
And come evening, in a world
bereft of other entertainments
(or distractions), what must it
have been like for them to gaze
up at the stars, and (for the yet
more intelligent among them) to
begin to note the patterns in the
waxing and waning of the moon,
the way individual stars seemed
to rise at slightly different times

and in different places along the horizon, the way such patterns aligned with the changing seasons—and then, completely out of nowhere, suddenly, one afternoon, to experience the world-upending spectacle of a total eclipse!

It might have been like that early scene in *2001: A Space Odyssey*, only minus the intervening aliens and their monoliths (unless aliens were themselves the ones—or maybe God, the One—who somehow managed to pull our moon into its uncannily unique alignment with the sun). Maybe I had *2001* on my mind because one of the congregants at the wedding was our friend Michael Benson, fresh in from Ljubljana—"I couldn't help myself: suddenly I just watched, spellbound, as my fingers typed in the plane reservation"—who'd just completed the manuscript for his fiftieth anniversary study of that film and its director, Stanley Kubrick, and author, Arthur C.

Clarke, due out in the spring of 2018, and we'd dallied a good part of the evening discussing his findings.

Anyway, so yesterday I mailed a synopsis of all this to another mutual friend, Walter Murch, the legendary film and sound editor and all-around polymath, who was the subject of my own most recent book, *Waves Passing in the Night: Walter Murch in the Land of the Astrophysicists*, chronicling his improbable excursions into a whole other branch of gravitational astrophysics, and I wasn't the least bit surprised (nothing about Walter surprises me anymore) to receive, by return email, the following:

> Yes, I agree. The beginning of *2001* actually begins with eclipse imagery, long before the monolith is ever introduced.

Walter continued his email with a journal musing of his own from October 2003:

If Earth had been cloud-covered, like Venus, would we have developed mathematics to the extent that we did? There is a proof somewhere of how humans could deduce the existence of stars even if they had never seen them. Perhaps we could have done so, potentially, but would our minds be predisposed to think in that direction? Does not the night sky pull our imagination off the surface of the earth and make it dream and speculate: what if? Then add the fact that humanity emerged along with the existence of perfect solar eclipses. The moon is moving away from the earth, so perfect eclipses didn't exist ten million years ago, and will not exist ten million years from now. Does not the eclipse light the imagination? Did it somehow help to create this wondering animal?

Walter's email went on:

Given the few humans alive one hundred thousand years ago, when language (or so we think) began to emerge, and the infrequency of solar eclipses, the ability of an eclipse to kindle the human imagination must be one of those crucial "singularities" in history (like the "eukaryotic singularity") when the event triggered a paradigm shift in one individual (or a small group) and then it spread outward from there, carried by language. Solar eclipses are not experienced "globally" by everyone at the same time (the way we experience lunar eclipses)—I have seen only one eclipse in my life (a partial eclipse in London in 1999). The total eclipse that the United States has just experienced is the first to transect the continental United States in one hundred years, more than the average human lifetime. And it was a thin line of totality, only a few miles wide. Imagine the world of one hundred thousand years ago, and how few people there were back then, and how many would have seen a similar eclipse, unprepared for it by any prediction. And without language how would they have spread the word? Partial eclipses are more common, of course. Much to think about…

Much to think about indeed. But what it all got me thinking about is where ideas come from. In this particular case, had I even come to this sudden supposed insight in any sense "on my own," or wasn't it perhaps rather the case that a prior set of influences in my immediate past (Kubrick, Clarke, Benson, Murch) had all lined up just so, perfectly, in such a way as to render that momentarily blinding supposition—*ha*! eclipses, monkeys, the jump-start toward subsequently cascading intelligence—all but inevitable?

Maybe all thought is just the world itself daydreaming and marveling at itself.

Anyway.

Love to all,

LAWRENCE WESCHLER
PELHAM, NY

DEAR MCSWEENEY'S,
This week, on a work trip, I somehow witnessed two situations in which a husband referred to his wife as a "big pain in the ass." These very publicly made statements occurred when their coupledom was threatened by physical separation: one over a spot on a film festival shuttle, and the other in the C-group of a full Southwest flight. I can't remember the first incident well, because of the abundant amount of free alcohol from the afore-mentioned film festival, so let's discuss the second. It happened on a flight from Las Vegas to Ontario.

My paranoid self got the aisle seat and a middle-aged straight couple was separated, the wife next to me in the middle seat, the husband across from me in the aisle seat. When I asked the gentleman if he'd like to switch, even addressing him with the collegial "boss" at the end of my inquiry, he said, in the middle of a full plane, among his C-group brethren, "Nope, she's a big pain in the ass. She can stay over there!" and laughed. The foreign country that was now row 26 raised its flag in that moment, the wife laughing and saying, "I can't *stand* his ass," as I smiled and nodded along, which seems to be a skill that sharpens with every passing year. Their reaction came off as some type of well-greased theatrical performance. In interpreting the husband's comment as a performance of patriarchal ownership via detachment from his wife, I still couldn't understand this whole ass-pain thing. I feel as if the *Broad City* pegging episode that opened season 2 should've quelled the American male's fascination-turned-terror about their own butts. There needs to be a Pew study about the number of straight men who learned what pegging was that night.

Anywho, these same anti-ass-pain jocks are more than

happy, it seems (and this is a projection), to involve themselves in the pain of other people's butts. Double standard much? And if these are examples of Americans' modification of the original phrase "a royal pain in the arse," then the man's statement on the plane also declined to grant his wife, to whom he has dedicated his life, some notion of projected royalty. Regarding whether these guys are actually good husbands, who knows, but it was striking, the sheer amount of gall behind it all. There's something honorable about the comedian who—because of their sharpened sense of intent and purpose—doesn't have to say "motherfucker" every five seconds, and so in this same way, humor that entertains the idea of a jilted couple in need of a time-out could, and should, be executed with a greater level of wit in lieu of always equating marriage with eventually hating your partner, a.k.a. your ball and chain, a.k.a. your old hag. I'm reminded, McSweetness, of something my friend said at a bar last week: "Why do great people sleep with terrible people?" I still don't know the reason for people's illogical acts—from marginal partners, to self-sabotaging, to voting abominably—and I am not exempt from failure's humbling gut-punch—but I do know Sigourney Weaver dumped Bill Murray in *Ghostbusters II* for calling her his "old ball and chain," and that shit cannot and will not happen to me.

Yours,
JOSÉ VADI
OAKLAND, CA

DEAR MCSWEENEY'S,
Whenever I see three question marks in a row, I think about getting divorced. I met my husband, whom I'm now separated from, when I was eighteen and in college. We had our first date a year and a half after we met, at the library, and it was all asking. What's that book you're reading? Why don't you like Burger King? Is that a birthmark? What was it like traveling to South Africa? Is that Randall Cunningham jersey your favorite shirt? I had so many questions, but the beautiful thing was that he did, too! I finally had someone who wanted to really know me. I fell in love with him because he cared deeply about my interior life.

Then, after eight years together, our relationship was suddenly marked by uncertainty. Our questions devolved into a roll call of harried pleading. Why don't you want kids? Will you go to therapy? Will you please go to therapy? Why won't you go with me? Are you cheating on me? Can you give me a year to figure this out? Please? It turned out we hadn't been all the way truthful with our answers, or hadn't asked right, or just changed too quickly. Eventually, the conversations had become one-sided, and the gentle querying turned passive-aggressive. Every question had a sigh or a shrug built into its grammatical structure. We grew and grew until we grew apart, and someone put a period on the whole thing.

That experience has attuned me to the affront of three question marks in a row. We used them in texts and emails near the end, and so even when we spoke I heard them in our voices. The consequence of my romance's transformation into a den of emotional hostility is that I now see more than one question mark in a row as the grim reaper's scythes. They recall the doom of "read" receipts, of bed death, of what happens when someone you love gets tired of you. In my mind, triple question marks are an emblem of angst, an emoji of exasperation.

As a collective symbol, three question marks are a signal of impatience, a confusing way to elicit information. Rather than suggesting a hunger for knowledge, as the repetition may appear to imply, they connote chaos, someone jamming a keyboard in frustration. The identical marks bring to mind metastasis. Their curvature is the arc of raised eyebrows, their order the time-lapse of a defeated person, grief and habit hooking the spine into bad posture like mine. Or the smoke curling up from too many blunts. The older folks in my family have a saying: "Death comes in threes." So it was ironic that the communication patterns I'd previously bragged about in my new age, fifty-fifty relationship eventually affirmed that old-school sentiment.

Of course, three question marks can be fun. My friends know I hate three-in-a-row so they use them to make me laugh. Sometimes three can mean pure bewilderment, or excitement. When you use three question marks at the end of good news, like "We got Markelle Fultz???," they can resemble the fuzzy-wipe effect of an onscreen dream sequence. They are more whimsical than exclamation points and more mysterious than animated icons.

Lynne Truss, that multi-hyphenate writer and commenter on grammar, described an early application of the question mark, *Punctus Interrogativus* of the eighth century, as a "lightning flash, striking from right to left." One question mark no longer looks that way, but three shocks me to my core. In a 2011 article for *Wired* magazine, dating expert Sam Greenspan cataloged several common grammatical symbols as they pertain to text-speech. "Question marks have a tendency to stack onto each other. And with each stack the meaning changes," he writes. For example, "What time do you want to meet up" accompanied by one question mark is "simple,

unassuming, and friendly. Gets the point across, elicits a response, but also drives toward a solution." Two "looks like a typo." Three, on the other hand, "feels impatient, childish. It's an aggressive question: It demands a response, and suggests that the response had better be to your liking."

Which brings me to my point. Last week, I finally decided to reenter the dating scene. After months of saying no to this guy who works at my local Ethiopian bakery, I gave him my phone number. We agreed to meet for a drink after his shift ended. Fifteen minutes before the date, he texted to say that something had come up and that he would be twenty minutes late, and did I have time to wait??? Of course I had time to wait. I'd been single for a year and a half. The only thing on my agenda that night was refereeing a literal catfight that popped off in my kitchen between my roommate's two domestic kitties and her newly adopted street kitten that owns the hallway after dark. But when I saw the blitzkrieg of the three *???*s I recoiled and wrote back that I had work in the morning, sorry. I'm afraid I'm unduly traumatized by these signs. Will men think I'm anal-retentive if I explain why I really, really hate seeing such symbols stacked together? Is it too much to reveal when you first meet someone? I'll have to figure this out. Anyway, I just wanted to write a letter of appreciation to you, McSweeney's, for not clotting up your pages with superfluous punctuation. Your grammatical discretion bespeaks an inner strength I find attractive.

Yours,
NIELA ORR
PHILADELPHIA, PA

DEAR MCSWEENEY'S,
I am writing to you from Paris, where I spent much of the day being photographed. One photographer took me to an old hospital and another to a famous cemetery. Jim Morrison was somewhere, Simone de Beauvoir, too. The cemetery photographer used film. I could hear its clicking and sliding. I leaned against a mausoleum and watched the aperture open and shut, a spiral eye blinking. It was amazing and I wondered whether I would look amazed in these photos, or if my amazement was private. "This is a ceremony," the photographer said, noticing me noticing. Film made him pay attention, he said, to the light, to the texture of the stone, to everything. I think he liked this part of the process best, the paying attention. I saw that he could see things that I could not. Later he gave me a book of his portraits. I have it with me now. There is something hypnotizing about this book. I have spent a lot of time with it, looking closely at the writers he photographed. I can see them,

their houses. Some of them are already gone. Where to? They would have heard what I heard in the cemetery, the click and slide. We have undergone the same ceremony. I look closer, looking for wonder. I try to see if I can see them seeing him seeing. I think I can.

Sincerely,
CLAIRE VAYE WATKINS
PARIS, FRANCE

DEAR MCSWEENEY'S,
In the course of my adult life I have voted only once, a fact I attribute to having played rugby at school.

It was not a choice. We were forced into shorts and scratchy blue jerseys. The field, in the dark of the English winter, was hard as rattan and frequently covered in frost. Adjacent to the field was an abattoir. When the wind was favorable, the smell of roasting animal flesh would drift our way in clouds.

The teacher was a bald-headed victim of testosterone poisoning who would have been at home on either side of a prison yard. His face was as red as a suckling pig's. Rumor had it he once won a drinking competition by quaffing forty-two consecutive pints of beer, leaving his opponent, a fellow teacher, naked and singing sea shanties on a bridge. He always wore a yellow tracksuit with a whistle around his neck, which he would blow and yell, "Get stuck in, lads." If you did not, he would stride over and scream heteronormative insults into your face.

The school had three teams, a first fifteen, a second, and a third. The rest of us belonged to the "rejects," which meant we played for only eighty torturous minutes every Wednesday. I was not an aficionado of the game. There was no escape from the cold, which, with my South Indian genes, I was particularly vulnerable to. I would try to keep warm by scraping my hands against the sides of my pocketless shorts, my teeth chattering, my cheeks tear-stained. If the ball came my way I would pull my sleeves over my hands and handle it as I would an ice sculpture, presenting it to the nearest player, regardless of which side we were on. Sometimes a boy would tackle me anyway, slamming me into the ground, which felt like being struck in the flank by a stampeding boar. On occasion I would take advantage of a distracting moment in the game by making a run for it into the woods, where I would hide until the final whistle sounded. Once in a while I would forge excuse notes from my parents, claiming an ankle injury or a chest infection.

Being a nonplaying player, I did not care which position I was given so long as I did not have to step inside the "scrum," a moving, cannibalistic beast comprised of sixteen boys with interlocking heads who push, kick, bite, and butt until someone succeeds in knocking the ball backward to a member of his team. One team starts on the left, the other on the right. Both fight with all their brains, brawn, and sinews to gain ground, sometimes only inches. The aim of the game is to transport the ball to the opposite side of the field in order to win five points, which is termed a "try." At any moment, one can ascertain which side is in the ascendancy from the position of the ball, which could be near the center, or on the left, or the extreme left, or the extreme right. The ball is everything. The ball is power.

We rejects were encouraged to support the first fifteen, to wear its colors, to cheer its members. We had little choice in our affiliation: it would have been bizarre to cheer for the opposition, though I am sure there were a few renegades throughout the years who adopted such an approach. Theoretically, at least, that option was always available: rugby is not a dictatorship wherein one person sits on the ball while his teammates shoot the spectators. There are rules, a referee, governing boards, coaches, managers, experts with expert opinions. And, of course, one is free not to participate at all, to ignore the entire world of rugby, as I did, and focus on other endeavors.

But herein lies the problem. At school, rugby was the only game there was. We were told that it was good for us, that it would make us strong and fit. Many boys loved it, would speak contemptuously about those who showed little interest. To them it was *our* game, *our* team, *our* school. The school had given us rugby and it was our duty to give back to the school. The finest and most enthusiastic boys of all became

team captains, deciding selection and strategy, wrote match reports. Others, less skilled or athletic, played their parts by donning the school uniform on Saturdays and cheering for their classmates, rejoicing when their fellows were proved victorious.

As for the rest of us, the rejects and cynics and losers and wimps, we were voiceless, faceless, and silent. Although it was true that we had chosen to reject the game, it was also true that rugby was the only game in town, a circumstance that had been decided for us, before us, in spite of us, by the school, something else none of us had chosen to go to. This, too, was something we had been born into. If we didn't go to school, we were punished and publicly shamed, forced back into line.

As I grew older, it became clear to me that the same was true of politics. In politics, the state was rugby's equivalent. There were two sides, one on the left, one on the right. Most of the players were people I would never have become friends with. They had far more in common with each other than with my peers. But every four years we were asked to declare our loyalty to one side, the ones in blue or the ones in red, and if we refused we were labeled irresponsible and ungrateful. Even if, at times, I became distracted by the spectacle of the game, when the final whistle sounded I was always left with the same singular truth: I had not chosen this game. It had been imposed on me. And whether I voted or not, this would always be the case.

Some years ago I learned of another game played for centuries in the Amazonian jungle. As in rugby, there are two teams. Each forms a line and lifts a heavy tree trunk onto their shoulders. Thus burdened, the two teams run toward the finish line, moving as fast as they can. If one team is struggling, however, a member of the opposing side crosses over and assists them. The aim is for both teams to finish at the same time.

Had I been born into a society that played this game, I suspect I would have had more interest in politics. I would have joined in gladly, even enthusiastically. I would have participated; I would have cheered; I would have played. But this is not the way it works. We do not get to choose the games we play. We can opt in or we can opt out, but the game is fixed.

Sincerely,
RAJEEV BALASUBRAMANYAM
BERLIN, GERMANY

THE INTERVIEW

by NICK ARVIN

ONE WAS SITTING at the conference table when Two came in. Two sat, and they looked at each other.

One tapped a mechanical pencil on the table. "What're you here for?"

"Interview?"

"To interview? Or be interviewed?"

Two said, "Be interviewed."

One said, "Me, too."

"You're doing the interview?"

"No."

Two said, "Well, I'm not doing the interview, either."

"I guess we're both here for the same thing."

Three came in and looked at One and Two. One said, "Hello."

"Hi?" Three said. "Is this part of the interview?"

Before anyone could answer, Four came in.

One said, "I guess we wait here to be called for interviews."

Three said, "This isn't the interview?"

Four said, "None of you are the interviewer?"

Five came in. The door closed behind him. He looked at the others. He looked at the door, then again at the others. "Why," Five said, "did she take my phone?"

One said, "You're not the interviewer."

Three said, "So she's taking everyone's phone?"

Six came in. He looked befuddled.

One said, "Interviewer?"

Six said, "What?"

Three said, "Well, he's not the interviewer."

Six said to One, "You're the interviewer?"

One said, "We're asking you."

Seven came in. He stopped and stared. "Are all of you here to interview me?"

Everyone laughed, except Seven.

One, waving airily, said, "Have a seat."

More came in. All of them were young, just out of college. All of them were men. When Thirteen came in, the eight chairs at the conference table plus the four along the wall were full. Thirteen appeared extremely confused. Everyone could see that he was not the interviewer.

One said to him, "The interviews should start soon." He added, "You can have my chair, if you want," although he remained sitting in the chair.

Thirteen shuffled to stand in the far corner.

One said, "I guess we're all interviewees."

Cynthia returned to the reception desk, retrieved her coat, took the elevator down—pacing a circle as it descended— then strode through the lobby, pushed outside into the shocking cold, stopped, and took a breath. The snow came down so fast that she could hardly see the buildings across the street.

It had begun falling at lunchtime, and the engineers and other staff were quick to shut down their computers and flee; by four o'clock, only Cynthia was still in the office. The interviewees began arriving around four thirty, and she knew instantly that she had made some colossal error. If the office manager knew—or the engineering manager, or the HR manager, or any manager—she would be fired. But no one knew, yet. As long as no one knew, she wouldn't be fired.

With these thoughts in mind, she made some decisions. Instead of telling the interviewees there had been a mistake, she showed them where to put their coats and bags, and, because the email invite to the interviewees listed her boss's phone number, she asked them to leave their cell phones with her. She said that the engineering manager hated distractions. She was ready to make up a story about how he had once punched a guy who was texting in a movie theater, but the interviewees handed over their phones almost eagerly, as if to demonstrate their willingness to do whatever a prospective employer might ask.

She led them to the back conference room, which was sometimes referred to as the Assay Room. She didn't know why it was called that. The door closed with a soft *whoomp* and a tiny click. As soon as the interviewees were all in there, she wanted only to get away.

On the sidewalk she hesitated a moment, then turned and set out, kicking a path through the drifting snow.

* * *

Nine said, "Did you see anyone out there?"

Seven said, "The receptionist."

Four said, "Other than her? I didn't see anybody."

The interviewees looked at one another.

One, spinning his mechanical pencil between his fingers, said, "They must know we're here. The receptionist knows."

Three said, "Why'd they schedule interviews at the end of the day on a Friday, anyway?"

Five said, "Receptionist could've assumed the others know we're here, but actually they all went home, due to the snow."

One said, "It does us no good to speculate. There are facts. We were asked to come interview. The most likely explanation is that this is part of the interview. Jobs are scarce. They can be picky. They're creating a situation. Applying stress. Seeing who does well under stress and who doesn't."

Three said, "Speaking of speculating."

Five was peering closely at One. One said, "What?"

Five said, "Maybe you're here to observe, or whatever. Like, you're the interviewer, basically."

"Me?" One laughed. He sat straighter. He seemed to consider the possibility. "But no. I'm actually not."

Three snorted.

Five said, "Could be that that's what the interviewer is

supposed to say. According to the script, or something."

One said, "Ha-ha. But no, I'm not. So."

Cynthia had forgotten her hat and gloves. After only a block she began to shiver, so she crossed the heaped snow and slush in the street toward a glow of neon. As she pushed through the door a humid warmth and the smell of beer embraced her. At the glossy wooden bar she ordered a hot toddy, extra hot. She sat watching it steam, her thoughts turning quickly but going nowhere. She needed to do something, but she couldn't think what.

She had been sitting for several minutes when the man next to her said hello. She turned uncertainly, feeling as if perhaps someone had hailed her from far away. He said it was none of his business, she should tell him to go away if she wanted, but she didn't look well, and he wondered if she was doing all right. She looked more closely at him, and he blushed. He said his name was Gerry, by the way.

Cynthia hesitated, then in a rush began to tell him what had happened.

Three announced that he was going out to look, which started an argument, mostly between Three and One.

One said, "You can't just make a decision like that for all of us."

Three said, "I'm making a decision for me."

Twelve said, "We'll vote."

Eleven cried, "A vote!"

Nine stood and went to the door.

One said, "Wait!"

Nine said, "I have to go the bathroom."

He jiggled the doorknob, tugged, pushed. It was locked.

The back conference room had once been a small lab, for the assay and spectral analysis of hydrocarbon samples. Due to the risk of fire or hazardous fumes, the lab had been built with concrete walls, ventilation, no windows, a steel door, and a digital lock that even the engineers who used it every day had never completely understood how to use. As the company grew, a larger space was needed, and the lab was moved to a building in the suburbs. The back room was lightly refinished, and a conference table and chairs were brought in.

Cynthia had been working the front desk for only a few weeks and didn't know any of this.

Some sort of auto-mailer mistake, she told Gerry. She had

entered some text and the auto-mailer was supposed to fill in names and times and send emails. Who did interviews at five o'clock on a Friday? Why hadn't they called to see if there had been a mistake? Why hadn't they called to reschedule when it began snowing? She made a strangled cry of fury and despair.

Gerry looked a few years older than she was, a tall, dog-faced man with messy hair, glasses, watery eyes. He said he had worked at one time in a metal-fab shop, and the engineers there had been like that, all about following directions even if they led you off a cliff. But, he said, you shouldn't lose a job over a simple mistake.

Well, she admitted, there had been others—wrong documents sent to the wrong people; left some important dude on hold a couple of times; forgot the weekly doughnut order. She made mistakes when she grew bored, and this job was a bottomless sewer of boredom. She hugged herself and told Gerry about her five-year-old daughter, Jaden, shy child, friend of bugs and gnomes. Jaden was with her dad. Cynthia had already fallen behind on her rent, and Jaden's dad—who was a self-righteous asshole philanderer, by the way—wouldn't let Cynthia have her time with Jaden if she was out on the street, which, maybe she couldn't totally blame him, and, on top of that, generally these days she felt depressed and like total shit. She could never get ahead, only further behind, like trying to climb an endless down escalator. She was a terrible mother.

Gerry laughed, kindly. He said he was sure that wasn't true. He said he knew that her daughter was beautiful and that Cynthia was a good mother, just by listening to how she talked about her girl.

This made Cynthia feel warm, happy. But she did need to go back. Soon they would come out, looking for their phones. She didn't know what to tell them, except that the interviewer was running late, but then what would she do?

Gerry said maybe he could go with her, for moral support?

She grabbed his arm. Maybe he could do even better.

Nine, who had been wincing and shuffling in place, barked, "I have to pee!" He lifted his chair.

One said, "Do we want to be associated with destruction of property?"

Nine said, "I'm going!" He glared around.

One said, "Okay. Okay." He raised his hands. "On your own recognizance."

Nine swung the chair, hard. With a short, sharp noise,

it bounced off the door. He swung again, and a couple of times more. A chair leg flew off. Where the door's paint scraped off, it showed steel beneath.

Others grabbed chairs and attacked the walls. Eleven succeeded in knocking away a patch of plaster—it revealed solid concrete.

Ten said, "Oh."

Six said, "I had plans for tonight."

Nine said, "I really, really have to pee." He jogged in place.

Twelve said, "We'll have to pee in our shoes."

One said, "Could be it's a test, to see how we approach the problem of getting out."

Three said, "Don't be a moron."

One said, "No one just forgets thirteen interviewees in a locked concrete room."

Three said, "You think you're logical, but you're not."

Seven said, "Well, we're all just doing our best."

Freezing air surged into the bar, and an elderly woman in a soiled denim jacket appeared in the doorway.

Cynthia had been telling Gerry that he totally looked the part of an interviewer, and Gerry had begun speculating about how he could give the impression of being an interviewer without lying exactly. Cynthia was pulling on her coat and trying to encourage him to do the same.

The woman in the doorway peered around, open-mouthed. She let the door swing shut and wobbled forward with an icy, furry something in her arms.

Cynthia couldn't see what it was at first, but the woman—by a series of turnings, reversals, and lunging movements—carried it to the bar. It was an animal, a puppy, hardly larger than a loaf of bread, fur crusted with ice and snow, limp, maybe dead.

One said, "Probably they're watching to see how we respond." He glanced at Three. "And they're definitely keeping track of who's being a dick."

Three said, "Think they'd rather hire a dick or a moron?"

Nine yelled at the door, "I don't want the job! Someone else can have it! Just let me pee!"

Four said, "Let's set off the smoke alarm."

But no one had a lighter.

A minute later, Nine took off his left shoe and stood in the corner to pee in it.

*　　*　　*

The elderly woman said to the bartender that she had found this puppy in the alley. She seemed dazed, or drunk, or high, or perhaps naturally mentally precarious. She wondered aloud what she should do. The bartender lifted his chin and backed away. She turned in a circle. The frozen puppy's legs dangled awkwardly from her arms.

Gerry started talking softly to the puppy. He glanced at Cynthia. Cynthia shook her head. But to her dismay, he asked the woman if she needed help with the pup.

In reply, the woman shoved the animal into Gerry's chest. He barely caught it. She turned and left.

Eleven, the tallest, climbed onto the table. Using a house key, he turned the screws around the vent and removed the frame and louvers. He stood on his toes to look into the opening. He said, "It's pretty small. I don't know if anyone will fit. I can't."

Everyone ended up looking at Eight. Eight was bony-thin and scarcely five feet tall.

Eight blushed.

One said, "You want to try?"

Eight said, "I might fit. I don't know. It's just, I'm not, like, super enthusiastic about small spaces."

Seven said, "You don't have to." He looked at the others. "He doesn't have to."

Eight sighed. "I guess I'd better."

Gerry wanted to drive the pup to a vet, but that would take forever, and Cynthia felt her only hope lay in getting Gerry to talk to the interviewees, so she wrapped the puppy in her coat and persuaded Gerry to let it warm up for a minute, and maybe it would be fine. The bartender glowered at them, but they finished their drinks and see, Cynthia noted aloud, already the puppy was doing better—as the ice melted out of his fur, he opened his eyes and looked around. He appeared less like a bedraggled puppy, more like a small, scruffy dog, dirty, mangy, some sort of mixed-breed terrier.

Yet Cynthia felt her own prospects dying while they waited for the dog to revive. This was taking far too much time. She jumped off her barstool. Gerry, she suggested, should bring the dog to the office—it would be perfect, actually! He could use the sickly dog to explain why he was so late for the interviews. Gerry nodded along, and the dog was certainly doing better, twitching his ears and glaring. Cynthia put some money on the bar, Gerry held the dog, and together they stepped through the door into the cold, which, because Gerry still had the dog wrapped in her coat, passed instantly through Cynthia's blouse and pimpled her skin.

Gerry wondered aloud at how long the interviewees had been waiting—they might be cranky—but Cynthia said it would only make it easier to convince them that the job at hand was a terrible one, and they should never come back.

Meanwhile the dog began clawing and growling. Perhaps he was trying to jump down. As Gerry fumbled, the dog twisted and bit his arm, hard.

By the sounds of creaking metal and gasping breaths, the others could track Eight's location in the duct. His voice came out muffled and tinny. "This is super tight. Not like the movies." When he came to the place where the duct pierced the wall, he stopped.

One shouted, "What's happening?"

Eight's voice was faint: "I'm coming back."

Four shouted, "What do you see?"

Eight didn't answer. He worked backward at a creeping pace.

Three said, "Fuck."

*   *   *

Gerry screamed. Cynthia shrieked. The dog jumped. He rolled in the snow, bounced up, scampered into the street, and there, in the thickly falling snow, in a strangely gentle event, a car ran him over.

Cynthia turned first to help Gerry, but he stared aghast at the place where the dog had been—it seemed the dog had vanished. Now another car was coming, so, cursing, Cynthia ran into the street and located the dog in the slush and snow and lifted out the sodden, trembling animal. She brought him back to Gerry, and Gerry told the dog he would be okay.

The dog did not look like he would be okay, and Gerry's forearm dripped blood.

Cynthia carried the dog, and they walked four blocks to Gerry's car, an old Honda, carpet crusty with spilled soda. Gerry was pale and his hand trembled as he gave Cynthia the keys. The veterinary clinic was just two miles away, but the Honda could only crawl through the storm. The dog breathed unsteadily on Gerry's lap. Cynthia told Gerry that she admired his kindness toward the dog, especially after the dog bit him. She admitted that if it had been her, she might have thrown the creature in front of another car or two.

Gerry shook his head, smiled, and said he doubted that. It frightened and dazed Cynthia—it had been so long since anyone had expressed faith in her.

Eight dropped onto the conference table, shaking, panting, smeared with black dust. "It's really tight. I kind of maybe freaked out a little. There's no way forward. On the other side of the wall, the duct turns straight down. I couldn't see how far. But I got the feeling it goes pretty far."

Ten asked, "Did you yell and listen for an echo?"

"No."

Four asked, "Did you drop something and time the fall?"

"I didn't have anything to drop."

Three said, "You'll have to go back."

Eight said nothing.

Three looked around at the others. "He'll have to go back."

One said, "No, he doesn't have to."

None of the others said anything. A couple of them glanced at the shoe in the corner leaking pee.

Seven said, "Could you do it again?"

Eight contemplated with pursed lips and bulging eyes. "I guess? The vertical duct is bigger. I could slip into it pretty easily, if it doesn't go down too far."

Three said, "Got to try."

One said, "What if we make a rope?"

Eight rubbed vaguely at the dirt on his hands.

One said, gesturing to indicate everyone, "Take off your shirts."

The vet glanced at Gerry's arm. He gave Gerry a bandage to wrap it and said it would need stitches. Gerry asked him if he would do the stitches, but the vet said he could not, because he was a veterinarian and Gerry was a human. Then the vet took the dog away to a back room. The dog didn't look good.

The little waiting area had only two chairs. In the window, the falling snow glowed in halos around the streetlights. Gerry had stopped trembling, and he had some of his color back, but now, to Cynthia's surprise, he began to cry. He said that he had only ever made mistakes in his life, and here he was, no job, no health insurance, bleeding in a veterinary clinic for a dog he didn't know. How was he going to pay for the dog, the stitches? He was estranged from his family, his car was dying, he was lonely, had no friends, was lazy, boring, had weirdly shaped toes… Cynthia stopped him, hugged him, said into his ear that he was obviously a good person because she'd seen what he'd done, who he was. The rest didn't matter. She had started crying, too. She told Gerry about Jaden, how Jaden didn't like to go into a crowded room, didn't like strangers talking to her or even looking at her. If someone new came into the apartment, Jaden hid under the bed. But when she and Jaden were alone! Jaden talked nonstop—every thought or question that entered her mind came out her mouth. If she wasn't talking, she was giggling...

A tech came into the waiting area and said the dog would be fine, just a couple of cracked ribs, evidently the car had squeezed him into the snow as if into a pillow. Cynthia and Gerry laughed and cheered.

A minute later, when no one was looking—because neither of them could afford a vet's bill—they left.

Twelve said, "Pants have more structural integrity than shirts."

The others let the observation pass in silence because they preferred to keep their pants on. Most of the interviewees were wearing undershirts, but Three, Five, and Nine were now bare-chested. Three had a sprawling, mordant graveyard scene tattooed across his back.

They knotted the shirts together and looked at Eight.

One said, "Ready?"

Eight sat gazing at the floor.

One said, "It's okay if you can't do it. It'll be fine. We'll just hang out until they get back."

Three said, "Pissing into our shoes."

Eight said, "I just need to catch my breath."

The others watched him for a minute and another minute, but he didn't move.

Eight said, "I'd feel better if we had some food."

One said, "People can live three days without water and three weeks without food. And, actually, if it comes to it, it's okay to drink your pee. Pee can cycle through your kidneys a few times before it gets to be poisonous."

Six said sadly, "My dog hasn't been out all day. He's probably freaking."

Twelve said, "I'm trying to decide whether to pee into my right shoe or my left shoe."

Eleven said, "I'd feel better if I had my meds."

One said, "In a situation like this, we sure learn a lot about one another, don't we?"

Eight rose and with an attitude of unenthusiastic determination climbed onto the table. Seven handed him several quarters. Eight looked up at the duct. "Lift me."

*　　*　　*

The interviewees would surely have given up and left by now, Cynthia thought, and Gerry's arm was still seeping blood, so she volunteered to drive him to a doctor. The wheels turned with muffled noises. The snow cut streaks through the headlights. The city lay smothered; the streets seemed abandoned.

In a strip-mall urgent-care clinic, a physician's assistant put sutures in Gerry's arm without event. Afterward, two of Gerry's three credit cards were turned down. He took the driver's seat and turned the key, but the car only wheezed. He said, "Oh boy." He climbed out, opened the hood, and began hitting things with a tire iron.

The groans that Eight made as he progressed eventually arrived at the place where the duct pierced the wall. He called, "I'm going to drop a quarter."

Everyone stood listening. They heard nothing. Eight said, faintly, "Uh, I can't feel my hands, because of having my arms out in front like this. I kind of dropped them all."

Four yelled, "But how far did they fall?"

"They were rattling around all over. So I'm not sure. But I think it goes down pretty far."

One shouted, "We'll get you more coins to drop."

"My arms are stuck out in front of me. I'd have to come out again."

Three called, "You have the rope! Go down!"

One said, "Shut up, asshole."

Three glared at One. Eight said nothing. But he could be heard breathing.

One called, "Come on out!"

Eight called, "I'm going down."

One said, "You can't!"

"This vertical duct is much bigger. It must branch to other floors." Eight spoke slowly, with little moans and grunts between phrases. "It's easier to go forward than backward."

One called, "Come back!"

Three said, "Don't yell at him. He knows what he's doing."

One called, "You can come back!"

Eight said, "I'm going to try it." They heard him start moving again.

Gerry hit things over and over with the tire iron, and every so often he shouted that Cynthia should turn the key, but nothing happened. It seemed evident that Gerry didn't know what he was doing, so she suggested options—tow truck, cab, bus—but he shouted for the key again. Shockingly, the engine ripped to life.

When she tried to back out of the parking space, the wheels spun down into the snow. Gerry pushed while Cynthia worked the gas and brake to rock the car, careful not to stall it, until it was free. Then they made the slow drive back downtown in the furious falling snow.

Eight called, "Going down now."

The rope of shirts, which they had tied to a bracket, twitched, tightened, and shook.

The interviewees were silent. They rubbed the secret places on their hands, tongued the gaps between their teeth, clenched their toes.

Eight shouted something, which resonated weirdly.

One said, "What did he say?"

Seven said, "He said, 'Got it!'"

Nine said, "No, it was 'What's that?'"

Three said, "I heard 'Ah shit!'"

The rope of shirts had stopped moving.

One called, "Are you okay? What do you see?"

They listened.

Eleven stood on the conference table and tugged on the rope of shirts. "It's completely slack."

One said, "He must have gotten out on the floor below." No one contradicted him. He said, "Help will be here soon."

Cynthia gave Gerry directions to where her car was parked, and when he asked about the interviewees she said they had to be gone by now. They'd get in touch with her boss. She'd lose her job. Gerry didn't argue. She said she didn't know what she would do. He reached over and gripped her hand.

They exchanged phone numbers, and Cynthia kissed him on the cheek, climbed out, and waved. Only after he pulled away did she remember that her keys were still on her desk. She considered calling Gerry to circle back and drive her, but she didn't want to look like a complete idiot, so she started trudging to the office.

She felt cold and depressed. She tried to think where she would live, what she would tell her ex.

Four said, "Seems like he should've been able to get back up here by now."

Eleven said, "Maybe he got lost."

Two said, "Maybe the elevator doesn't work."

Three said, "Guys, he fell."

Seven said, "He didn't scream."

Three said, "People don't always scream when they fall."

One said, "It could be that that was a part of the interview."

Someone laughed; it was hard to tell who. Most of the interviewees were looking hard at nothing. But Three glared at One.

As the elevator rose, Cynthia's phone pinged. A text from Gerry: he'd liked meeting her so much, felt a soul kinship, she was such a good and honest person, could they possibly get dinner tomorrow?

It made Cynthia deeply happy. But she did think he was awfully hasty and perhaps seemed desperate. He was by his own admission kind of a fuckup. Yet she suddenly felt a little hopeful.

The elevator doors slid open, and she stepped out.

Three said, "He's lucky if he isn't dead."

One said, "You told him to go."

Three said, "He wanted to, you bossy, know-it-all idiot."

One said, "Stop."

Three said, "An engineer has to able to see the things that can go wrong. You've chosen the wrong career."

One, his face purpling, said, "You told him to go!"

Three mimicked him, whining, "Shirts off, everyone."

One shouted, "Shut up! Shut up!" In a spasm he lurched forward and swung a fist.

Nine said, "Oh!"

Twelve said, "That's bad."

One, backing away, said, "I'm sorry. Oh, fuck. I'm so sorry."

Three said, "What?" He looked down. One's mechanical pencil was stuck in his stomach.

An obscure noise from the rear of the office caught Cynthia's attention. For the first time it struck her that the interviewees might be there, miraculously, waiting. She opened a desk drawer: the interviewees' phones were there. In the closet, their coats and bags lay untouched.

They would be unhappy, of course, but surely she could explain to them, with humility, her situation. If they got to know her a little, they would understand. She started back through the empty cubicles. She would tell them about Jaden. How the two of them liked to go to the park, where Jaden could wander for hours, picking up interesting pieces of grass, poking at the fat black ants, skipping around the overflowing garbage cans, chattering all the while.

The cubicles lay in darkness, but the overhead fluorescents were on motion sensors. As Cynthia walked they silently turned on, lighting the way ahead.

THIS IS
A GALAXY

by CHRIS DENNIS

WHEN HIS FATHER WAS only nineteen he moved to the United States from Turkey. The only things he brought with him were a black-and-green embroidered apron and a stolen library book titled *The Universe.* Some of the first words his father learned in English were words he'd read in the book. He sometimes used words from the book to describe random things: this or that was a supernova. A coworker was a black hole. The day's electromagnetic energy was off. A room had too much gravity. The neighbor's dog was a red dwarf. That guy at the deli, what a quasar.

Tamer sometimes pictured his father on an airplane wearing only the apron, holding the book in his lap. He had real memories, too, though. His father reading in bed, wearing his orange afghan like a cape. His father standing in front of the bathroom mirror, pulling his robe tight against his meager body while he sang along to Fleetwood Mac or Sezen Aksu, the queen of Turkish pop, sauntering demurely toward the mirror to give his reflection a little kiss.

Once, when he was maybe ten years old, Tamer used a box cutter and masking tape to make a flip book out of the yearly portraits his father had had taken of him at Sears. As the pictures flicked against his thumb, he imagined how it might feel to grow up in an instant.

When Tamer tore the flip book apart, his father asked, "What for? It was looking so good."

"I don't know," Tamer said. "I just wanted to." When Tamer stapled the pictures back together, he put them in the wrong order, so when he flipped through it again his face shifted between ages.

His father's bedroom was like the smallest antiques store, with a high four-poster bed in the middle and two walls of shelves on either side where he displayed his things: polished stones, finger cymbals, daggers with naked ladies carved into the handles, a model of the space shuttle *Atlantis*, many postcard photos of Stevie Nicks. The two of them lay in bed facing opposite directions, their backs touching. It was warmer that way. The windows were drafty. Tamer asked his father about a giant telescope in Arizona, then about an elevator in Ukraine that a person could ride straight down from a mountaintop overlooking the Black Sea, through the mountain to the beach below.

Sometimes he'd say to his father, "Tell me about the time my mother disappeared in the cave on Mackinac Island and was never seen again." And his father would tell him the story, or if he was in a bad mood, he'd say, "I never took her to Mackinac Island. We have never been there with her. The caves are shallow. You could not lose a ladybug in them, much less a lady."

Other times, if he wanted to change the subject, his father would say, "I could tell one story about a summer in Afyon when moss covered the south side of every tree." Looking down at the two of them from above the bed, Tamer imagined, it would look as if he'd grown from his father's spine. He imagined himself as a small twin hanging there, his legs dangling even as his father walked around town, made the beds at work, riffled meticulously through the knickknack aisle at the Saint Vincent de Paul thrift store.

His father sighed into the pillow. He said, "This is like a baby. A ten-year-old should not always go to bed with the father. He should sleep on his own."

"You always say that, but I'm still here," Tamer said. "And I'm not tired, and you know what else?"

"You want to hear how I cannot hold open my eyes?"

"No, about the time the people in Turkey quit their jobs to burn corn, when you said they looked at the sky and knew they had to set the cornfields on fire."

"It was wheat," his father said.

Tamer pictured the bedroom ceiling unfolding like the lid of a giant box, revealing a vivid collection of stars above the house. He pictured his father being vacuumed into that far-off glitter. He pushed his feet beyond the length of the blanket and his father rolled over, burying his nose in Tamer's hair. When Tamer closed his eyes again, his father had drifted even farther away into outer space—a single mote floating through the constant black.

"Okay, Tamer, the day your mother died I was in line at a bank, waiting. This was on Poplar Street, which is in downtown Detroit. She was crossing Second Street. That was maybe two blocks from the bank we were at. I was cashing my paycheck and she was run over by a moving van."

Tamer sat up. "Before you said it was a limousine. What was I doing?"

"It was an eighteen-wheeler. You were crying for a Dum Dum. You know, also, the saddest part, the day before she died we had a terrible fight and she cracked my favorite Diana Ross album, *Silk Electric*, over her knee. Like a stick! I had to throw it in the trash! It was the very next day she died."

Tamer had no trouble talking to his father or to himself or to his father's friend, Philip Point, but around anyone else his mouth seized—a blip traveled toward the back of his throat and scattered like a spark. The counselor at school called it a speech phobia.

"Oh, but at home you should hear his wonderful English," his father said to the counselor, misunderstanding the diagnosis. "He speaks as an adult!"

They each had their own disfluencies—a block and a bumble.

"Break your bread here, over the table or over the counter," his father said in the morning, "or don't break it at all and instead I will cut it in half for you with the bread knife if you will hand it to me. Let me see it."

"Put lots of butter on it and I'll eat it on the way to the bus stop," Tamer said.

"Look at you. Your shirt is inside-out."

Tamer put his shirt on the right way and took the bread and walked down the street to the bus stop, where the other children waited in their colorful jackets. He positioned himself just beyond the clutch of rowdy grade-schoolers and didn't speak. He stared down at the sidewalk, counting the cracks.

During the day, his father worked at the Sunrise Motel on Chase and Ford as a housekeeper and desk clerk. In the classroom at Lakeside Primary, rummaging through a pencil box, Tamer felt dull and forgettable as a stone. During recess he paced the perimeter of the gymnasium. Each lap was a segment he could clip from the day, an hour scored into strips until there was nothing left, until a voice came over the garbled intercom saying, "Bus seventeen riders, please report to the north entrance."

There were times late at night when Tamer should have been asleep when he'd hear his father's music and go into the living room to find him curled up on the couch, wearing his special satin robe with the long braided belt, laughing and telling jokes with his friend, Philip Point. Philip and Tamer's father would sometimes stare at each other for a long time, taking sips from the same bottle of Seagram's 7 until one of them turned to courteously exhale his cigarette smoke.

"Go into bed, Tamer," his father said at the sight of him in the hallway.

"I'm going to sleep with you," Tamer said.

"No, sir. Goodnight, please."

"Hello, Philip," Tamer said. "These pajamas are new. You can come in here and talk to me."

"No, he will not," his father said.

Philip and Tamer's father sat on the couch with their legs wound together, smoke rising from the overfilled ashtray on the table, Perseus or Gemini lighting up the sky outside the long bay window behind the stereo cabinet. The house lights were out but the moon and the constellations shone into the living room as Tamer ran his fingers across the raised pattern of the wallpaper, heading slowly back down the hallway in the dark. In the other room his father and Philip would whisper and laugh, and the bottle would clink against the ashtray while the music played, until Tamer finally lay in bed long enough to reenter a dream—to cross from thinking to sleeping like a cloud thinning out in the sky.

Then there was a situation at the grocery store. It was close to dark and the temperature had dropped several degrees during the half hour they'd spent inside. This is how Michigan is. Two men inside of Food Pride followed

Tamer and his father out to the parking lot. The tall one said, "Excuse me, ma'am, can we help with the groceries?" The heavy one laughed and a blast of breath rose from his mouth. They grabbed their crotches and blew kisses and the tall one said, "Listen, baby, what are you doing later? Where's your husband?"

"He's got lipstick on," the heavy one said, both of them erupting again into a fit of laughter.

When they reached the car, his father said, "Shut up, both of you. There's a child in this backseat. Just go from here!"

But the tall one reached out, touching Tamer's father on the arm, saying, "No one gives a shit if we're out here, baby. You're in America now. We just wanna look at you." The man leaned forward, bringing his face in close as if he were about to kiss Tamer's father right on the lips. "Sexy faggot," he said, "I can't stop looking at you. I'm lost in your pretty eyes."

The heavy one was standing by, smiling, then not smiling. He watched Tamer sitting there in the backseat holding the toy he'd gotten from the coin machine at checkout. The heavy one coughed into the shoulder of his jacket, thrust his hands deep into the pockets. Tamer's father got into the car and slammed the door. When he started the engine and began to pull away, one of them smacked his hand hard against the roof, making a sound like thunder inside the vehicle.

In the backyard Tamer would assemble ERECTOR sets, the structures eccentric and lopsided. He'd build them and take them apart, slipping unevenly, helplessly, toward adolescence.

One day a package arrived in the mail. "I waited for you to get here," his father said. It was from Tamer's aunt, his father's sister, in Afyon.

Years later Tamer would receive a letter from her, too. He'd notice how the aunt's Turkish script crept into her written English the same way it had into his father's, the barbed handwriting like black fingernail clippings thrown across the page. He'd hear his father in the letter, his voice with all its foreign blunders. Tamer would stand in the foyer of his apartment building, a grown man, facing the elevator. The elevator doors were old and wouldn't close all the way but the car kept going as he stepped forward, bracing himself on the frame so he could lean in and gaze up at the elevator ascending into the darkness. A bulb would flash, red, then dark again, filling the shaft like gas flooding a line. Partly it'd be the mechanism of the elevator, the tense roar of the engine, the pulsing light, the raw pink of dusk coming through the plateglass doors behind him, all of it making it seem like every door could be a portal into the past, every opening a chink in time where he could swiftly pass into that long-ago living room to sit on the couch next to his father. There'd be music playing in one of the first-floor apartments, and a woman by the mailboxes pouring vodka into a soda bottle. Outside would be the sharp climate of near spring in Detroit.

Before opening the package, his father explained to him that in Afyon there were no yards to play in, just miles of cramped buildings and houses and a castle built high on a hill of volcanic rock in the center of the city, every brick road sloping toward the countryside. He told Tamer about the restaurant that was also a library, from which he had stolen the book about the universe. "It was the only English book, hidden behind the others, but I like it most for the pictures." His father explained that on his nineteenth birthday he'd left the library with the book in his satchel, and how during the months that followed he'd applied for a passport, planning a trip to the United States with money an uncle had sent him on the condition he'd come to work at the uncle's motel until the debt was repaid. His father stayed working at the motel, even after a young American couple took it over and the uncle, claiming he was bored with the cheapness of Western lodging, returned to Turkey.

"Now we will open the mail! How exciting this is!" his father said, carefully getting at the box with a nail file, lifting out the contents and laying them on the table before Tamer as if he were presenting him with two precious heirlooms. Wrapped in orange tissue paper was a box of cookies and a videotape. There was a note attached to the video by a thick rubber band. His father read it aloud in Turkish, not even bothering to translate.

"Should we watch?" his father said.

"Okay," Tamer said. "And I'll eat the cookies?"

"Do you know what kind they are? They are special."

"So I can't eat them?"

"No, I was only saying they are special."

It was a grainy black-and-white recording. At the first sharp quivering of a clarinet, his father screamed, "Oh! It is Esma Redžepova singing 'Chaje Shukarije'!" He patted Tamer on the knee as they sat on the couch in front of the television, the light washing out his father's lean face. There was the long exhalation of an accordion, and a woman singing in a high, birdlike vibrato. Tamer's father sat very still on the edge of the couch, mouthing every word, wiping his tears with the corner of his apron. In this moment Tamer felt his father was not his father, but a stranger. The men on the videotape formed a circle around Esma Redžepova, swaying back and forth while playing their instruments, tilting in close to sing backup on the chorus. Tamer ate the cookies, which were crisp and rich, like sugared nuts, while his father stared dreamily. "What a stylish dance! This is a whole galaxy!" his father said. Esma Redžepova, with her many necklaces and round, serious face, was the first woman Tamer had ever looked upon and felt a kind of desire—a yearning to hold and examine entirely.

A dim cluster. A stolen library book. The slow excavation of a beginning. What is a memory? A sand-filled crater on the surface of one's most solid self? Decades later, Tamer would feel, each time he recalled something, the small, sad changes being made—like a hand disturbing a compact cavity of sand as he searched for the bottom.

By the time he was sixteen, stocky and disheveled, acne budding along his jaw, his hair unclean and long enough to hide behind, the once-prolonged *m* and those manic repetitions at the start of words had been rubbed from his voice, leaving mostly silence in their place. He was just back from the neighbor's house and throwing his sneakers toward the sofa. He was holding a paper sack full of old *Hustler* magazines that the neighbor boy had sold him for four dollars. In the kitchen the rug was unraveling, gathering around the legs of the table and the metal chairs, running under the refrigerator. His father was lying down, wearing his apron and a purple Nike T-shirt, staring up at the ceiling fan. The video of Esma Redžepova played on the television in the living room. There was the usual furious pumping of the accordion, the shocking timbre of Esma's voice, and inside the music, a ringing, until he moved closer to the kitchen, so that all the colors of the room shifted and it was not the rug, but something soaking through his father's shirt and apron, spreading out like thick, dirty water across the linoleum. He went into the room. The floor was smeared with blood. He got down with a dish towel and pressed it against his father's chest. The blood soaked through. He grabbed all of the dish towels. He yelled, "Wake up right now, motherfucker!" He heard his voice in the room and it was not like his own voice but instead like his father's when he yelled at the neighbor's dog. It was a cheap sound. It was the heaviest thing. His father had already stopped breathing. Tamer thought his own throat was going to close shut, too. He didn't want to leave the room to call the ambulance, but he made himself go to the phone. He pressed the towels one at a time until he found the exact place where the blood came from. It was a small hole. He could put a finger over it and make it disappear. He tore the flimsiest towels apart and tied a single long bandage around his father's chest. He sat there, holding the sticky towels in place, attempting a chaotic CPR until the paramedics came through the door and pulled him aside.

The suspects had left tracks from the door to Selden Avenue, one block south. They'd taken his father's shoes and pitched the gun, like litter, into a nearby drainage ditch.

"Why would they take his shoes?" Philip cried, hours later, after they'd left the police station. He pulled his car onto the shoulder of the Southfield Freeway, pounding his fists against the steering wheel. He couldn't stop crying. "Who are the police?" he asked Tamer. "Who am I? I am somebody. Who are they?" He was screaming. "You can stay with me, Tamer!" Philip's face was bloated, as if injected with something, all of his features seized by fear.

Tamer stayed at Philip's house in Dearborn Heights. He lay on the couch, staring at the TV, eating mixing bowls full of cereal, hiding in the bathroom, watching reruns of *Family Matters* or *Step by Step* or *ER*. There was no funeral service. There wasn't enough money for one. Or else Philip couldn't pull himself together long enough to arrange it. Late at night, hours after Philip had drugged himself with sleeping pills, Tamer would jolt from a half sleep, feeling as if he were being hauled viciously out of his own body—pulled into a black hallway, tugged under dark waters, dragged through a hole in the floor. Soon there was a wooden box on Philip's bedside table. Philip said, "What are we going to do?" But Tamer could only shrug and stare at the TV. A med student stepped away from a body. Dr. Doug Ross hovered with a scalpel. "Stop!" the visiting attendant said. "This lady is suffering from pulmonary edema!" Tamer would stand in Phillip's room and stare at the wooden box until he thought Philip might come in, then he'd go back to the couch. Early in the mornings Tamer could hear Philip in the sunroom, his spoon clanking against a cup as Philip sobbed in the high, ugly tone of a teenage girl. Sometimes, Tamer could tell, Philip tried to hold it in his chest until it sounded like he was gagging. "Ejder, Ejder," he said. It was surprising to hear. It was as if Tamer's father hadn't had a name until now, until Philip said it. Tamer could not bring himself to get up from the couch to go and comfort Philip. It didn't seem appropriate.

"I don't see any reason why you can't stay as long as you want and we'll see about getting your father's Oldsmobile over here so you'll have something to get around in. And I know you'll want his car, unless you don't?" Tamer was sitting on the back porch, thinking he'd drive the awful car, and he could stay with Philip. He decided Philip was the only other person who loved his father and maybe he wouldn't mind being here with him. No one from

Afyon called or wrote or came, though who, other than Tamer, could've told them what had happened? Philip and Tamer drove to the house on a Saturday and Tamer filled some boxes with all the things he wanted to take. He didn't look in the kitchen. The body was somewhere else. The body was suspended in time. The kitchen was clean as a tooth. They left the house and locked the doors and on the porch Philip gave Tamer the keys, dropped them into his palm. They planned on coming back in a week for his father's car, but instead the police came to Philip's house with a social worker, saying Tamer had to appear in court. Philip had it all wrong, he said to Tamer. He wasn't thinking.

They took Tamer in the back of the police car to a children's home where he slept on a cot at the foot of another bed. The next day he sat with a judge in a cramped office while the social worker read aloud from a folder of papers. Afterward, alone together in the men's room, Philip asked Tamer if he understood what was happening. Tamer said he did not.

"I don't think I do either. I've been too upset. You'll be eighteen soon, though," he said, "and we can sort it all out."

"That's more than a year from now," Tamer said.

Philip washed his hands at the sink and dried them. He

stared at his shoes. He said, "I wonder if someone is wearing the shoes? Do you think someone's wearing them?"

"How would I know?" Tamer said, the heat draining from his body all at once. He turned away from Philip's lifeless face in the mirror, and headed toward the door.

Philip drove Tamer to the foster family's house, but wouldn't get out of the car. Tamer walked to the steps to meet the social worker, who smiled while handing him her card and a piece of candy. "Their names are Patsy and Darryl," she said, "and their daughter's name is Cecelia." Tamer didn't turn around when Philip drove off. Instead he stared at the obnoxious wreath hanging on the front door, trying not to drop the heavy box he was holding.

They wanted to shake his hand. They wanted to take him out in the backyard to show him the basketball hoop. His room had a single bed and a large metal desk. They emptied the closet so he could put his things inside.

During the first days he ate his meals at the desk. The Buckleys used paper plates. They used plastic forks and plastic cups. It was hard being in the house. He felt paralyzed by the pressure to speak. In the afternoons, when the house was still empty, he went into the living room to watch television. He would come out of his room at night, to sit on the couch and watch *ER*. Cecelia said *ER* was boring but Patsy called it "a high-octane drama!" "We love it, don't we, Tamer?"

Patsy was loud and looked, always, as if she'd just returned from vacation. Her skin was flushed and bronzed, and her clothes seemed suited for someone much younger.

Twice he put on the videotape of Esma Redžepova. He mouthed some of the words. He looked at the black-and-white footage and wondered how she must look now—aged, or different, not the slight, agile woman on the videotape.

Tamer called Philip once a week, just for the chance to speak without having to dislodge every word like a seed from a straw. "Are they treating you nice?" Philip asked. "Do you talk?" Tamer didn't respond, which, of course, was his answer. When he closed his eyes he felt that every new movement he made left a blur, every new instance of stillness, a bright orb. It was as if he were tracking himself, like a satellite.

In the courthouse the judge had asked Philip, "What is your relationship to the father? You were friends?"

"We were friends," Philip said.

But it didn't feel like the truth to Tamer. What else could he have said? It was like he was being interviewed for a job he didn't want. He touched his face too many times, ran his fingers inside the cuff of his pant leg and repeated the questions back as if they were impossible to answer.

Darryl Buckley owned a butcher shop and said to Tamer, "If you want some extra spending money you could come and work after school or on the weekends."

Darryl and his wife stared at each other from across the dinner table. Patsy looked at Tamer but spoke to Darryl, saying, "Tell him what time to come to work."

"After school, Patsy. I already said that."

"He did," said Tamer.

Cecelia fished a bone from her mouth, laid it on the edge of her paper plate. "I'm sorry," she said. "It's a bone." Her hair was careful and made her look like an adult. She wore ugly clothes, too. "Business casual," she called it. Patsy and Cecelia both had large, glassy eyes like cartoon forest animals and together consumed many packages of chocolate almonds.

"I'm glad you're eating with the family, Tamer," Cecelia said. It sounded as if she had rehearsed it.

Tamer longed for a moment like the one in the video, where the camera panned to capture an overhead view of all the musicians in their huddle, their heads nearly touching, as if they were spokes attached to some hidden axis, their large, gauzy shirts brushing against each other as they rose up and leaned back to reveal Esma Redžepova. She lifted her arms above her head, twirled her wrists, and splayed her fingers. She turned to look at the camera while the men swayed and circled her, like many moons moving into alignment. "Hello, Esma. Hello, many moons," Tamer said to himself in the living room, unsettled by the sound of his own voice. The whole scene, with its perfect choreography, made him even more desperate for his father, for the now-lost moments in his life when every action was carried out with grace and inherent rhythm.

He was sitting alone with Patsy in the kitchen in his new basketball shorts when she reached over to put a hand on his leg, running her finger up his thigh. "You're a beautiful man, Tamer. I bet your father was a beautiful man. Are all Turkish men so handsome? You want to help me bread the fish?"

"No," he said, getting up from the table and walking out into the yard. He stood behind the garage, watching bees swarm an empty soda can.

In the butcher shop he stocked the shelves and ran the register until Darryl came in one afternoon with a set of knives he'd bought especially for Tamer. "I appreciate them," Tamer managed to say. There was a chart in the back room showing the animals and all their parts. Tamer stared gravely at it when there was nothing else to do. He would arrange and rearrange the animal parts on the cutting table.

He made the cuts along the meat, and each time the effort of his hand holding the knife seemed to lessen, or soften, so that eventually it felt as if every animal were designed to be disassembled. Darryl fried pork skins in the deep fryer and complained about the customers. Other times he hid in the office doing crossword puzzles. At the end of every week he paid Tamer his hourly wage and occasionally a little more. "To save," he said, leaving Tamer to close up alone.

Eventually he made Tamer shoot a cow. They drove to a meat locker in Hamtramck. Tamer watched as a man in rubber coveralls put a gun against a cow's head. The man gave the gun to Tamer and explained how to use it. He took Tamer's hand in his own and pressed the barrel to the hair between the cow's gelatinous eyes. Tamer pulled the trigger. The hand-gun made a quick, dull pop and after the slaughter Darryl explained how to dig the bullet from the brain. Tamer pushed a finger into the tepid smoothness, excavating a tiny shell.

He felt dislodged.

Cecelia found a dead cat on the carport and asked Tamer if he would help her bury it. "It's the right thing to do," she said, her hand perched insincerely on her hip. He couldn't help but wonder, too often now, what Cecelia looked like without her clothes on. The girls in his class were quiet or else they shrieked manically at one another from across the lunch table. While Cecelia was looking for a shovel Tamer put his mouth up to the cat's and blew.

"Disgusting!" she said, coming around the corner of the garage. "You're crazy! You're going to catch a feline disease." He looked at her in her elaborate sweater, a dire expression on her face. He looked back down at the cat. It lay there stiff as a doll. Wouldn't it be something, he thought, if the cat began to squirm?

After dark he went into the yard again. He'd been lying in bed just thinking about the cat. He was still in his underwear, and he knelt down beside the small grave. He brushed the dirt away. Move a leg, move anything, he thought. It felt as if so much time had passed—he was so different, he thought, each day. How long, he wondered, would that feeling last? It was as if time were passing too quickly and also not at all.

As he was falling back asleep his father came and stood at the foot of the bed. He opened his satin robe and showed Tamer his chest. His lungs looked waxy and crooked inside the open, raw cavity. His father slowly turned his head toward the bedroom door, then even more slowly back to Tamer. It was as if he were trying to say something. He had a guilty, exhausted expression. Finally, in a voice that wasn't familiar, his father said, "That was a nice thing to do, for the girl, Tamer."

"Thank you," Tamer whispered back.

Tamer had sex with Patsy Buckley on the Fourth of July while Darryl and Cecelia were at the levee watching fireworks. She asked him again, "Are all Turkish men like this?"

"I don't know," he said.

"You're a virgin?" she said.

"Yes," he said.

"I don't give a shit," she told him. "I deserve this. You deserve this. Look at me while you're inside me so I can see your beautiful face."

They were in the garage, in the backseat of the car. What he wanted to do, but was afraid to, was lower himself down to where he entered her, to examine the secret shapes of her body, to see how it all worked. But the whole situation felt involuntary and embarrassing, so he kept his eyes closed and allowed her to do most of the work.

He understood that his mother had left them all those years ago because she was living with a man who didn't need her, a man who couldn't help but stare at other men while waiting in line at the grocery store, the filling station, the park. His father loved to cut the sandwiches into triangles and wipe the bathroom mirror and steam the cushions on the couch—he adored steaming the cushions. Tamer wondered if all mothers were like Patsy

Buckley, hiding out in their garages at night with their rum and cokes, reading ragged copies of *The Thorn Birds* or *Kaleidoscope* until their husbands fell asleep watching television in bed.

Tamer lived with the Buckleys for a year and three months. He moved out two weeks after his eighteenth birthday. They had a party for him in the backyard. The smell of charcoal clung to their clothes; the icing slipped off the cake. Patsy spilled a daiquiri down the front of her sundress and sat with it dripping between her breasts. She insisted they sing "You Are My Sunshine" instead of "Happy Birthday." He quit working at Darryl's shop and used the money he'd saved to rent an apartment in Southfield. He got a job at Leonard's Meat Processing on Nine Mile Road and for the first time ever he was alone.

There's a rainbow sheen in certain cuts of meat. Tear it from the bone, hold it up to the window. Sometimes when light hits a side of beef it splits into colors. At Leonard's there was a system of tracks along the ceiling of the locker so the cows and pigs could be rotated and spun, like clothes on a rack. He could tear down a full-grown hog in less than an hour. He'd slide a bucket under the hog where it hung from the ceiling like a colossal coat. The blood spun down. The organs plopped. Hardly anyone talked to him.

The hog bled what little blood it had left and the bucket filled to the lip or overflowed onto the floor.

Tamer would not have said he was lonely, but he pulled a milk crate up to his living-room window after dark so anyone on the street could see him sitting by himself. Outside, Detroit hummed like a hundred faraway motorboats. He shaved his face and washed his body at the kitchen sink. He looked at the skyline on his walk to work in the mornings, watched the sunlight spread like a spill, watched the city soak it up like a rag.

Philip came by, eventually, with an old recliner chair. In Tamer's new apartment he emptied a bag of curtains onto the floor, insisting they should hang them up. "Everyone can see in," he said. He stood on the cushion of the unsteady chair and clipped the hooks over the rod. "My god," he said, "you're so high up." Tamer brought two beers from the refrigerator and they drank them on the living-room floor. "You shouldn't have these," Philip said, appearing uneasy and out of reach.

"I know," Tamer said, "but the clerk at the liquor store is Turkish. I wanted a reason to say hi."

"You could have bought a soda," Philip said. "Did you talk to him?"

"No," Tamer said. "And I wanted these."

The fluorescent light in the kitchen blinked off and on

and after a while Philip said he had to go. Tamer put his hand on Philip's shoulder in the doorway, the way he'd seen other grown ups do. Moments later he watched from the window as Philip got into his car and pulled out into the intersection. Tamer stood at the window with the new curtains wide open, watching the city grow dark. He could see Philip with his turn signal flashing as he moved out of sight. Across the street was another row of apartment buildings with the balconies lit up. If he leaned close enough to the glass he could make out the edge of Bouveric Woods, a tight mass of trees with limbs like many arms broken and healed incorrectly.

Tamer had come to a place where he could at least imagine what he might say to Philip or to anyone he wanted to talk to, even if he couldn't yet say the things aloud. He thought he'd like to say, *It's hard to stop being angry that he's not around. It's hard to stop thinking about him all the time*, or *I don't know how to stop wanting him around for no good reason other than to have him here*. He wanted to ask, *How much longer will it be like this?* even though he knew the answer was probably forever.

He worked, or watched television, or practiced saying simple things to strangers. He stood in the foyer of his apartment building watching the people on the street. He waited by the elevator as if he were about to meet someone, as if at any minute a conversation might begin. It was late summer when he received the letter from his aunt. The address was incomplete, and she had misspelled the name of the city. In the letter she explained how she had learned about his father's death through the manager at the motel, that months afterward the family had held a small service of their own in Afyon and how she wished Tamer could have been there. The aunt said she would someday like to visit him in "Destroy." Outside, two older gentlemen took each other's hands and stepped off the curb, beginning a slow walk across the street. The radio in the first-floor apartment went off, and the woman in the chair poured more vodka into her soda bottle. Tamer waved to her, and quickly turned back toward the elevator. He wanted to step through the doorway and into his old house.

Philip had never offered him the wooden box, but it didn't matter. What he really wanted was to return to the house with a box cutter and remove the rectangle of linoleum where his father had died. It was something he thought of often. He played it over in his head, drawing out the plot, precisely cutting through the material and peeling back the slick sheet so he could roll it up like a scroll. That was the moment. It was the last place his father had been, the last place he'd touched. He wanted to reach through the open elevator doors and into the kitchen, to find that smaller version of himself making a picture book, to hear the accordion bellows unpleat and watch his father dance to the music before lying down on the kitchen floor. It was strange hearing a song that many times and not knowing what it meant beyond the meaning he had made for it. He would put the picture book on the table and lay down on, the floor too. He'd ask his father for another story about his mother and it would be the truth this time. His father would sit up and look at him or lie his head gently on Tamer's stomach, pressing his ear in close. He'd have said something like, *Wait. I think I can hear something in there, Tamer. In your belly,* or *Hold, please. This is radio waves from space! It is from stars colliding. The noise has been traveling all these years from another, distant planet. And just now it has arrived.*

Tamer could imagine almost anything his father might say. He could arrange the words and his father would be there for a minute, in a lonely but consoling way. It was getting harder to actually hear his voice, though, to feel the deep-down presence possible only because of the sounds he made when he spoke, no matter what the words meant. He wasn't sure how he was supposed to feel about this, angry or lucky, that someday the sound of his father's voice would be gone for good.

CRAZY

by MIA MCKENZIE

THE DAY I DECIDE to kill a really famous old lady, I cook an extravagant breakfast. I've taken to doing this at least a few times a week. Sometimes it's apple-and-asparagus omelets. Other times honey-drizzled grilled salmon and cream-cheese bagels. This day it's Florentine crepes. Served on the china plates that used to be my mother's. Or, more accurately, the china plate. I only ever need the one.

I sit alone at my tiny kitchen table, chewing and

thinking. Not about the old lady, who I haven't yet decided to kill, but about my life. What I think about my life is this, exactly: My life is one of those lone, dirty, discarded socks you sometimes see in the street. The kind of thing you look at and go, How did that get there?

I sip my coffee and notice a strange taste. It tastes like coffee. I grab the bourbon and splash in some more. On the TV, there's a morning show playing scenes from one of my favorite 80s sitcoms: *The Golden Girls*. This piques my interest and I turn up the volume. One of the old ladies from the show is very sick with cancer. She's one of only two surviving members of the cast. The morning-show host reads get-well emails from the old woman's fans, people who grew up watching the show, for whom, even after many years, it still holds some nostalgic importance.

I wonder if, when I am old and dying, anyone will email me, care of the *Today* show, things like this: "You gave me years of laughter. That time you wore that nun's outfit, I almost peed my pants."

I get into my car and take a few seconds to consider driving to a nearby gun shop, buying a revolver, and shooting myself in the face. This is not unusual. Getting into my car always makes me contemplate suicide. I mean, it's not a bad car. It's a regular car, four wheels and everything. You know what it's not, though? It's not a 1969 Alpha Romeo, red, like that one Benjamin Braddock drives in *The Graduate*. Every day that simple fact makes me want to off myself. But I don't. Instead, I drive to work, where I die slowly, a little bit more every weekday.

The bank where I work isn't worth naming and the job I do there isn't worth describing. It's a plain old beige job in a plain old beige office, and beige really needs no introduction, does it? We all know beige, some of us better than others. Some of us are just passing acquaintances of beige. Others of us get dry-humped by the soft dick of beige every day.

Morning, Ashton, Ernesto says as I pass his cubicle. *Did you watch* Glee *last night?*

No.

Oh, you missed a good one! Kurt and Rachel sang a duet that Barbra Streisand and Judy Garland sang together on the old Judy Garland Show*!*

Oh, I say. *Well, I had a few friends over and we just drank wine and talked. Never even thought to turn on the TV.* Which is all a humongous lie. There were no friends; there was no wine. I did watch *Glee.* And that duet was mag-fuck-ing-nificent. But there's no way I'm admitting that, especially to Ernesto, who is some kind of proud man-spinster, always going on and on about TV shows and what's on sale this week at Walmart and never having the decency to be the least bit embarrassed about it. My life may be a dirty street-sock, sir, but I don't intend to go waving it around like a soiled surrender. At some point, I'm going to get my shit together, okay?

I haven't even made it into my cubicle yet and I already want to go home.

My cubicle has walls like gray carpet. If you try to tape anything on the walls, lint gets onto the tape and the tape won't stick. So you have to tack everything. All over the insides of everyone's cubicles, there are red and yellow and blue and pink tacks holding up calendars and unframed photos. In Ernesto's cubicle, held up by one green tack and three yellow tacks, is a picture of a cartoon baby cow, and above it are the words *Don't eat me.* Ernesto is not a vegetarian by any possible interpretation of the word. Not only does he eat meat at every single meal, but I have never once seen him eat a vegetable. Often, customers spot the cartoon and ask if Ernesto's a vegetarian and Ernesto says, *No. Why?* I can't imagine what he thinks that cartoon means.

On one wall of my cubicle there's a framed picture I took of a seagull with a bright yellow beak, standing on the edge of a pier somewhere on Muscle Beach, its wings half-opened as it prepares to take flight against a sky that is blue and hazy with promise. It's possible that one could make the same argument for why this photo doesn't belong in my cubicle as for why the baby cow doesn't belong in Ernesto's. Gratefully, no one has.

Felix arrives at nine thirty. From my desk, I see him through the glass doors as he pulls into the parking lot. He's hard to miss in his pristine red 1969 Alpha Romeo. Even in Los Angeles, it's a flashy car. I watch him set the alarm and saunter—Felix is a saunterer if I ever knew one— toward the entrance of the building. As he reaches for the door handle, I imagine, as I do every day, that the door is somehow suddenly electrified, and that when he touches it a current like a lightning bolt will surge through his bony body, burning him to a dark gold crisp, like a french fry. When that doesn't happen—when he enters unelectrocuted and is greeted by the hearty good-mornings of our co-workers; when he sees me and smiles and says, *Hey, Ashton, don't forget about lunch;* when I smile back, nodding, saying, *Yep. Can't wait;* when he goes into his office, which is a real office with a door and walls you can tape shit on—I look at the photo of the seagull with its half-opened wings and I wish I could find it, kill it, and eat it. Fucking bird.

I'm slacking off, commenting on my friends' Facebook statuses—and by friends I mean, of course, all the random people I have met over the last several years with whom I spend no time in real life but whose daily activities I am privy to intimate details of, including the anxiety and fear they are experiencing while waiting for scary test results or that their mother is in town and that bitch is driving them crazy—when Adina from the bakery across the street comes in with their morning deposit. She is wearing her knee-high leather boots, the ones I sometimes have lucid dreams about, and new glasses with thick black frames. She smells like autumn on the East Coast, always, even in summer, like crushy leaves and wood fires, somehow, and that smell fills up the tiny bank. Ernesto looks over at me and raises his eyebrows, whispers, *Your girlfriend's here*. I whisper back, *Shutthefuckup, Ernesto*. Well, I don't, really, but I want to. Because she's not my girlfriend. I don't even think she knows my name. Even though I see her every day while wearing my name on a shiny tag pinned above my left tit. Even though we've interacted twenty-three times.

Since we know her, and since her boss, the owner of the bakery, is a really rich, influential dude, one of our most important customers, Adina doesn't have to wait in line like any old asswipe. Whenever she comes in, she gets helped by one of us, one of the account managers, whichever of us happens to be free at the time. Because she is so lovely, and because she smells like autumn, all the men want to assist her. Even Ernesto, although in his case it's because he wants to be her best friend and watch *RuPaul's Drag Race* with her. As Adina bypasses the customers waiting in line and heads for our little cluster of cubicles, Ernesto calls out, *Hey Adina, Ashton can help you over here*, and points at me.

I very much regret telling Ernesto about my crush on Adina. It happened only because I was drunk. One day at lunch I had two or six sakes with my sushi and came back plastered and spilled my guts to him over the low wall that separates our cubicles. It went something like this:

Me: *You know that woman from the bakery?*

Ernesto: *Elizabeth?*

Me: *No.*

Ernesto: *Adina?*

Me: *Yes. I think I love her.*

Ernesto: *Ohhhh. Well. Isn't that an interesting development? So, you like ladies?*

Me: *Have you seen her thighs, Ernesto? Have you looked at them? I mean, really looked?*

Ernesto: *She's certainly beautiful.*

Me: *Shut up! Everybody says "beautiful" about everything all the time! It doesn't even mean anything anymore!*

Ernesto: *Sorry. Jesus.*

Now he's grinning at me as Adina makes her way over to my cubicle.

Here's what I like most about Adina, more than her autumn smell and her thighs: she's not here for your bullshit. Like, one time on my lunch break I saw her out walking and this guy yelled across the street at her, *Damn! Can I get some fries with that shake?!* Which, first of all—*really?* What are we, in tenth grade? Anyway, she stopped walking, looked right at dude and yelled back, *Eat my dick, you fucking sleaze.*

Morning, she says, taking a seat on the opposite side of my desk.

Hi. Making a deposit?

She nods, unzips a burgundy money bag, pulls out a stack of cash with a deposit slip on top, and holds it all out to me over the desk.

While I process her deposit, she sits there looking distracted, her eyes, which are large and deep brown, scanning the room. I wish just once she'd look at me. Like, really look.

I wish just once she'd notice. I want to say something, something like, *you have lovely eyes.* I want to be that girl. But I just enter the bakery's account number and keep my mouth shut.

Ah, the lovely Adina. It's Felix. He's smelled pretty-girl pussy and come sauntering. He leans against my cubicle, grinning, arms folded across his chest. He looks like he's posing for a Newport ad. *We missed you last week.*

I was on vacation, Adina says. *In Santa Fe.*

I love Santa Fe. I tell myself I'll retire there one day, spend my golden years writing stories in a little adobe house with a view of endless red clay and cacti.

Lucky girl, Felix says. *It's beautiful there.*

There's that word again. *Beautiful.* It's a word people say when they can't be bothered to think any harder, to conjure a word that really fits.

It's breathtaking, I say, before I even realize I'm saying it.

Adina looks at me. And for a few seconds, I know I'm really there. She looks into my eyes, at my nose, at my mouth. Then at my nametag. She says, *Ashley. It is breathtaking. That's just what it is.*

And I think: Whoever this Ashley is, she's lucky. I wish I were her.

*   *   *

We drive to lunch in the Alpha Romeo. Felix says there's a great Ethiopian place he wants to take me to. It's not my first time in this car, not by a long shot. In high school, when the car still belonged to Felix's dad, Felix would sometimes steal it and take me for rides. I've known Felix since I was fourteen and he was fifteen. I'm not sure if I ever loved him. There were times when I thought of him almost like a brother. But I don't really love my actual brothers, so that's not saying a whole lot. I know for sure that at some point I wanted to be him. I remember standing in front of the mirror when I was fourteen, with my hair tucked up inside a backward baseball cap, a roll of socks in my underwear, my arms folded across my chest, and a grin on my face as crooked and self-assured as his. He had a girlfriend, Alana, who was the subject of every erotic thought I had between the ages of fourteen and fourteen and a half. Felix would often bring her along on our joyrides in the Alpha Romeo. She was Afro Puerto Rican, super-dark coffee-bean brown and the kind of curvy that made me stutter sometimes, and when we rode with the windows down, her thick, wavy hair whipped my face, clung to it so it was hard for me to breathe, but I didn't mind, because even at fourteen I understood that this was a good way to die. Felix's right hand would move between the gearshift and Alana's knee, and I would close my eyes and wish it were my hand. Sometime during senior year, I gave up on being Felix, or even being like him. I made peace with the presence of my vagina, and even grew to appreciate it.

What kind of old woman do you think you'll be? Felix asked me once. We were at his house, smoking weed and watching *The Golden Girls*.

I shrugged. I didn't like to think about myself being old.

According to this show, you have four choices. Slutty, dumb, mean, or... well, mean.

Well, if those are my choices, I guess I'll go with mean.

Bad choice! Mean people don't live that long. All that meanness gives them cancer and they die long, drawn-out, horrible deaths. I bet those two die first, the two mean ones.

None of them are going to die. They're just characters on a TV show. The show will eventually get canceled and those characters will live forever in reruns.

I guess. But let's just say that the characters and the actors are the same. Just for the sake of argument. Who do you think lives longest? The slut or the dummy?

I don't know.

I say the dummy. 'Cause some people are just too stupid to die.

No. The slut. The slut has more to live for.

We giggled and passed the bowl. Felix took a long, long drag.

I'll bet you, he said, a minute later.

I had already forgotten what we were talking about.

Bet me what?

That the dummy lives the longest.

I shrugged. *Okay. What are we betting?* I searched my pockets, pulled out some crumpled cash. I got fifteen dollars.

Felix searched his own pockets, produced nothing but lint. *I'll bet you the Alpha Romeo,* he said. *Against your fifteen bucks!*

I laughed, shaking my head. *That car's not even yours.*

It will be one day, he said.

I thought about it. The clearest thinking I'd done all night. I imagined myself at the wheel of that car, imagined Alana, or any girl I wanted, beside me, my hand on her knee. I held out my hand to Felix and we shook on it.

We pull into the small parking lot across from the Ethiopian restaurant and I'm reaching for the door handle when Felix puts his hand on my shoulder. He's been making small talk the whole way over, but now he looks at me very seriously. *Are you doing okay, Ashton?*

I really don't like it when people get serious all of a sudden like this. It makes me nervous. It makes me feel like something is coming that I can't handle. *Yeah,* I say. *I guess. Why?*

You've been acting weird the last few weeks.

By whose standard of weirdness?

By the universally agreed-upon standard.

I shake my head. *No such standard exists.*

Felix takes a deep breath. *You're acting like you did before you ended up in the psych ward. Like, antisocial and... I don't know. Disconnected.*

You know what? No matter how many weeks of your life you spend outside of the psych ward, all anybody ever wants to talk about is that one week you spent *in* the psych ward. Jesus.

I'm fine, Felix. Totally fine. Which is maybe a lie, but whatever.

Felix just stares at me, with that look Oprah always gets when she knows somebody's bullshitting her, and I quickly get out of the car, saying, *Come on, I'm starving.*

Once we're seated and eating, Felix says, *I'm just saying, you could have a much better life if you tried.*

What's wrong with my life? I ask through a mouthful of injera.

Well, for one thing, you get no pussy.

I get pussy.

When? When was the last time you got any pussy?

Like a few weeks ago. It's such a bad lie that we both feel embarrassed by it. It takes a minute for us to recover and be able to look each other in the eye again.

All I'm saying is, you're a dime when you try.

Yeah? In what ways am I a dime?

Well, first of all, you're the smartest woman I know.

The smartest woman? You know men who are smarter than me?

He thinks about it and after a few seconds he shakes his head. *No. I don't, actually. You are the smartest person I know. Plus, you're cute. And funny. I'm telling you, you could get any woman you wanted once she got to know you.*

You know when people say things about your life as though they know, as if they have any fucking clue what it's really like to be you? It's annoying. But worse than that, it's a trick. Because if they say it with enough certainty, they get you believing it, even if only for a few minutes, before reality reappears and punches you in the head.

Back at the bank, Felix parks the Alpha Romeo in his spot, and as we walk to the entrance I see Adina crossing the parking lot. I watch her thighs, remember her screaming *Eat my dick*, and think about what Felix said, about how I could have any girl I want.

Wow, is that your car? Adina calls out to Felix.

He stops and smiles at her. *Sure is.*

It's just like the one from that movie, right? I love that movie.

It was one of my dad's favorites. I watched it with him a hundred times when I was a kid.

Felix holds the door to the bank open for her. She smiles and starts to go past him into the bank, but he puts a hand on her shoulder and says, *How about we grab some dinner later and you can tell me all about breathtaking Santa Fe?*

Son of a—

Adina hesitates and for a second I think she's going to say no. I'm sure of it. I watch her mouth form the *n*—her lips parting, her tongue curving up against the roof of her mouth. But then she hesitates again, and after a half a second she says, *Sure.*

I look at the Alpha Romeo. A feeling like ice water runs up the back of my neck and a shrieky voice in my mind says: Kill the old lady. Get that fucking car.

I spend that evening drinking screwdrivers and googling like crazy. There are only two surviving Golden Girls. One of them—the slut—is sick with cancer. The dummy has a new TV show, which is surprising, because she's, like, ninety. But whatever, good for her. I find out where the show is filmed and then email my cousin Blake, who works at that same studio, as a staff writer on some cop show I can never remember the name of, and ask if I can visit. Three hours later he writes me back, and even though he sounds annoyed, he says okay, but not until next week, when he'll have some time to show me around. I write back and say that I don't need him to show me around, that I can show myself around. He writes back that he's sick of his cousins getting in touch only when they want to get on the lot and stalk TV stars or whatever, and never because they actually want to see him. I write back that he's a big fucking baby and always has been and never mind then. He writes back fine, he'll put my name on the visitors list, but I owe him now, and he'll be expecting an actual Christmas gift this year, and not a donation in his name to some charity he's never heard of that he suspects does not really exist.

The next morning, I call off work and at eight on the dot I drive to Burbank. I feel a little out of it, probably mostly because of all the vodka, but also there is this subtle vibration inside my head, like buzzing bees but quieter. It's the same vibration I felt before I set all of my neighbor's birdhouses on fire. It occurs to me, briefly, that I am once again doing something crazy. But then I'm like, *Nah*.

*   *   *

My cousin has left my name at the security gate. The guard gives me a visitor pass to wear around my neck, along with a map of the lot. The buzzing in the back of my brain gets louder as I follow the map to the right sound stage. There's a red light on outside the door. I know from TV that this means they're filming inside. I enter really quietly. I stand at the back of a small group of extras waiting to be useful. I see the old lady. She's doing a scene with a couple of other actors. I feel pain in my face and I realize I'm gritting my teeth. I loosen my jaw. I roll my tongue around. I think I'm sweating. I wipe my brow with the back of my hand but there's no moisture. When the scene ends, some guy yells, *Lunch!* and everyone starts to wander off. The old lady heads in my direction, past the group of extras. Many of them take the opportunity to tell her how great she is. How much they've always loved her. She smiles at them, gracious, and thanks them.

After the group lets her pass, I see there's a young guy with her, maybe an assistant. I follow them as they exit the set and step out into the sunlight. I'm right on their heels. The old lady must sense someone behind her because she suddenly turns and is looking at me. The high-pitched voice in the back of my head shrieks: *It's now or never.*

I take a step toward the old lady. And then I stop. Because, as it turns out, and much to my surprise, I have no idea how to kill somebody. Sure, it looks easy enough in the movies—a quick neck snap or whatever—but when you are actually standing in front of a person, it doesn't seem so *bing-bam-boom.*

The old lady cocks her head to one side. *Hello, dear. Do you need something? Would you like an autograph?*

Then guess what fucking happens? I explode in tears. Ex-fucking-plode. I stand there, sobbing like a goddamn lunatic, tears streaming down my face, snot collecting in thick puddles inside each nostril, as I sniff and sniff, trying to keep it from oozing out, while the old lady and her assistant—or whoever the fuck he is—watch me, their faces full of confusion and pity.

Are you all right? the guy asks me.

I shake my head no. Taking a few steps backward, I lean my body against a wall and slowly sink down onto the ground. I lean my head back against the wall and just bawl. I bawl for a younger me, one who deserves a better existence than this, one who really should have better shit to do.

Should I call someone? the assistant asks, more to the old lady than to me.

No! I say, through sobs. *I'll be okay. I'll be fine. Not everybody is supposed to have a big dick and an Alpha Romeo.* Did I mention Felix has an enormous dick?

The old lady looks around, like she thinks maybe someone is playing a celebrity prank on her. *A… big dick?*

I shake my head. *You wouldn't understand.*

She shakes her head, too. *Probably not. But, look, should we call some—*

When I was young, I thought I had all these choices, I tell her. *I thought there were endless possibilities. Or, at least, you know, a whole lot of them. But it turns out there were only a few. You know what I mean?*

She just looks at me like she doesn't.

I sigh. *It's just that nothing's turned out like I hoped it would.*

She laughs, kind of a little snicker. *My dear, life never turns out the way you hope it will when you're young. And thank god for that, because you don't know what really matters and what doesn't. It takes getting old to figure that out.*

How old? I ask.

Seventy-five, she says, *eighty.*

Well, fuck.

She comes closer to me, ignoring the assistant's *stranger danger* expression. She bends over a little, looks uncomfortable, then straightens up again. She grabs hold of the wall and tries to lower herself to my eye level, but when she does that the joints in her knees make a cracking sound, so she gives up on that and says, *Stand up, young lady,* while extending her hand to me. I take her hand and lift myself up off the ground.

One thing you might try, she says, *is thinking about the time in your life when you were most happy. That might give you some idea about what's really important.*

I try it. After several seconds I say, *I don't think I've ever been happy.*

She frowns, like she's ready to give up on my crazy ass.

I think some more. *Well, I used to like watching your show, with my friend when I was a teenager.*

She shrugs. *That's something, I guess.*

I think maybe it's more than *something*, maybe it's significant, but by now my brain is tight and fuzzy, like a sweater that's been through the dryer, and I just want to go home and make myself an elaborate breakfast. Or shoot myself in the face. Whichever.

That night when I get into bed, I expect to lie awake for hours, kept conscious by the question of happiness. But the minute my head hits the pillow, I'm out. I wake up starving. Literally, I'm hungrier than I can ever remember being before. I consider a few different extravagant breakfasts: almond-crusted French toast with strawberries, bacon quiche Lorraine, apple cinnamon ricotta pancakes.

But instead, I grab a bowl and proceed to eat half a box of Cap 'N Crunch. It is more delicious than I can describe.

I'm at work an hour before Felix saunters in. When I see him grab the door handle, for the first time in maybe a year I don't envision his death by electrocution. Instead, I observe that his hair is graying at the temples more than I've ever noticed. I think about how old we're both getting.

How was your date? I ask him when he stops at my desk.

What date?

With Adina.

He acts like he's trying to remember who I'm talking about. *Oh, the bakery girl? Yeah. Didn't happen.* He's shrugging like he doesn't care, but I can tell that he does by the way he keeps folding and unfolding his arms.

Why not?

She called me like an hour before we were supposed to meet and canceled.

I grin at him.

He frowns. *That's the first time I've seen you smile in, like, a month. Thanks a lot.*

I'm still grinning as he saunters away to his office.

On cue, like in a movie, Adina comes in with the bakery's morning deposit.

Morning, Adina. Ashton's available, Ernesto says.

I'm smiling at her, thinking about her canceling on Felix.

Hi, Ashley. You look happy today, she says.

It's weird, because I sort of feel happy, too. Not like super good, but kind of okay, you know? Like I don't want to shoot myself in the face at all. How often can you say that?

Instead of saying that, though, I'm all, *Yeah, I guess so. How about you? Are you happy?*

She says, *So-so, I guess. I mean, I went a little crazy earlier and almost murdered this asshole in the bakery.* Then she looks like she really didn't mean to say that. Like she's embarrassed. *I mean, not* really *murder him. I'm not crazy crazy.*

Oh no, of course not. Me, neither. Not at all.

She shrugs. *But I guess everybody's crazy sometimes, right? Isn't life just a whole bunch of going crazy and a whole bunch of coming back, over and over again?*

I want to hug her, and possibly pleasure her orally if she was into it, because that's maybe the truest thing anyone has ever said. I want to ask her about her crazy, what it looks like, how it feels, whether it involves high-pitched voices at the back of her head or the stalking of octogenarians. Instead, I say, *I've always wanted to retire to Santa Fe.*

She looks really interested in that and says, *Yeah? Tell me.*

A DISPATCH
FROM MYANMAR

WHAT I LEARNED
ABOUT FAKE NEWS
IN SOUTHEAST ASIA

nonfiction by R J VOGT

L ET ME START BY saying I had no business being
there. I mean, of course I was honored to be there,
which in this specific instance meant clinging to
an iron gate outside of a Mandalay polling booth alongside
hundreds of yelling Myanmar men. This narrow ledge was
a front-row perch from which one could witness the country
sometimes known as Burma—one of the world order's last

holdouts, on the level of Cuba or North Korea—transition to a real, live, messy, dirty democracy. As a journalist for the *Myanmar Times*, I was downright thrilled to be there.

To be clear: I had few qualifications. Other than a flimsily laminated press credential and my camera, I was just a bespectacled white guy on the sidelines, sweaty and overwhelmed. I spoke little to no Myanmar language, had less than one hundred days' experience in-country, and could hardly handle the dented Honda motorbike I'd rented—let alone decipher the intricacies of Myanmar's first national election.

And yet there I was, peering through the bars as an official began counting the votes out loud in the compound courtyard. The crowd cheered every vote for the oppositional National League for Democracy (NLD), softly booing those for the ruling regime's Union Solidarity and Development Party (USDP)—cheers outnumbered boos three to one and grew louder as the count dragged on.

By the time I left the township, it was clear democracy had won the neighborhood. By the time I filed my story later that evening, it was clear democracy had won the entire country.

And by the time I quit the *Myanmar Times*, fifteen months later, it was clear to me—democracy can be manipulated. You can't believe everything you read in the news.

*　　*　　*

What happens when a nation long mired in dictatorship transitions to a democracy? What's it like to witness a country blossom, from closed off to opened up? These were not questions I was pondering when I took the job at the *Myanmar Times*. Myanmar was low on my list of prospective countries to work in—to be honest, I couldn't have placed it on a map—but I was twenty-two years old and eager for any gig that didn't include "social media coordinator" in its job description.

When I accepted the offer, Myanmar was set to hold its first-ever national elections in six months. I'd be there to help cover them, working for an organization billed as "the country's oldest independent English-language daily" newspaper. Current and former employees gushed about their experience working there, and Southeast Asian news junkies considered it one of the best rags in the region. For a kid from Suburbia, Tennessee, with a degree in literary journalism, the appeal of working alongside seasoned foreign correspondents and some of Myanmar's top journalists outweighed the concerns of moving to one of the least developed countries in the world. In retrospect, the fact that the publication had endured years of military censorship and was currently owned by a military-friendly businessman should have alarmed me; in reality, it only made the offer that much more exciting.

I arrived in Yangon during monsoon season, dazzled by streets teeming with rickshaws and off-brand Japanese cars and fried-cricket vendors, everyone ever-dripping from afternoon rain. The city overwhelmed me: rats skittered between grandmothers with machetes who squatted, flat-footed, over slabs of chicken; street dogs prowled through trash, pausing only for fighting or fucking; everywhere, monks padded quietly by with their alms bowls, accepting donations with bowed heads. Pablo Neruda, who worked in Yangon (then called Rangoon) at the Chilean consulate in 1927, wrote that its streets "engrossed me and drew me gradually under the spell of real life." Nearly a century later, it seemed little had changed.

Then again, everything was changing. The price of a single SIM card had come crashing down, from $1,500 under the military junta in the mid-2000s to $1.50 by the time I got there, in 2015. Cheap Chinese smartphones had erupted into ubiquity, tucked into the checkered *longyis* wrapped tight around the waist of every man, woman, and child. With internet access came Facebook accounts, and suddenly the citizens of one of the most isolated countries on the planet were sharing selfies and memes of funny-looking farm animals. It wasn't just technology—the Western world was entering in other ways, too: a flood of Kentucky Fried Chicken and German tour groups and, once, a Jason Mraz concert.

The staff of the *Myanmar Times* captured these changes in print from a proud old office on one of downtown Yangon's most prominent street corners. The paper's name is boldly printed in four-foot-high black letters, stark against the white paint flecking off the walls. A portico out front bears the slogan "Heartbeat of the Nation."

During my early days at the paper, it really did feel like the heartbeat of the nation. Each morning I stepped over the office's snoozing street dogs and climbed a grand wooden staircase to reach the newsroom, an entire floor of renovated urban decay dedicated to editorial. My co-workers included award-winning editors and some of the best local reporters in the country, most of them spending breaks blowing cigarette smoke out the window of the drafty third-floor lounge. Stub the butts and back to our desks—sure, there was fluff in the twenty-four-page tabloid the team pumped out each night, but it ran alongside some of the most trustworthy political and national news in the country.

The tail end of a Bay of Bengal cyclone had flooded much of the country the week I arrived, and just a few days later I was sent to cover the relief effort, bouncing wildly through the Ayeyarwady River delta on a jerry-rigged bus of volunteers. The country of 54 million people is largely agrarian, and once we left the Yangon metropolis we entered a verdant world of rice paddies and bamboo houses. After sixteen hours we reached our destination, a flood-ravaged village desperate for food and fresh water. In between interviews with community leaders and local residents, I remember looking around and realizing, Wow, there are no other Western reporters working on this story.

That trip led to a front-page story on how Aung San Suu Kyi, the beloved human rights icon and NLD leader, was illegally campaigning before the election season had kicked off under the auspices of donating rice to flood victims. Our translation team translated the English version for the weekly Myanmar-language edition, ensuring more people would read the story: the *Myanmar Times* was covering real news, publishing truths that nobody else would.

Monsoon season petered out and campaigning officially started. Mango stands turned into avocado stands; the news cycle grew hectic. I was dispatched to cover the election from Mandalay, the country's second-largest city. When Aung San Suu Kyi and the NLD won by a landslide, my coworkers and I interviewed revelers dancing in the street.

Back in Yangon, the staff swapped stories of watching old women weep outside voting booths after casting the first vote of their lives. The Myanmar language does not have a word for "democracy," so its people have simply co-opted the word: suddenly I began to hear it dripping from everyone's mouth.

In hindsight it's hard to believe how quickly the newspaper's optimism unraveled: within a few weeks of Aung San Suu Kyi's remarkable electoral victory, the *Myanmar Times* had begun to lose its grip on independence.

We weren't always so independent, I learned from the senior staff. They told me how the paper was founded by an Australian media magnate named Ross Dunkley in 2000, in partnership with Sonny Swe, the son of a general in the military intelligence unit. Some critics accused the Aussie of getting in bed with the junta to make a buck, but he told one film crew, "I'm not in bed with anyone. Not even my wife."

Despite its early reputation for toeing the military line, the *Myanmar Times* turned a corner in 2012, when the reformed military government lifted prepublication censorship laws. By then the Aussie and the general's son had suffered arrests, imprisonment, and targeted media attacks—partly due to military purges, partly due to

Dunkley's penchant for mischief—and within two years, majority ownership had fallen into the hands of U Thein Tun, a prominent beverage magnate.

Around the office, U Thein Tun was called "The Chairman." All I knew about him was that he had brought Pepsi into the country during the early 1990s and maintained connections to every beer produced in-country. My colleagues said he owned the newspaper just so he could say he owned the newspaper.

The Chairman kept such a distance from its day-to-day operations that I did not experience his influence over the staff until a month after the election. We had published a story about twelve men convicted of training with the "Myanmar Muslim Army" (a dubious, unheard-of threat) and our coverage ran on the front page, above the fold.

[A too-brief Myanmar political history: Buddhists and Muslims don't always get along, especially when it comes to the Rohingya. A Muslim ethnic group from the far west of Myanmar, near the border with Bangladesh, the Rohingya make up roughly 2 percent of Myanmar's total population. Records from the eighth century attest to their presence in the Arakan kingdom nearly a thousand years before the Burmese kings conquered the region (now called Rakhine State), but the Myanmar military government has long denied them citizenship and claims they are Bengali immigrants. (Bangladesh, with its own substantial crowds of impoverished people, wants nothing to do with them.)

Over the past year and a half, the United Nations and other humanitarian agencies have accused Myanmar's military of the mass systemic rape, pillaging, torching, and murder of the Rohingya based on interviews with refugees and satellite footage of razed villages. Hundreds of thousands of Rohingya have fled on boats operated by human traffickers, risking slavery rather than death at the hands of soldiers. Many others, mostly children, have drowned in river crossings at the border.

Despite its ranking as "the world's most charitable country," Myanmar, with its 90 percent Buddhist majority, harbors no pity for the Rohingya, with military officials claiming that "the Bengalis" (the government refuses to use the word *Rohingya*) set fire to their own villages to earn undue media sympathy. In fiery sermons, nationalist monks stoke fears of an Islamic terror attack, injecting even more hatred and vitriol into the narrative. Tensions between Buddhists and Muslims, even non-Rohingya Muslims, were a consistent part of our coverage in the months leading up to the election, even before the "Muslim Army" story broke.]

Considering the circumstances, the "Muslim Army"

Mandalay, November 8 2015: A voting official displays a vote for the National League for Democracy to the crowd.

Mandalay, November 8 2015: Young voters sit on the courtyard walls of a polling station to listen to officials announce the election count live over a megaphone.

Yangon, November 5, 2016: A trishaw driver takes a midday break to read the day's news in one of the *Myanmar Times'* rival Myanmar-language publications.

Sidoktaya village, August 9, 2015: Aung San Suu Kyi delivers aid to flood victims in the Bamar heartland—and also campaigns for the upcoming national election.

တပ်နှင့်ပြည်သူလက်တွဲ၍ ပြည်ထောင်စုဖြိုခွဲသူမှန်သမျှ ချေမှုန်းကြ။
TATMADAW AND THE PEOPLE, COOPERATE AND CRUSH ALL THOSE HARMING THE UNION.

Mandalay, October 8, 2016: The south wall of Mandalay's Royal Palace still sports a billboard from the old military regime.

Sidoktaya village, August 9, 2015: Crowds of supporters crush forward to get a glimpse of Aung San Suu Kyi.

allegations were big news—if true, they proved that the Tatmadaw, Myanmar's military, had evidence of an imminent insurgency. If they were false, as was more likely the case, the news showed the former junta leaders rounding up innocent Muslim men on trumped-up charges. It was obvious front-page content.

A few days after the coverage ran, the Chairman told us not to use the word *Muslim* on the front page ever again. He extended that decree to anything "religious," apparently incensed to discover that our paper was considered "pro-Muslim" in some circles. The demands came in a list, bullet-pointed and signed by our British CEO, an affable old businessman with an eye toward retirement.

The editorial staff was stunned. Just as a nationwide democratic transfer of power had finally taken hold, our owner wanted to regress and censor a major news story? A few of our veteran leaders—including some who'd endured years of government censorship during the previous regime—fired off a response. My favorite excerpt comes from an early draft:

> We were informed at our meeting with the CEO and COO that the *Myanmar Times* was a "pro-Muslim" newspaper. This allegation is false. Neither official could, when repeatedly

asked, provide the slightest evidence to support it. The fact is that much—but by no means all—mainstream Bamar/Buddhist opinion is anti-Muslim, a sentiment not shared by the editorial staff of our newspaper, nor, we believe, the huge majority of its readers. We believe the self-contradictory, inept and unrealistic instructions contained in the December 14 Notice would, if widely known, lead to a significant drop in the number of readers who now trust our newspaper to provide them with impartial, factual, balanced and well-researched information about what is going on in this country.

The showdown felt like a big deal to me, the newest member on staff, but then the office closed for a week between Christmas and New Year's. In absentia, tensions diffused. No newspapers were printed; no rules were followed or not followed. When everyone returned to work in January, we tentatively eased back into the way things used to be.

One strange thing about the *Myanmar Times*: the paper didn't have a true editor in chief. A beloved managing editor with a calm demeanor tended to make final calls, but each beat editor worked with their staff to oversee their individual section. It was organic and ad hoc.

In the heart of the dry season, the Chairman ended that tradition and brought in a Malaysian man named Bill Tegjeu to serve as our new editor in chief. The incoming supervisor's CV revealed that he'd worked at a Malaysian newspaper in the early 1990s before leaving for a stint in advertising. There was a restaurant/pub/beach resort he ran for four years. That flamed out, apparently, leading to a few years of freelancing before the most alarming résumé entry: helping an online news site hire "an entirely new back-end operations team, including the subs desk."

The expat editorial staff swapped conspiracy theories over milk tea at the sidewalk tea shop. Some of us were convinced he'd been hired to fire us all, but the most logical conclusion was that the Chairman had hired Tegjeu to gain a tighter grip on editorial control in response to the Muslims-on-the-front-page ordeal. I wondered how the local reporters would feel about the new supervisor.

He arrived in February, a scowling man of few words who spared little time to communicate with us. Nobody knew how he was supposed to fit into our editing workflow, and uncertainty blossomed into scarcely concealed frustration. One of our most experienced editors kicked a desk after Tegjeu pushed to keep a religion story off the front page—in the end, the story was buried and our editor limped off a broken toe.

Meanwhile, the world outside the newsroom looked sunnily upon Myanmar's ongoing democratic transition. Aung San Suu Kyi, imprisoned for fifteen years over a twenty-one-year period due to her role in the democratic uprising of 1988, was technically barred from assuming the presidency due to a clause in the military-designed constitution; in a clever twist of semantics she simply declared herself "state counselor" instead and appointed a puppet president in her shadow.

Though it retained an effective veto in Parliament, the military peacefully handed over power and accepted its electoral defeat, giving the woman they'd once confined to house arrest the reins to run the country. Myanmar-language newspapers on every street corner trumpeted the positive changes to come, with photos of the national heroine on every front page.

The changes inside the newsroom continued to dismay us. By April, our managing editor had resigned to work at a new rival publication. Tegjeu hired a friend from Malaysia to replace him—a man with no Myanmar experience and uncertain editing skills. Then the editor who'd kicked the desk quit, fed up with our ebbing independence after Tegjeu forced us to print an unmerited apology to one of our owner's friends. His position went unfilled. When our CEO finally retired, exhausted by all the personnel decisions, the Chairman named Tegjeu the CEO, awarding him financial control to go along with his grip on editorial content. The new CEO/editor in chief immediately promoted our chief Myanmar political reporter to chief of staff, effectively pushing one of the country's most well-connected reporters out of the game.

The skeletal remaining staff was shocked, but we kept reporting as best we could. A watershed moment came in October, when a major Rohingya story broke: military sources were reporting that a band of Muslim insurgents had killed nine border guards in northern Rakhine State. In response, the Tatmadaw kicked off a scorched-earth counterinsurgency campaign in the area where most of the nation's Rohingya live. As the military carried out its hunt for terrorists, our special-investigations editor wrote about dozens of rape allegations leveled at the soldiers by Rohingya women.

It was an explosive piece. Over the weekend, the spokesperson for the puppet president weighed in on the story via Facebook, viciously attacking the author's reporting and ethics. Soon, Myanmar's equivalent of the far right was calling the *Myanmar Times* "fake news" on Facebook. The presidential spokesperson even posted a photo of the article, circling the author's name and photo in red. We were horrified: a representative of Aung San Suu Kyi's administration had targeted one of our own.

Tegjeu and a newly hired COO—a former spook in the ministry of information—met the editor at a downtown bar four days after the story ran. They fired her on the spot, citing a clause in our contracts that prohibited "behavior that brings ill repute to the brand." The entire staff was also reprimanded, and instructed not to report on the ongoing security operations, Muslims, or the military.

We all wanted to, but only the business editor rage-quit in response. The rest of us struggled with what to do. On one hand, none of us wanted to be complicit in the cover-up of outrageous human rights abuses. But on the other, nobody wanted to abandon our paper, or our local coworkers, to this new standard. We'd entered the realm of full-on, government-driven muzzling of independent press—a relapse into the years of military dictatorship. Fight-or-flight instincts kicked in.

By the end of 2016, more than a year had passed since the landmark election, and the NLD was slowly establishing control in Myanmar. Aung San Suu Kyi, awarded the Nobel Peace Prize in 1991 for her nonviolent activism against the military regime, had tried to plough ahead on a peace process to end the country's decades-long civil war. The United States had lifted the last of its sanctions on certain members of the elite "crony" class, many of whom had been blacklisted due to connections with the former military regime. Tourism companies routinely listed Myanmar as one of the hottest destinations for the intrepid wanderluster.

And yet the country's new leader remained largely silent on the Rohingya issue, refusing to grant journalists access to the region, denying reports of abuse, and defending military protocol. The *Myanmar Times* remained mute, too. I participated as needed, filling the sports pages with updates on the national team's soccer matches.

One former editor would later point out the irony of watching a newspaper that had endured so much hardship under military rule being reduced to rubbish at such a promising time. The *Myanmar Times* had survived an official censorship program (complete with redlining government officials and last-minute front-page redesigns), a major cyclone, two different military leaders, and a monk-led revolution—censored or uncensored, it had always maintained a singular and independent mission, bent on covering the news it could. But just as freedom of the press seemed more assured than ever, we lost all semblance of editorial independence.

I realized then that truth doesn't depend on who runs a country; it depends on who runs a country's newspaper.

Morale dried up as more staff left. The newsroom, once electric with the hum of gathering news, lost its buzz. The pages grew thinner on local content and heavier on wire-service material that we simply copied-and-pasted into print. Subscribers began to pull out.

I stayed on longer than I should have. I needed the money and the job was easy. The paper was no longer "the heartbeat of the nation"—or maybe it was, and the nation just didn't have much heart for news about the Rohingya. Regardless, I'd long since abandoned my wide-eyed idealism. Facebook was right: we were fake news, the dregs of what's left when you omit the real story.

In January 2017, a reporter turned in a carefully

researched two-thousand-word feature story on military land-grabbing near the Thai border. By then, so many editors had left that I—with less than a year and a half of experience—was running the weekend features section. Knowing Tegjeu would want to see it, I ran the piece by him. He barely skimmed the text and handed it back with a shake of his head: "Nothing negative about the military."

That was the breaking point for me, and I turned in my notice. There was only a handful of native English speakers left at that point, holding up various pillars of the old news beats, but we dropped off one by one. Our best Myanmar-language reporters left as well, some to better journalism opportunities at wire services and others to less-scandalous careers: the reporter who once covered rebel armies now runs a small convenience store on the outskirts of Yangon.

A few replacement native-English-speaking editors have finally been hired, and the paper continues to come out daily. Tegjeu quit not long after I did, citing family reasons. If he'd been hired to clean house, it seemed he did his job well: only two of the original fourteen foreigners who'd worked at the paper when I arrived remained after I left, and both jumped ship not long after.

The Chairman has hired a new editor-in-chief from Thailand, one with a surprisingly good reputation in the industry. Respect for him is falling fast, however, as he recently seemed to equivocate newspapers with propaganda. "The government wants to construct the Myanmar narrative, which is still absent," he said in an August 2017 panel discussion. "You need a massive [number of] people to believe the same thing."

The print edition still appears on newsstands, with misspelled headlines and stories about generals donating huge sums to monasteries. On some days it rivals the state-run *Global New Light of Myanmar* for its willingness to ignore any stories that reflect poorly on the Tatmadaw. Nobody I know takes the *Myanmar Times* seriously anymore.

And the Rohingya crisis the newspaper refused to report on has only grown more dire. In August 2017 an armed group claiming to be Rohingya attacked Myanmar border patrol agents in a strike reminiscent of the October 2016 attack. Twelve soldiers died, and, once again, the Tatmadaw responded with a scorched-earth campaign that has left multiple villages in flames despite the season's heavy monsoon rains. More than sixty thousand people fled in the first week after the attacks, and scores turned up dead, many drowned, in the exodus. At the time of this writing, the

UN estimates that the refugee population in Bangladesh could exceed three hundred thousand in a matter of days.

Once again, Aung San Suu Kyi refused to let international media into the area where the Rohingya live or even attempt to rein in the Tatmadaw. Days before the attack, her office released a statement accusing international aid groups—including the UN—of aiding and abetting "terrorists" inside the country. More and more of my Myanmar friends have begun sharing articles and status updates that warn about Western media "propaganda" and label any accusations of Rohingya mistreatment "fake news." These days, the *Myanmar Times* doesn't get the criticism it used to.

I ended up sticking around Yangon for a few months after I quit the paper. Hustling for airline magazines and the occasional online story, I attempted a career as a freelancer—but without a firm grasp on the language, I began to wonder if maybe these weren't my stories to tell. This country needs trained Myanmar journalists, I thought. Not another foreigner trying to make a name for himself.

It wasn't long before I purchased a one-way ticket home. My days became a blur of goodbye dinners and packing boxes; I found myself dreading my departure as much as I looked forward to it. The truth is, for all of Myanmar's rough edges, it remains an exceedingly hard place to leave behind.

I flew out of Yangon on a typically rainy July afternoon one hundred weeks after I'd first arrived, landing in Nashville two days and nine thousand miles later. The reverse culture shock rattled me at first: all the country music, and American excess, and central air-conditioning.

But for the most part, it's been pretty easy to assimilate. There's plenty of fake news 'round these parts—and at least I have experience.

LESS

by IACOPO BARISON

(Translated by Gregorio Magini)

{ - }

WHERE'S MY SHIRT?"
I looked at her, didn't know what to say.
We were three feet apart, far away, and in the middle there was the end of the world. We waited.

PLUS

by IACOPO BARISON

(Translated by Gregorio Magini)

{+}

WHERE'S MY SHIRT?"

The English girl from Bristol is pretty revved up because she lost her shirt and she's been looking for it and her bra is a size too small, so a couple of pretty healthy guys surround her and try talking to her but the music is too loud; no one's able to communicate.

Anyway, I have an eternal headache and the weed is starting to take effect and it's raining and there's a swimming pool, but it's covered. I guess it's empty. I've been here for half an hour and I still haven't figured out whose party it is. Maybe some colleague of mine, a director of political sci-fi, or a production company, or maybe nobody in particular, and the party just took form from a spark on its own, heedless of the world, then people started talking about it and sharing invitations.

I leave the English girl where she is—she's in tears now—and the DJ is playing Katy Perry and a boy of about twenty or so, bearded, short hair, approaches me and says: "Hey! I know you."

I don't know what to say. I keep walking and mumble: "Yeah, of course," and he loses interest and turns and repeats an identical sentence, same words and same inflection, to someone else.

I didn't really want to come, but I knew I had to, so I put on some clothes at random and the early evening traffic drove me here, to this nobody's party, and now I do my best to smile but I can't. Tomorrow morning I have an interview.

There's a guy in the bathroom. He says that a friend of his (a totally honest guy, he specifies) told him some unbelievable story, and he's trying to sum it up, but it's not easy. It sounds like a fairy tale. A friend of this friend of his, according to the story, discovered that every night his parents got into his PC and deleted bits of his thesis, here and there, like ten thousand characters at a time, and he was too absent-minded and too full of prescription drugs to notice and so he kept writing, and the thesis would never end, remaining an unfinished draft eternally.

"Andromache's shroud, you know?" says the guy in the bathroom, and I wash my face and keep listening.

He kept writing the thesis for a couple of years, then he finally realized what was going on. Writing, by then, had become a condition of life, a sort of second nature. He lived with his parents. They were rich, and had a beautiful house. Completing the thesis, presenting it, graduating, would have had a number of consequences, a loss of privileges. It was how his parents managed to keep him young, under control.

"If he finished it, this friend of this friend of mine would have had to look for a job, a place to live, a whole new emotional dimension. Which was what his mother, in particular, wanted to avoid, and his father followed in her wake," he tells me, and I walk out of the bathroom and check the time and realize it's late—maybe I should go.

Leaving the villa, my clothes get drenched in the rain. A girl in shorts and an Arcade Fire T-shirt opens her arms and then her mouth and tries to catch the falling drops. I say: "Watch it. You're going to slip."

"No, I won't," she replies. I step forward and say: "Humans have been around for eleven thousand generations. How would you feel if ours was the last?"

"Uh," she muses, "probably better. You?"

I look at the sky. Before we broke up, my girlfriend wanted to go to the Natural History Museum. It was Saturday, we were trying to find some diversion. There was a small-scale replica of an asteroid. It was perfectly convincing. It was about to hit Earth, somewhere between France and Russia. We were simultaneously intimidated and fascinated and the museum was almost empty. I pulled out my smartphone, took a picture.

"So this would be the apocalypse?" my girlfriend asked.

I looked at her, didn't know what to say. We were three feet apart, far away, and in the middle there was the end of the world. We waited.

VANISHING POINT

A MÖBIUS ATLAS

story and photos by MERRILL FEITELL

Then there was the winter I spent living in my parents' basement.

I'd just stopped by for a quick summer visit, but it was December and I still hadn't left.

My father was dying in my childhood bedroom and I was caught without the job, lease, partner, or kid that would've qualified as an excuse to leave.

If I sound insensitive, it's because my father had been dying for as long as I could remember, even back when he was a young, healthy man.

He liked to get us all dancing around him, frothing with worry until we turned on each other.

I still wonder which part he liked best: the three of us dancing around him or the fact that we'd do this and then invariably turn on each other—but we all skated this switch seamlessly, our family Möbius strip

I grew up facing west. There was a lot of yelling and the family dog was always vanishing under the beds.

You could trust her animal instincts; the sound of her clawing out from beneath a box spring meant the coast was clear, the rage had passed. After she died, there was no way of knowing.

From my childhood bedroom, I could see two possible vanishing points: you could go west or you could go down.

And there I was again, almost forty, with my own dog in tow, dancing full-time around my dying dad.

Suffice it to say these were bleak days.

With an ambivalent non-boyfriend in the West and my own ambivalence toward my dying family in the East, I hadn't committed to much more than freelance gigs and sublets on either coast.

But I'd committed myself to the dog.

I'd rescued the dog from the terror of a high-kill shelter; how could I subject him to my family? There was always someone yelling: *Just let me die already*; someone slamming the blender around; slamming a door; someone hurling a dripping urinal right at your face.

I had to get him out of there; he was too big to hide under a bed.

I'd catch myself looking out at the familiar childhood view, considering—*theoretically*—which would be less cruel: to jump with the dog or to leave him behind?

I knew there were places I'd wanted to go
but I couldn't remember what they were
anymore. Besides, desire alone was never
good enough reason.

The best I could do was borrow a book
on meditation from the public library.
The only exercise I tried was called "The
Ideal Image."

The instructions were to imagine my
meditating self reflected in a mirror—and
then to imagine the world beyond the self,
the lush fields and snow-capped mountains, et cetera.

Do this for four minutes, the book said.

The dog and I kept at it for years.

What choice did we have? We could
go west, or we could go down. We started
out west and just kept going.

Since 1872, we've had photographic proof that a running horse does, in fact, lift all four feet off the ground at the same time.

Whether you're looking at horse, dog, or human, in Eadweard Muybridge's freeze-frames it's plain to see that the animal in swift motion experiences a moment of suspension; with its feet off the ground, it appears to be flying.

In other words, with its feet off the ground, the flying animal can't help but lose all contact with the earth.

We often lost all contact, which was never the point, but sometimes I mistook this for vanishing.

Is it any wonder I so often drove at night? If you can blot out the vastness, it's possible to forget just how alone a creature can be.

The only other antidote for such emptiness is to keep moving.

Motion was its own illusion of safety—like a fully charged phone, useless and searching for signal; like a big-barked dog afraid of plastic bags and wind.

Motion was hope and hopelessness in the same disguise.

Pick a place, any place! I just couldn't.

Put an ant on a Möbius strip and it'll keep crawling the endless, one-sided loop.

Sometimes I'd think about the pioneers, wondering if all those settlers were just settling.

Did they stop their wagon trains because they'd reached the ideal place? Or did they simply wake up one day no longer driven to keep on driving?

The world is vast, I once read on a treasure map posted on a rest-stop wall. *You need purpose to land, a missing treasure you're seeking.*

What's our missing treasure? I asked the dog, who, bored by the heartland, likes to snooze through it in the backseat. I drove all night, waiting for his answer.

Every trip we run out of road, but the dog and I are just like any other pair of objects in motion: likely to stay in motion until acted upon by an outside force.

Sure, there were outside forces acting upon us all along, but most of them just pushed us onward.

Once, at the hospital, I spent nearly an hour trying to convince my dad it was okay to shit in the bed.

I sat holding his hand, trying to undo the training his own mother had put into effect eighty years prior. It was going about as well as a horrible thing can.

Sometimes he'd listen to me, the seldom-seen daughter.

I tried to be a good citizen of our family—dancing around, frothing with worry, cooing until, at long last, my catheterized and constipated father crapped, as we all knew he should. But then came the turn—the seamless family flip—from citizenry into something ready to explode.

Whatever happened that day was humiliating enough that I bolted—like any object accelerating in direct proportion to the magnitude of net force applied. I ran out of the room and down the hall, toward the elevator and the dog, who'd been left alone in my parents' apartment.

I could hear someone chasing me and assumed it was my brother. He'd finally absorbed so much of our father's rage that he'd begun, periodically, to emit it. I was less afraid of what he might do to me than I was of how little it mattered—except, I reminded myself, whatever happened to me would matter to the dog.

But the person chasing me wasn't my brother; it was the wife of the man behind the curtain who shared a room with my dad. *You need to know this*, she said.

I stood there like a headshy stray as she held onto my arm, trying to get me to face her. *You were doing great in there. We were listening. That wasn't about you. What happened in there, it wasn't about you.*

She did not say the familiar things: *Who the fuck do you think you are? Who does she think she is?*

She was this angelic outside force testifying in the hospital corridor and what she said was: *Go. You're right to get gone.*

Forget the discomforting fact of losing contact with the earth. Four out of five animals will tell you the same thing: *Who cares what you lose? Nothing feels better than flying.*

I once asked the ambivalent non-boyfriend in the West where he'd go if he could go anywhere. *Morocco*, he said.

I was impressed that he had an answer. I'd driven all those miles and still couldn't name a specific place. Forget "The Ideal Image"—my meditative practice was momentum and not giving a shit.

But somehow the rear view starts to soften and there I am, heading back to start the dance all over again.

Oh, the pity of my father's sad, scrambled brain! He could be so funny when he wanted to be, and he so loved the dog. His demented rage was different—but we all knew the song and we kept dancing to it.

I let him lead me: across a park to a river's cool, muddy banks; to a senior center's porch where, I imagine, he must've been doted on and treated to treats.

Then I drove to the pound, where the state grants five days of shelter before the stray is to be *humanely destroyed*.

The facility director explained that she tries to buy time for any stray who strikes her as adoption-worthy; she has to do the rounding-up and gassing herself. Years had passed, but the dog clearly remembered her.

I could relate to the profound ambivalence with which he greeted his savior/captor.

On the way out of town, I pulled up to the animal dropbox, left the car running, and stood there taking pictures, the dog's eyes gigantic with terror as he sat subjected, cowering in the backseat.

I did this. And I kept at it until dark. I suppose I was just dawdling, trying to buy another night before arriving at my parents' place.

I'll tell you this, Muybridge: the animal in terror also experiences a moment of suspension. The breath halts; the eyes get huge; the animal in terror appears frozen in place. You can get rid of the photos, but you end up haunted just the same.

There we were—two creatures paralyzed by the proximity of a childhood home.

A vanishing point is defined as follows:
1. *the point at which receding parallel lines appear to converge*
2. *the point at which a diminishing object disappears altogether*

Here's what I've learned about the vanishing point: No matter how hard I gun it, I never get there and nothing ever altogether disappears.

Where are you? my father kept asking until he couldn't anymore. *Where are you now?*

At first, just the states in the middle confused him, but eventually there were only two places he could fathom: one could be *Here* or one could be *Gone*.

Where are we going? Where have we been?
Two questions; same answer. It's like we
really are stuck on a Möbius strip.

Once upon a time, I hot-glued a camera
to the dash. Now I sift through the pictures
as if a sequence of fragments might explain
all this motion, revealing how many hooves
we've had off the ground and everything
else that's impossible to see in real time.

Our first trip was in winter and hectic;
I was trying to outrun a convergence of
storms. The dog was so scared, I feared he'd
bolt to resume his life as a stray. But he
didn't. *Come, sit*, I said. That's all it took.

Now look at us: two citizens of nowhere
maintaining a mutually beneficial iner-
tia—I'd go anywhere on Earth if it meant
this dog would stay forever.

Where are we now? the dog asks when
the late-night deceleration is enough to
rouse him, his big head suddenly overtak-
ing the rear view.

When I say, *Let's go home*, he heads for
the car. It's like we're living a riddle: Pete
and Repeat went out on a boat; Pete fell
overboard. Who was left?

CRUMB CAKE

by ETGAR KERET

(Translated by Sondra Silverston)

FOR MY FIFTIETH BIRTHDAY, Mom takes me to Fat Charley's Diner for lunch. I want to order a pancake tower with maple syrup and whipped cream, but Mom asks me to order something healthier.

"It's my birthday," I insist, "my fiftieth birthday. Let me order the pancakes. Just this once. Instead of cake."

"But I already baked you a cake," Mom grumbles, "a crumb cake, your favorite."

"If you let me eat pancakes, I won't even taste the cake," I promise. After thinking for a minute, she says grudgingly,

"I'll let you eat pancakes and cake, too, just this once, only because today's your birthday."

Fat Charley brings me the pancake tower with a lit sparkler on top. He sings "Happy Birthday" in a hoarse voice, waiting for Mom to join in, but all she does is shoot the pancake tower an angry glance. So I sing with him instead.

"How old are you?" Charley asks.

"Fifty," I say.

"Fifty years old and still celebrating with your mom?" He gives an appreciative whistle and goes on, "I envy you, Mrs. Piekov. My daughter is half his age and she hasn't wanted to celebrate her birthday with us for ages. We're too old for her."

"What does your daughter do?" Mom asks without taking her eyes off the pile of pancakes on my plate.

"I don't exactly know," Charley admits. "Something in high-tech."

"My son is fat and unemployed," Mom says in a half-whisper, "so don't be so quick to envy me."

"He's not fat," Charley mumbles, trying to smile. Compared to Charley, I'm really not fat.

"I'm not unemployed either," I add, my mouth full of pancakes.

"Sweetie," Mom says, "organizing my pills in a box for two dollars a day doesn't qualify as a job."

"Congratulations!" Charley says to me. "Hearty appetite and congratulations!" and backs slowly away from our table as if he were retreating from a growling dog. When Mom goes to the restroom, Charley comes back.

"I want you to know," he says, "that you're doing a really good deed. By living with your mom and everything. After my father died, my mother lived alone. You should have seen her. She burned out faster than the sparkler on your pancakes. Your mother can gripe till tomorrow, but you're keeping her alive, and that's a good deed right out of the good book. 'Honor thy father and thy mother.' How are the pancakes?"

"Fantastic," I say. "Too bad I can't come here more often."

"If you're in the neighborhood, you're always welcome to drop in," Charley says and winks at me. "I'll be glad to give you more. Free of charge." I don't know what to say, so I just smile and nod. "Really," Charley says, "it would make me happy. My daughter hasn't eaten my pancakes for years. She's always on a diet."

"I'll come," I tell Charley. "I promise!"

"Great," Charley says, nodding. "And I promise not to say a word about it to your mother. Scout's honor."

On the way home, we stop at a 7-Eleven and Mom says that because it's my birthday, I can choose one thing as a present. I want a bubblegum-flavored energy drink, but Mom says

I've had enough sugar for one day, so I ask her to buy me a lottery ticket. But she says that, on principle, she's against gambling because it teaches people to be passive, and instead of doing something to change their destiny, all they do is sit on their fat behinds and wait for luck to save them.

"You know what the chances are of winning the lottery?" she asks. "One in a million, even less. Just think about it: we have a better chance of being killed in a car accident on the way home than you do of winning." After a brief silence, she adds, "But if you insist, I'll buy it for you." I insist and she buys it for me. I fold the lottery ticket twice, once along the width and once along the length, and shove it into the small front pocket of my jeans. My dad died in a car accident on the way home a long time ago, when I was still in my mother's womb, so go figure.

At night, I want to watch the basketball game. The Warriors are really good this year. That Curry is so hot on the three-point shots; I never saw anything like it. He shoots without even looking at the basket and the balls drop into the hoop one after another. Mom won't let me. She says she read in *TV Guide* that there's a special about the poorest places in the world on National Geographic.

"Can't you skip it for me?" I ask. "After all, today's my birthday." But Mom insists that my birthday started yesterday and ended at sunset, so now it's just a regular day.

While Mom watches the program, I go into the kitchen and organize her pills in the box. She takes more than thirty pills a day. Ten in the morning and twenty-something at night. Pills for blood pressure, cholesterol, her heart, her thyroid. So many pills that just swallowing them makes you full. Really, I don't think there's a disease in the world she doesn't have. Except for AIDS, maybe. And lupus. After I finish organizing the pills in the box, I sit down next to her on the couch and watch the program with her. They're showing a humpbacked kid who lives in the poorest neighborhood in Calcutta. At night, before he goes to sleep, his parents tie him with a rope so he'll sleep bent over. That way, the narrator explains, his hump will get bigger, and when he grows up, it'll make people feel really sorry for him and give him a strong advantage in the tough competition with other beggars in the city. I'm not someone who cries a lot, but that kid's story is really sad.

"You want me to switch to basketball?" Mom asks in a soft voice and ruffles my hair.

"No," I say, wiping my tears with my sleeve and smiling at her. "This is an interesting program." It really is an interesting program.

"I'm sorry I said mean things about you in the diner," she says. "You're a good boy."

"It's okay," I say, and kiss her on the cheek. "It didn't bother me at all."

The next morning, I go to the eye doctor with Mom. He shows her a chart with letters on it and asks her to read them out loud. She shouts the letters she can see, and insists on guessing the ones she doesn't, as if a lucky guess will help cure her. The doctor adds another pill to her collection, to be taken once a day, for the glaucoma. After the doctor, we go to Walgreens to buy the new pill, and so I won't forget, I add it to the box in the compartment for the night pills as soon as we get home. Then I change into my tracksuit, take my basketball, and go out to the children's court. I'm not a great player, but if the kids there are young enough, they're sure I'm a god.

A few years ago, I had a run-in with a redheaded mother with tattoos who got stressed because I was playing with her son. The minute she saw me on the court with him, she told me in a really loud voice that I shouldn't dare touch him. I explained to her that, according to the rules of basketball, you're allowed to touch your opponent when you're guarding him, and she had nothing to worry about: I knew I was bigger and stronger than her cute little son, and anyway, even when I'm guarding, I do it carefully. But she, instead of listening, got even angrier. "And don't you dare call my son 'cute,' you pervert," she screamed and threw her paper cup of coffee right in my face. Luckily for me, the coffee was lukewarm, but still, it stained my clothes.

After that incident, I didn't go back there for a few months, but then the playoffs started, and when you see good games, it makes you want to play, too. I didn't want to go back there, because I was afraid the redhead with the tattoos would be there and start screaming again, so instead, I asked Mom if we could buy a basket of our own and hang it in the yard. That was the first time I told Mom about what happened on the basketball court, and she got very quiet, the way she always does when she's really mad. Then she told me to put on my tracksuit and take my basketball, and we left the house.

On the way to the court, she told me that all the parents of the children who play with me there should thank me because there aren't many grown-ups in the world who still have enough gentleness and goodness in them to play like I do with children and teach them things.

"Sweetie," she said, her voice cracking, "when we get to the court, if you see that stupid tattooed monkey again, you tell me, okay?" I nodded, but in my heart I was praying that the tattooed redhead wouldn't be there, because I knew that even though Mom is old, she could easily smash that woman's head with her cane.

When we reached the court, Mom sat down on a bench and checked out all the other parents like a bodyguard trying to spot an assassin. At first, I had an empty half-court to myself, and just dribbled and shot baskets alone, but very quickly the kids on the other half of the court asked me to join them because they were missing a player. At the end of the game, when I made the winning basket, I looked over at Mom, who was still sitting on the bench pretending to be reading something on her cell phone, and I knew she'd seen everything and was proud.

Now, when I reach the court, there are no kids there and I just take some lazy shots that miss the basket, but after about fifteen minutes, I get bored. Fat Charley's Diner is barely a five-minute walk away, and when I get there, it's almost empty and Charley is really glad to see me.

"Hey, hoop star," he says. "Were you playing basketball?" I shrug and tell him that there was no one on the court.

"It's still early," he says and winks at me, "but by the time you finish the mountain of pancakes I'm going to make you, there will definitely be a few people there." Charley's pancakes are really fantastic. When I finish eating, I thank him and ask again if he's sure it's okay for me to eat there without paying.

"Whenever you want, hoop star," he says. "The pleasure is all mine."

"And you won't tell my mom about the pancakes, right?" I ask him before I leave. "Don't worry." Charley laughs and pats his big stomach. "Your secret is buried deep in my potbelly."

The big lottery drawing takes place on Saturday nights. Mom reminds me about it right after she takes her pills.

"Are you in suspense?" she asks. I shrug. She tells me again that my chance of winning is less than one in a million, and then asks me what I'd do if I did happen to win. I shrug again and say I would definitely send some of the money to that humpbacked kid we saw on TV. Mom laughs and says the film was made more than ten years ago and it's very possible that the humpbacked kid is now a humpbacked grownup and he's begged so much that he doesn't need favors from anyone. Or maybe he died from one of those diseases those people get because they don't wash their hands.

"Never mind the children from National Geographic," she says and ruffles my hair the way I like her to. "What would you want for yourself?" I shrug again, because I really don't know. "If you win, you'll probably move to a big place of your own and buy a season ticket to sit in the VIP box for all the Warriors games, and hire a stupid Filipina to organize my medications instead of you," Mom says, giving me a not-very-happy smile. I actually like organizing Mom's pills for her; it relaxes me.

"I don't like going to games," I say. "Remember when we went to visit Uncle Larry in Oakland and he took me to a game? We stood in line for almost an hour and the ushers at the entrance yelled at everyone who went inside."

"Then no season ticket," Mom says. "So what do you think you'd buy?"

"Maybe a TV for my room," I say, "but a really big one, not like the one we have in the living room."

"Sweetie," Mom says, laughing, "the first prize is sixty-three million dollars. If you win, you'll have to think of something else besides a large-screen TV."

This is my first time ever watching a lottery draw. There's a kind of transparent machine full of ping-pong balls and each ball has a number on it. The woman operating the machine is blond and she smiles nervously the whole time. Mom says that her bust isn't real and you can see right away that she's had Botox injections because nothing on her forehead moves. Then Mom says she has to go to the bathroom. This year, she's developed a serious problem with her bladder and that's why she has to go to the bathroom every half hour.

"Good luck, sweetie. If you see that you've won while I'm peeing, give a yell and I'll run out with my underpants down," she says with a laugh and gives me a kiss before she gets up from the couch. "But don't yell for no reason, you hear me? You remember what the doctor said about my heart."

The blond with the nervous smile presses a button that turns on the machine. I look at her forehead. Mom's right: nothing moves there. The first ball that drops out of the machine has the number 46 on it, which is the number of our house. The second one has the number 30, which is the age Mom was when my dad died and I was born. The third ball has the number 33, which is the number of pills Mom took every day before she got the prescription for the glaucoma pill, and the fourth ball has the number 1, which is the number of sparklers Charley lit on my pancake tower. It's weird how all the numbers the blond with the frozen forehead chooses are connected to my life and Mom's, and how all those numbers are written on my ticket. I don't even check the last two numbers; I just keep thinking about what could make a woman inject herself with stuff that paralyzes her forehead and how sad it would be if Mom and I had to live in separate houses instead of together.

When Mom comes back to the couch, I'm already watching the sports channel, but she insists that we switch to Fox because it's time for the evening news broadcast. The newscasters talk about a suicide bombing in Pakistan that killed sixty-seven people. They don't mention the name of the city where the bombing happened and I just hope it isn't Calcutta. Mom explains to me that Calcutta is in India, and Pakistan is a different country, even worse than India. "The things that people do to each other," she says as she gets up and starts walking slowly toward the kitchen. Terror attacks on TV always make her hungry. Mom asks if I want her to make us scrambled eggs and I tell her I'm hungry, but not for eggs.

"Want the last slice of the crumb cake I baked for your birthday?" she calls from the kitchen.

"You'll let me eat something sweet even though it's nighttime already?" I ask. Usually she's very strict about things like that.

"Today's a special day," she says. "Today is the day you didn't win the lottery. You deserve a consolation prize for that."

"Why are you so sure I didn't win?" I ask.

"Because I didn't hear you yell like you promised," she laughs.

"Even if I screamed you wouldn't have heard. You're half-deaf," I say, smiling back at her.

"Half-deaf and half-dead," Mom says with a nod as she puts the last slice of cake on the table for me. "But tell me the truth, sweetie, do you know anyone else in the whole wide world who can make a crumb cake as delicious as mine?"

CUTTING HORSE

by LATOYA WATKINS

THIS HORSE BEING IN my backyard got me in some kind of trouble. That much I know. Since I got home from work, I been sitting back here flipping between news channels, watching this woman, her dude, and the laws on the national stations and folks looking for this horse on the local ones.

It was seven horses got out the gates of them stables around the corner, but she the only one still ain't back with them. Now they saying she been stolen. Say they received reports that the suspect, a black male, holding the horse in the area. The Rowlett police chief told the cameras they got to proceed with caution 'cause they don't want the horse life in no more danger than it already is.

And I'm thinking, Who put horse stables in the middle of the suburbs anyway? When me and my cousin Moochie stacked our paper long enough to buy our land, we went out past Lubbock city limits, out there by the hog pens, and built our stables and shit there. You do that to give the horses room to roam, to feel wild, to feel kind of free. Ain't no room for all them horses on that little patch of land around the corner. All it is is a little corner. Not even two acres. Our horses never ran, closed gate or open. Forty acres of land was enough for them to feel free.

Them sirens, the way they going off in the distance, don't make me move from my loveseat, from my special place under the tarp-tent I set up last spring. My tarp-tent ain't nothing real neat or special. It's more like a sloppy fort that I done set up in the middle of the yard. Got four sturdy wooden beams from the hardware store and just draped the blue tarp over them, nailing it to the top corners and letting the rest hang down like a pharaoh hat. Like I said, it ain't nothing special, but I like it and it's mine.

Instead of getting up and running, trying to get where

somebody need me to be, do what somebody need me to do, I take a drag of the blunt I rolled earlier and keep my eyes focused on the TV screen. This weed make me cough, though. It's some good shit. Them boys on Parker Circle always got good shit.

Through all that, the sirens and the coughing, I keep my eyes on the woman on the TV screen I got sitting on the stand right in front of me. She yelling at the police that's hovering over her. She mad about how they done slammed her and her dude down on the cement; she got her arms spread out, her hands flat against the ground, and her mouth going. Her dude got the side of his face to the ground and his hands already bound behind his back. He quiet. Mouth closed. Almost like he dead, but ain't nobody been shot yet.

"See. You see my hands? They on the ground. Don't shoot," she saying to the police officer that just cuffed her dude's hands. "We unarmed, y'all," she say to whoever videoing the whole thing. "We ain't done nothing. They messing with us for nothing."

The camera zoom in close to her man face. His eyes look empty. Look shook, like while all these scared men drawed on him, he scared, too, like he remembering what happed to Michael and Eric and Alton and Philando and all of them. I'm remembering them, too. Looking at him all scared, I'm remembering them, too.

I turn my eyes to the blunt, mostly 'cause I know what happen next. Hold it out in front of me and look at it like I can't believe I got it in my hands. I'm looking at it like I ain't roll it myself, like I ain't never seen one. "Damn," I say. "This some good shit." And I mean it.

I work hard loading them packages part-time for UPS every morning, and this here, this blunt be the best part of my day. This the part I work to get to all morning long. This the part where I connect with me, with who I used to be. Every day, I can't believe I survived and made it to this part.

I hear the sound of gunshots firing from the TV, but I don't turn my head back to it. I don't want to see it. It's the real reason why I turned my eyes to this blunt. I done watched this ten times today already and I don't want to watch it again, especially when I think about them sirens out on the street. How they looking for me.

Instead of looking at the screen, I look out to the corner of the yard at the horse, and think about how a hour ago this beautiful beast just pranced up to the orange tarp I put up on the side of the fence I tore down. She a liver chestnut color, and her coat shine like rusty pennies. That shine, that mane, all of it remind me of home.

I think about my cowboy hats and how people used to laugh 'cause I was part gangster, part cowboy. How I loved breeding horses but I needed the game to do it. I think about what I gave up to be here. And I wonder what all this mean. Why this horse brought all her trouble to me.

A hour ago, I sat on my loveseat, tugged at a blunt with my teeth, and spat paper speckles on the ground. I heard my wife car start up from the other side of the fence, the side that's closed in, and I kind of froze. Sat there holding the blunt between both my index fingers and thumbs, like a taco, until I heard her car back out and drive off.

Cole, my wife, ain't come outside to tell me she was leaving. In fact, she ain't come and look for me at all after she made it in from work a few hours earlier, but that's a normal thing these days. She mad with me and I'm tired of her. She want to finish undoing me so I'll be like she want me to be, but I won't let her. I quit peeling parts of myself off after I realized I was the only one doing the peeling. She was keeping herself. Everybody around us keeping theyself. I'm the only one can't be me.

I don't know where she left to. She try to make her storming out mysterious most days. She might've gone blazing toward the baby day care to pick him up before it close or to the grocery store to get something to cook tonight.

I know her lips was poked out and steam was flowing from her ears. And I know she probably called her momma to complain that she sick of me. That she should of married up, not down. That I ain't never gone be the man she want me to be.

When I was sure she was gone, I licked the edges of the blunt and curled it tight into itself. Then I picked up the lighter from the lawn table I pulled under the tent last spring, and I held the blunt under the lighter until it was dry. That's when I smiled. Right after that, the horse pranced up.

This horse that done made her way to my yard got a shiny coat. Somebody take good care of her, but that don't mean she don't know she captive. She been working on that same patch of grass since I opened the gate and let her back here. She ain't no gypsy horse like the ones I loved breeding. Them still the most beautiful beasts to me. All that mane look like ponytails all over they bodies. And we kept ours looking fresh, like they was for shows or something. We pay the hood beautician, Lulu Shepherd, good money to come out and style and condition they mane every week and we fed them like kings. But they wasn't no real show horses. We couldn't be part of that world. We just rode them and showed them off in our hood. Riding the kids, Juneteenth parades, and birthday parties on the East Side. They made our folks happy. Feel like somebodies sometimes. The illegitimacy of our business might of kept us out of the show world, but it didn't keep them good old boys from buying my gypsies. My horses was everything.

This one look like a quarter. Them some nice horses, too. News folks say all seven of them cutting horses. I wonder if these city news reporters even know cutting about more than competitions and stuff. I wonder if the owners even know how important cutting was out on the open range. Folks around here think cutting all about sport, but that ain't where it started.

Cutting horse born to judge, to discern, and most folks, like them around the corner, got them sitting under some panel being judged. Cutting horse know which cattle need branding or sick or any other thing a cow can't open his mouth and say. Know how to read other beasts and move they minds, master them. My granddaddy used to say you make your horse your friend, not your servant. That way they want to do stuff for you. Horse don't want no master 'cause they masters all on they own. Specially cutters. Them folks, the ones looking for the horse and the ones reporting it stole, don't know how much this here horse know, how much she discern. They don't know she know *they* hearts.

I wonder what made them horses leave the way they did. On the news, they played a video somebody took. Them horses crossed Rowlett Road, and that ain't no low-traffic street, but they crossed it without a care in the world. I mean, they busted out that fence and ran pretty to the empty lot next to the Shell gas station across the street from they ranch. Them cars was going crazy, too. Pulling over. Getting out. Snapping pictures like they ain't never seen no horse.

I didn't find out nothing about it till she was already in my yard, lost in that patch of grass. She showed up just like that, in the middle of my watching another black person die before the whole world. From the gap between my fence tarp and the ground, I watched her hooves prance up and then come on around the side to my closed gate and wait for me to open it, like she knew exactly where she was going. When I opened it, she come in like she was invited or something. Come right in and walked by me and went to that very spot she stuck in. I left the gate open for her to leave, but I ain't cut the yard in a while, so she still busy grazing.

"Guess you ain't going back to your people," I say to the horse from my loveseat. She don't look up. She just keep with the grazing. "All right then," I say. "That's what you want."

This my first time ever living in a white neighborhood, and I knew I hated it when my wife looked at the Realtor, smiled, and said, "Yes, Aimee. This is it. This is the one we'll make an offer on." She took one look at how the steps of the front porch ascended and said, "Wow. First time I've seen something so breathtaking. I feel like royalty. Right, Ridley?" When we finished the tour of the inside and was spit out the back door to the backyard, I nodded my head. Something about the smallness of it, thirty-by-thirty in all, made me think I could live in this place. Be happy in this place.

Now I can hear the police sirens out on the street. I can't see no laws yet, though. Not from the alley. Not from behind the fence tarp. They ain't made it to me yet, but I know they coming.

Cole hate how much time I spend in the backyard, but she don't never give me credit for how it used to be. How I was for her that year we was dating and them first two years of our marriage. She don't never thank me for how quick I stopped selling drugs after we met. For how I stopped wearing cowboy hats and boots 'cause she didn't like it. Thought it was country. She don't never talk about how I had my gold teeth removed and got implants in the front to cover up the smallness of my teeth from where they had been filed down for the golds.

I do anything she wanted back then. She was everything to me. Didn't matter that she snore like a freight train or snort when she laugh. I ain't care about her turning her nose up at folks when we rolled through the hood. My sister called her bougie and my boys thought she was poison. And it pissed all of them off how she called me Ridley instead of RJ or Don Juan, like everybody else did. But ain't none of that shit matter to me. I ain't ask her to change nothing about herself. I ain't never wanted her to either. Them pretty brown eyes and that sugar-brown skin was everything to me. She talked proper and knew random shit and all that had me lost in her. She don't talk about none of that, though.

She hate how I done pitched this tent. How I took the loveseat she threw out last spring, covered it with thick plastic, and put it under my tent. She don't like that I spent almost a thousand bucks on a waterproof TV and put it out here with me. That I run cords from the back porch and stay out here most of the time. That I bought a space heater to keep myself warm through the winter and a high-powered fan for the summer. I pass most of my time sitting out here watching animal channels and black men die or reading books about animals and black men dying. She think all I be out here doing is smoking, but she don't know. That she think that mean she don't know at all.

In my mind, I done spent too much time trying to change myself for Cole. Trying not to be Ridley Johnson from West Texas. Ridley Johnson who hustled his way to the ranch he always wanted. Who everybody knew as Don Juan the gypsy horse breeder. Who everybody knew sold the best shit in Lubbock. Who everybody knew always loved horses and ranches and who hustled, honest and fair, till he had his own.

Dude on the TV crying and snot running out his nose, and I'm having a hard time seeing him broke down like that. He trying to talk, tell his story, and his eyes look even more shook than they did when he was lying down for the police with his girl. His eyes sit far apart, like they trying not to be on the same face, and his tears coming back just as quick as he wipe them away and he stuttering out, "We wasn't doing nothing. Creshia talk a lot. Fire off at the mouth, but she a good woman. Don't deserve to die 'cause she say what she want."

A woman, a older one, rubbing his back and telling him it's gone be okay. But dude crying and saying, "We was just walking our baby to school. We ain't got no car, so we got to walk her to school. We wasn't even doing nothing to make them slam us on the ground in the first place. Now she gone. She gone."

Now I'm sitting here watching this news and this beast, waiting for the sirens to reach me, and trying to figure out how to make this world work for me. I followed Cole from West Texas to here after she got the degree her parents sent her there for. Didn't nothing matter that day but her smile and how she was wearing it for me.

She'll be back soon. Gone flip about the horse being back here if she see it. She flipped when I tore the fence down two years ago. That was right after Eric and Mike. That's when I started trying to find myself. Trying to see myself without her. Without thinking about how anybody outside of me see me. Trying to go back to before I was born and be who I was fore any of this.

When we bought the house, the whole fence was some

kind of western red cedar privacy thing. Couldn't see nothing that was going on with the rest of the world from our backyard, so I tore the back of it down, the side that face the alley, with plans of replacing it with a low chain-linked thing. But I liked it open. Better than the closed walls in the house even. So I started moving out to the back little by little. After that, my rebuilding plans just kind of tapered off and I bought the orange tarp and nailed it across the wooden beams from the fence to shut Cole up. The tarp being there ain't really bother me none. I put it up just high enough that I can see the bottom of things. Ain't completely blocked in. I can see some of the world happening.

After she left an hour ago, she called. When my phone vibrated on that table and I watched the seeds and stems I'd separated from the good herb vibrate with it, I knew it was her without even looking at the picture she set for herself when she bought me the phone.

I thought about not answering it. After she leave the house, she like to call and nag me about being in the backyard. She say arguments less uncivilized when she can at least hang up in my face.

But I picked up the phone, wishing she just let me find my peace in peace.

"Yeah" is all I said when I answered.

"You at home?" she asked in a voice, in a language I know she don't use when she at work with all her other accounting people. She sound black, like she used to when it was just me and her, like she used to when I'd take her to my black world and make her forget anything else out there.

"Cole, you saw my car out back. I'm sure you heard the TV when you got out your car after work and when you got back in to leave just now. You know I'm here," I said to her, and I could hear the irritation in my own voice.

I heard the sound of her sucking her jaws, a thing I used to like when we was still new. It made her seem so sassy. So in control to me. That's what I liked about her the most when I met her. That's what made her stand out.

When I first met her, back when I lived in Lubbock, back when I was with my people on the East Side, back where things made sense, she'd do it all the time. The first day I met her, at the taco place on Ninth Street, when she was still a Texas Tech student and didn't know the East Side existed, I stepped to her, licking my lips like I was gone eat her, and said, "Excuse me, Ms. Lady. Can I holler at you for a minute?" She sucked her jaws and it turned me on in a way that none of the East Side chicks ever had.

That was before she knew me, before I begged her to marry me and promised to be a better man. That day, she sucked her jaws and rolled her eyes and said, "Young brother, you'll have to approach me better than that. Now, because you are so very handsome and possess so much potential, I'm just going to turn around and pretend to stare at the menu. That simple act will give you a chance to rewind and speak to me in a manner suitable for a woman of my stature."

The fat girl with her laughed, but I took the opportunity to bandage my ego and try again. I talked her into going out with me that night. At first, I just wanted smash because she'd tried to embarrass me in that public space, but after we went out to that bookstore for coffee, my first time going to a bookstore for some coffee, I wanted all the cats from the hood to see that I was moving on up.

"Yeah, I saw your car, Ridley. Smartass," she said. "I didn't see you, though. I called your name. No answer."

I exhaled but didn't say nothing. I knew where the whole conversation was going. It happened every day. It was her way of breaking me down.

"Let me guess, you outside." And then she added, "Smoking." She spat that last part like it was something disgusting. Like she hated it. Like she hated me. And I just sat there with the phone to my ear for a while, until I realized that she had hung up.

*   *   *

We live on a street of nothing but split-level houses. Cole liked that most about the neighborhood when we was new. Don't usually find nothing like that in Texas. Said it make her feel like she living up north or something. Like she was something else. Somewhere else. Somewhere better.

Anyway, all the split-levels in this neighborhood got second-floor decks and folks like to hang out on them on nice summer evenings and look down on the neighborhood they think they done made. Everybody see everybody backyard from they deck. Sometimes, I come from under my tarp and see Cole and all the other neighbors looking down around me but not really looking down at me. They be shaking they heads, like they disgusted, but all the time they be trying to keep they eyes off me. They been complaining about how they hate looking out at our backyard. How "unappealing" the tarp and the untamed yard is.

I was in the house filling up my water jug the first time the HOA dude pushed the doorbell and complained. I was minding my business at first. I wasn't even gone go in there. Cole done made friends with a lot of the neighbors. I don't know none of them, though. So I usually stay out the way when they drop by.

"Hi, Nicole," dude said. "You got a minute? This is kind of pressing." I recognized dude. He lived on the corner and was always jogging through the neighborhood in colorful bike tights. Real skinny dude with a red face from always lounging on his deck in one of them beach chairs, like he on a real beach or something. When he opened his mouth he sounded like a man trying to sound like a woman. And I thought maybe that's why he was there. That maybe him and Cole cool 'cause they got a lot in common.

Cole stood there with her hand on the door and looked down at her yoga pants and T-shirt, like she was ashamed of herself. She shifted her weight from one leg to the other, and I knew she was embarrassed, so I walked up behind her to support or protect her or something.

Dude's blue eyes shifted up to me, like he was really looking at me for the first time, and then he dropped his eyes to the clipboard he was holding in his hands.

"Sure," she said and opened the door wider. "Of course. Come in, Justin."

"No. No, thank you, Nicole. I'm fine out here," he said all nervous.

After that, he said folks was complaining about the tarp and the backyard and my wife face almost slid off with embarrassment as she tried to explain that we was renovating. I just walked off. I wasn't gone stand there and listen to her lie. Listen to her explain herself like he was the law and she had been caught selling drugs or something.

When dude left, I came back to her. Tried to put my hand on her shoulder. Tried to remember the times we used to touch each other and make each other feel good. Like the time I took her to my land. Let her ride one of my gypsies. She had never been on no horse. I held my hand firm at the softest part of where her hip and ass meet. She was trembling a little bit, but she kept looking down at me saying, "Don't let me go, baby. Don't let me fall." And eventually she stopped trembling. Stopped being scared. My hand on her made her feel safe that day and that's all I wanted to do after HOA dude left. But she pulled away and said, "See, Ridley? See?" Her brown eyes was watery and she looked like she wanted to cry. "We don't live in this neighborhood alone. You have to do something about the backyard. We're supposed to blend in, not stand out. I mean, the TV outside, the weed..." She sighed like she was tired. "It's like you do all these things to ask for trouble."

I ain't scream at her that day. I had already done enough the day I stood up for Mike. I just shrugged my shoulders and told Cole, "Fuck them white folks. Fuck a HOA, too.

We paying for this house just like they paying for theirs," and that was the end of that.

I'm sure some HOA member done called the laws about this horse. I'm sure they done seen her, recognized her from the news. They done looked down here and thought the worst. Thought I was a thief and called the laws on me. That's why the sirens stop and doors slamming right outside my tarp.

I hear all this going on, doors slamming and crowds forming, over the TV news showing black folks marching for the girl that got shot this morning, the one I been watching die all day. I hear all this and still sit there thinking about how I ended up here.

My momma brought me up in the church. Did her best to raise me right. She was a single momma, just like most of my friends' mommas. And I know it broke her heart into pieces when she found out I was selling drugs. She didn't never criticize me, though. I'm sure she prayed for my deliverance. That's just how she is. But she ain't never criticize me or slap the money I give her out my hands. I think she knew the conditions that conditioned me, so she bargained with God and let me be. She named me Ridley for her father, the one she hated, and she let him teach me to ride and appreciate horses. She said they was always gone be the thing I could look away to. Always said black boys need two things: a man to help form them and something they can look away to. I'm gone always be thankful to her for that. Always.

She was glad when I fell in love with Cole. She called her "a good girl." Said she was what she always prayed for me to have. And I guess Cole *is* a good girl. I mean, as long as I was peeling away the layers of myself, things was perfect between us. I guess she thought she was helping make this world safe for us. But I should of known nothing was gone be right after that stuff with Trayvon. I should of known all our differences was just too much. That her parents being college educated and where I come from clashed, like a desperate clucker mixing the wrong drugs together.

"What they doing to us?" dude on TV yelling. "Why they killing us? This got to stop. Creshia Boyd. She ain't deserve it. Her name Creshia Boyd." And I get a really good look in his tired eyes fore the camera switch back to the blond-haired news lady.

His eyes make me think about how losing your woman like that, not being able to protect her or make her feel protected, is unnatural. How I been watching men die for years now, but Creshia Boyd done died fore her man.

How he on TV crying 'cause he couldn't do nothing. Can't do nothing, and ain't nothing more unnatural than that. Think about all the black women that the camera missed dying. All the black women that's alive and still dead. All the black women like Cole. All the black women like mine.

"Creshia Boyd," I say soft. And then I say it again and again till I'm yelling it over and over, and I don't stop until I hear somebody yell from the other side of the tarp.

"This is the police. Come out with your hands up." I use the remote to switch off the TV, put my blunt out in the ashtray on the table, and stand up. I stretch my body, like I ain't been off the loveseat in years, and I let out a loud growl 'cause my body feel good letting go of itself like that.

I look out toward the horse and step from under my tent. She ain't messing with the patch of grass no more. She standing there with her eyes on me, like she want me to do something. Like she expecting me to. I see her eyes asking me, *Ridley, what's the plan?*

"I ain't done nothing wrong, officer," I say, walking toward the horse. "This horse come here on her own."

And then I hear Cole voice asking what's going on, like she out of breath, like she just run up. I think about Creshia Boyd and how she talked at them police with her face on the ground. How she was louder than her man. How she looked like she had had enough.

"Ma'am, you need to get back," I hear somebody command.

"This is my house," my wife yell in her voice for white people. "My neighbor called…" and her voice trail off, like she can't think of nothing else to say. "Ridley. Ridley? Baby, you back there?" she yell all of a sudden.

Her voice panicked and I want to smile because I think about what she said about Trayvon and his hoodie. How we sat on the couch together watching the news, me with my arm draped around her. We was both shaking our heads and I thought we was thinking the same thing, and then she said, "These young boys better get it together. He shouldn't have been wearing that thing on his head." After she said that, we debated. I lost 'cause I still loved her. Even then, I still loved her and stayed with her and her wrongness.

"Get back, ma'am," an officer yell, like he her daddy and done had enough of her mouth. Like he gone grab her throat and see his whole life behind him. Like seeing her can make him disappear into the past. Like she everything he hate about the world. Like she ain't nothing, and that make me want to defend her 'cause she mine and she black and his voice ought to remind her of that. And then her voice gone and I don't hear her no more. She ain't Creshia Boyd. She done moved to a spot where she can blend in. Be dead.

"We ain't done nothing," I say again. "You ain't welcome back here. This my property," I say. And I hear radios and cops telling each other to move.

My mind go back to Cole and how she done listened to that law. How she wanted to listen to dude at the door that day. How she want to obey 'cause she think that's safe. 'Cause she think she ain't got no choice. I imagine her standing back with her hands smashed together like she saying a prayer. Tears in her eyes. Hoping I make the right choices. Hoping we be all right.

And I think about the day with Trayvon and how I let it go, but how I stood up when she said Eric selling cigarettes was criminal. That he shouldn't of being doing it. That he'd be alive if he'd made better choices. I told her it didn't matter. He didn't deserve to die. I almost put my hands on her that day. I *did* put my hands on her the day she said Mike didn't comply. When she said he didn't really put his hands up so he got what he had coming.

I couldn't believe she believed what she was saying. My beautiful wife. The one I'd shed anything for. But when she narrowed them brown eyes, pursed her thick lips, and gritted her teeth and said, "What do you know? You not even an educated Negro," I lost it. That's when all the stuff I peeled flashed before my eyes. I grabbed her neck that day and watched her eyes bulge and thought about my gypsy horses and all the drug money that bought them and the drug money that was washed clean by me breeding them.

I thought about saying goodbye to my horses and handing them over to Moochie and following her to a job where wasn't no horses. Where I *am* the horse. And I thought about my granddaddy and how he taught me to click my tongue to move them forward. How he taught me to rub my fingers in little circles just above they nostrils as a treat. How he taught me to steer with my legs if I ain't had no reins. How he always said, "Don't never try to break them wild, RJ. You find a wild one, you let him be."

When I let go of her throat that day, I let go of her. We tipped around each other, until I eventually moved out to the backyard. I guess it was wrong of me to let go of my son, too, but I don't know no other way to be at peace about all this. To let all this go.

I walk toward the horse, close up the space between us, and I run circles with my finger on the space just above her nostrils, and I swear she smile like my gypsies used to do.

"You come to me for something? Huh?" I ask. "Walked

by all these houses and come right to me." And I let my hands slide down her soft coat. She muscular like my granddaddy colts and paints used to be. She letting me touch her, but she watching me from the corner of her eyes.

"I don't want you to peel none of yourself off," I whisper.

I let my hand go back to her mane and grab a little piece of it while I coo at her. "I just want to mount you. Get us out of here. Get us free."

And I'm a little scared at first. I ain't been on a horse since Cole and me married, but seem like the horse nod her head at me. Tell me it's okay. She gone let it be easy. I step one leg back and throw the other one over her in one good jump, and she don't move at all. She sit there, waiting for me to tell her what to do, and I look up and see all my neighbors watching and pointing and taking me in from they decks. I feel like they all seeing me for the first time ever.

I smile, wishing I had one of my hats, hoping I look something like my East Lubbock self. Like Don Juan the gypsy horse breeder. I want them to take pictures of me looking this way. I want them to think of me like this if they ever want to think of me at all. All I been in this place is some part-time worker getting took care of by his wife. I want them to always see this part of me.

"We're coming in," a voice yell from the other side of

the tarp and the plastic start rattling like they cutting through it or something. I click my tongue against the roof of my mouth and gently tap my heel into the horse side. Soon as she start to move I release my heel from her. Let her know I ain't trying to rule. Let her know she free. I steer her toward the open gate with my legs, almost asking her to take me there. Trying hard to let her know I ain't commanding nothing from her. Then I let my heel sink into her flesh hard enough to let her know we need to run, and she nod her head, understanding ain't no turning back.

When we shoot out the gate, I see all the police cars lining the alley from the corners of my eyes. Seem like they don't know the gate open on this side 'cause ain't no laws under the carport. They all surrounding the tarp in the alley, but me and the horse making our way round the side of the house to the front. By the time we got they attention and they start chasing us, yelling for me to stop, threatening to shoot, the horse hooves hitting the street like heaven. I'm on her back, looking to her, and she taking the street with a smile on her face, like this always was our plan.

THE
SUMMER FATHER

by LAURA ADAMCZYK

THE FATHER ARRIVES EVERY dead summer to
drive the girls west. No destination named, only
a direction and the promise of mesa, mountains,
stone-dry heat. Two weeks—the longest uninterrupted
time they spend with him all year. They pack sleeping
bags and pillows, Roald Dahl books, T-shirts, and bathing suits. It is the four of them in the cab of his truck,
the short trailer hitched behind. A tape deck and three

tapes. The shift from mother to father is swift. *Do you have everything you need?* A hug, a hug, a hug, and a wave.

At rest stops the girls imagine a mirror family on the other side of the highway, except they envision a father and a mother, a son or daughter or both at the end of her hand or hands. The girls do not need to say or even think that a father with his daughters is not like a mother with her daughters. At the rest stops, losing him for minutes, they coalesce, become a team. Three girls among women washing their hands, three girls among women's bodies, the air thick and hot, the sweet smell of a stranger's shit. In the lobby they look at state maps set behind glass, the red YOU ARE HERE dot. *We've gone this far, are going to go this far.*

In the afternoon, the father gives the oldest a thin fold of bills, and the girls run into a gas station to gather Corn Nuts and Twizzlers, Milk Duds and fun-size bags of chips. They each choose the same kind so regularly that the father made a song of it. Or the father made the song and the girls oblige it. When they return to the truck he snaps his fingers and whisper-sings: *FRI-tos / CHEE-tos / And po-TA-ta chips.* They like the way he defines them, even arbitrarily, even through slippery plastic bags of processed corn and sodium. *This is who you are, who you can continue to be.* He isn't there at home. He doesn't know how the middle daughter has been taking hour-long showers at night, how nobody knows what she does in there for all that time. How the oldest, only twelve, came home from the movies with a hickey not two weeks ago, and then sulked at the family party in the backyard, eighty degrees and she red-faced and sweating in a turtleneck. The youngest, the mother has determined, will need braces, despite having quit sucking her thumb last year. He no longer day-to-days it with them, never really did even when he was in the house, and so the jingle. My little *munch*kins, he says, getting back on the highway, as though tickled at being a father, at having these three separate pieces of him beside him reading books, housing secret desires and preferences each her own. He sets the cruise control and turns on the music, a favorite song with funky piano and brass. Hey, he says, and bobs his head until the youngest and the middle join in. It's like this, he says, gesturing with his hand, and they mimic him, as obedient as backup singers. The oldest, only twelve, nearly thirteen now, sometimes sullen, sometimes pouting, looks out the window, crosses her arms over her breasts, breasts she's been hiding under big white T-shirts, breasts whose sudden existence has the father calling the girls' underwear *unmentionables*: Don't forget your *unmentionables*. I've washed your *unmentionables*. C'mon, the middle says, pushing at the oldest's shoulder. She hates how the oldest must now be convinced to participate, hates her creeping sense of power, as though her presence were a gift and one to be doled out judiciously. They have to make her forget the girl she's becoming at school, the girl who quietly gets straight As but who hangs out with the tan, popular girls, *is* one of the tan, popular girls now, girls getting new bras, girls who let boys suck on their necks in the back row of their small town's single-screen movie theater. At home her sisters try to coax her into her previous self, an old dress that still fits but that she is sick of. What's wrong with it? her mother would say. You used to love that dress. C'mon, the middle says, and bumps her again. The middle shakes her shoulders, as though the oldest—only twelve yet moving exponentially beyond her ten-year-old sister—merely forgot how to do it. Cut it *out*, she replies, and the middle says, Fine, geez, and keeps dancing. Her movements are more contained, now only pretending to have fun, so as to show the oldest she doesn't need her.

The middle sister was there that night at the theater. She sat up front with her best friend, who, a third of the way in, nudged her and whispered, *Look*, and the middle turned to see her sister in a far corner with some skinny, freckled boy on her neck, her face stiff, eyes open. The middle looked back to the movie, now lost as to who the characters were, why they were doing what they were doing. The middle did not tell the mother, though she wished for her sister's punishment. She watched her mother discover the thing on her neck the next morning, breathing the oldest's name like a curse, and dig out the turtleneck so she could play ping-pong and eat potato salad and sit on the backyard swing staring into nothing.

When the song ends and the father rewinds the tape, the intro building again, the middle says, *Come on*, one last plea that's no longer pleading, a tone that says, *I know what you're doing, I know why you're doing it, but isn't this more fun?* The oldest angles away from the middle then looks back over her shoulder. She smirks and moves her eyebrows up and down. The middle snorts.

Stop it, she says.

What, the oldest says. I'm dancing. She shakes her shoulders slyly.

Dance normal.

I *am* dancing normal. She closes her eyes and shakes her head back and forth, hopping in her seat, her hair whipping around her face. It's a real freak-out! the oldest says. Seeing her, the father hams more. He closes his eyes and uses his fist as a microphone. The middle joins in as the brassy payoff returns, and for a moment, they all coordinate, punching their fists in time to the chorus. This will be the last summer like this. Next year, the oldest will insist on cheerleading camp and the father will instead have them for a week at his house. There will be trips to the park district pool, where the girls will eat nachos and Italian ice and look at boys and call their father to delay when he'll pick them up. The music is just louder than loud and it opens up a good feeling inside the middle's chest. It makes her uneasy. Like on the last day of school when she and her classmates had written their names and addresses on slips of paper tied to balloons and released them in the parking lot. She watched her balloon rise—one among the dozens—up to the tops of trees and beyond, a shrinking yellow dot.

They drive through the night. The father buys coffee; the girls run into gas station bathrooms—tired yet alert and giggling—the dull yellow lights swirling with mosquitos. The girls go into the back of the capped truck, where the dad has laid out a futon and a pile of blankets. The highway lights run one after another over the truck as though propelling it forward. The middle loves the late-night driving hours, hours usually kept away from her. Fifteen years later, after the father completes his slow, early death, the middle sister will think of those together-yet-separate hours on the night drive: she and her sisters dozing, her father up front, a slit in the window for his cigarette smoke to slip out of. Always there will be the same wonder: What did he think in those adult hours? Who was he then?

In the morning they stop at a small-town McDonald's, eating outside in the bright, early sun. The street, lined with trim, green lawns, leads to a stoplight and a row of antiques shops and bars. After they eat, the father lights a cigarette and spreads out the atlas. The oldest, sitting at the next table, leans over her book.

The middle takes the youngest a block down the street to a park, clambering up the curving metal slide, running across a wobbly wooden bridge. They climb on top of the monkey bars and crawl on hands and knees. She sends the youngest back, watching her dash across the empty street, and walks over to the swing set on the other side of a tall, needle-thick pine. They learned it as an accident, at the beginning of the summer at the playground across the street from the mother's house. A swing set with a metal trapeze bar hanging from two chains. The oldest sister and her friends would, one at a time, wrap their legs around the angled support beam and slide up, so they could sit on top of the high bar and swing. After a while they stopped going for the bar, only sliding up then down the beam. It tickles, one said, and the others laughed, the middle standing, watching. Three weeks, three bored summer weeks while the babysitter and the youngest sister stayed back home under the ceiling fan, eating ice-cream sandwiches and watching music videos. Then the oldest sister and her friends stopped going to the park. There was a girl down the street with a pool and a mother who worked nights. You can't come, the oldest said and bought a bikini with her own money. The middle sister felt betrayed but knew she would have repeated the betrayal to her younger sister if she'd been allowed to join them. The next week, on the night of the movie, the oldest and the middle stood outside the theater, waiting, and when the oldest sister's friends arrived, she joined them in a circle—arms crossed, their long, thin legs sprouting out from bright cotton shorts. A girl one grade ahead of them passed by, a girl with big brown hair and a cropped white shirt, with pink and purple beads at the ends of its tassels like a jeweled curtain. She walked with one hip out ahead of the other and it made her look at once filled with attitude and injured. That girl is a cunt, one of them said matter-of-factly and the others snorted. The oldest looked behind her, and the middle, leaning against the theater's brick exterior, turned her head to pretend she hadn't heard. The unknown word put a blood-taste in her mouth. Metallic like the smell of the support bar she leans her body on now. She closes her eyes. Her breath is slow and quiet, the only sound she hears but the wind in the trees, the distant whisper of a car. She slides herself up the bar until the tickling feeling leaks out of her. She slides down, her feet crunching into the bed of pebbles, and her older sister is behind her saying, You shouldn't do that.

She turns. A shameful heat opens in her stomach so fast it's like she's wet her pants. The sun is bright around her sister, the upward slope of her small, tanned nose, her brown hair hanging at her shoulders, but she looks like someone different. The middle's heart beats big inside her throat.

I wasn't doing anything, she says.

Yeah, right. That's gross.

It's not gross, the middle says, but there's no conviction in her. She cannot feel good about a thing she doesn't have a name for.

It's time to go, her sister says.

Back on the highway, the middle starts crying. Silently at first, but her heavy breathing gives her away.

Are you crying? The father leans over to look at the middle sister. He does a triple take between her and the road. She turns away from him, and her shoulders start to shake.

No, no, no, what's wrong? No, it's okay.

What? *Really?* The oldest looks at her, leaning in. Are you kidding me? She sighs and looks out the window.

The middle hangs her head, trying to make it so that neither her father nor her sisters can see her face. What's the matter? the youngest asks. The father fumbles with the tape deck.

Hey, c'mon, he says.

Everybody's attention gets her going harder and louder.

Oh, geez, says the oldest.

I miss Mama, too, the youngest says, putting a small hand on her shoulder, and it is like when the middle is sad at home and their border collie noses her cheek. Her face crinkles and the youngest starts up, too. I wanna go home, the youngest says.

C'mon, don't you start now, the father says, hitting PLAY on the stereo. The music comes blasting out in the middle of the song. He turns it up louder than before and the two cry harder.

Hey, hey, the father says, motioning with his hand, a bigger version of the dance they did earlier. The youngest moves deeper into the crying until it gets away from her. The father turns off the music and the middle stops abruptly, wiping her face with the back of her hand. She swallows and the father reaches over to mess her hair.

The drive, time, goes on and on. Flat, open, dull. An anxious, geared-up lull. It crackles and breaks once they enter the park, as soon as they see the brown official sign announcing its name in white, carved-out letters. The father tells the girls to hop out. One on either side of the sign and one at the bottom. The middle and youngest put their arms around it, as though it were a fifth family member. They collect these photographs the same way people buy magnets or badges or tiny spoons with the park seal stamped on them. They don't have the money for these trinkets, and though the girls secretly, separately, desire them, they have come to view them with disdain, as a frivolity they don't want anyway.

They follow the park road up the mountain, one side in shadow, sunlight pushing through fat clouds on the other. The campground is on the north rim of the canyon—dry pines, shadow and sun, pale dirt. A handful of colorful tents dot the spare forest. The girls don't see any other children, just middle-aged couples scattered among the dozen spots—men with gray beards, women wearing bandanas over their long hair. They make a slow circle around the sites, then take a spot on the edge. The father backs the trailer into the thin slice of tar pavement, then clips the pay stub onto the signpost, claiming the spot as their own. Some people have wooden plaques with their names in burned-out letters hanging from their trailers. THE JOHN-SONS. THE WARNERS. These are the same people who put potted geraniums outside their trailer doors, who roll out a carpet of fake grass beneath their striped awnings. A home away from home. The middle sister never saw her parents kiss or hug—nothing like it—and now there are only listless waves from cars or front porches, flat-toned telephone conversations in which the mother tells the father that the girls shouldn't eat so much candy. When she is twenty-five, the middle, alone in an art museum in Toronto, an otherwise unremarkable, unmemorable muse-um—a large, modern thing—will walk through a curving hallway into a white, open room, completely empty but for a man and a woman on the floor kissing. Their bodies longways on the blond, lacquered wood. The man will be on top of the woman, their bodies rubbing against each other with a slow, deliberate intensity. She will think their passion is a performance, some unmarked exhibit. Even so, a heat will swell in her stomach and her face will grow red, suspended in the eroticism of no possible relief or release. Stopped, standing in place, she will resume her slow walk at the edge of the room, so as not to appear taken, affected, anything. She will keep the couple in her periphery. The woman, blond like her, her jeans tight around her ass, the man's hands at her waist. Nothing will stop them; they will give no sign they know she is there. The middle will carry the memory of the couple for years but won't tell anyone, won't remember anything else about the museum or the pair except the careful distance she kept between herself and them.

The first step inside the camper shows everything shifted, disrupted and wrong, as a house recently burgled. A cabinet door open, a box of cereal on the floor. They put it in order. They take the cardboard box of newspaper off the floor, place it out next to the fire pit. The middle and the youngest unroll their sleeping bags on the bunks by the door.

What are we going to do after this? the middle asks. Are we going to have a fire tonight?

Of course we will, the oldest says.

They drive to the visitors' center. They wander through an exhibit on railways, another about how glaciers formed the canyon thousands of years before. They see the area's animals, stuffed and behind glass. A chipmunk clutching a branch. A mountain lion hunched on a high slab of rock. They read about what they eat, their prey and predators, where humans might see them. They play a game matching the animal to its tracks and droppings. The plaque reads, THEY'RE ALL YOU'LL EVER SEE OF SOME SPECIES.

Returning to the site, the father climbs onto the trailer's bottom bunk to take a nap. It is the hot, quiet slump in the day and the cars and trucks are missing from the other sites. The oldest reads at the picnic table and the middle and youngest hang together in the hammock.

When are we going home? the youngest asks.

We just got here, the oldest says, not taking her eyes off her book.

Two weeks, the middle says. Like last summer.

I want to talk to Mama.

You can't talk to Mom, the oldest says.

Why not?

The pay phone is all the way down at the entrance. It's too far.

I want to talk to her.

We can tomorrow, the middle says.

The youngest wedges herself out of the hammock. The middle watches her walk to the trailer and step up on its metal step.

What are you doing? the oldest asks.

I want to see if Dad will take me.

He's sleeping.

I want to talk to Mama, she says more insistently.

You'll hurt Dad's feelings, the oldest says.

The youngest crosses her arms and sighs, stamping over to the fire ring and huffing down onto a fat log. Her face crumples and her chest heaves.

Hey, c'mon, the middle says. Don't cry.

You guys are such babies, the oldest says.

The youngest puts her thumb in her mouth, her brow knitted, angry and concentrating. She wraps her other arm around her stomach. She closes her eyes and her mouth starts going, her face softening. Her mother did so much to get her to stop last year. At night, she duct-taped socks over her hands. She rubbed fishing-lure gel on her thumbs, but they would find her in the morning with the socks torn off, the gel smeared around her mouth like melted ice cream. The mother kept socking her hands and the youngest kept ripping them off. Stubborn, stubborn, then she stopped cold, and it seemed like that was that. Around this time, the youngest started bringing her toy vacuum cleaner into the bed to sleep with her. Nearly the length of her body, a white, smooth plastic, its base a clear dome inside of which whir tiny Styrofoam balls when it's pushed. She calls it by the neighbor boy's name, a boy with a head of tight blond curls whom they see out at the beach club the mother's family belongs to. Her sisters tease her whenever they see him, draw out the syllables of his name in a long *Oooo*. At night, she wraps an arm and a leg around the toy, and the mother, worried about the youngest's teeth, lets her keep it in her bed, as though it were nothing more than a stuffed animal.

The youngest's cheeks hollow and fill, making small sucking noises.

Stop it, the oldest says.

The youngest's eyes stay closed.

Hey. The middle says her name.

Stop it, that's gross, the oldest says again.

Just let her, the middle says. Seconds ago she was tempted to get up and pull her sister's thumb out of her mouth herself, but she feels her allegiance turn sharply on its heel.

You used to, the middle says.

Yeah, well, I stopped because it's gross.

It's *not* gross, the middle says, standing up, her arms stiff at her sides.

No, it *is* gross. It's disgusting and she shouldn't do it.

You're a cunt, the middle says, her eyes quaking.

You don't even know what that word means, says the oldest.

Yeah, I do.

Oh, yeah, what?

It's someone who's *mean* and *slutty*.

Like that the oldest is up and on her, pushing her into the hammock, leaning over and punching her skinny arms. The middle puts her arms over her face and kicks out with her legs. The youngest sister stands and wails, her eyes closed, arms loose at her sides.

The middle rears back and kicks her older sister in the chest—a bony, dull thump—and she falls into the dirt. Her face is a mix of pain and anger, reared up, then—just as fast—restrained and put away. The middle stands up and moves away from her, the oldest says, I hate you, the youngest wails, and the father throws open the door of the camper, screaming, What the hell is going on, goddammit, shut up.

*　　*　　*

They wind down to the park entrance and find a pay phone, each of the girls taking a turn. The youngest sniffles, says she wants to go home, can't the mother come and get her, and then she goes silent, listening. She nods and nods, bucks up, and gives the phone to her sister. The middle says, She started it, says, She's so mean, I never want to be like her, and the oldest cries, finally, silently, turning herself toward the brick exterior of the liquor store. There is a liquor store, a gas station, and a closed antiques shop on this stretch of road and nothing else. A grassy field behind a barbed-wired fence and beyond that the mountains they came here to see. Be good, the mother says to each of them, not Be good for your father, just, Be good. The oldest and middle are made to apologize to each other before the father takes the phone, his voice a tight whisper.

They drive to the grocery store. The father's is a summer birthday and, in the fluorescent lights of the aisles, the girls go off on their own, find a boxed cake mix and the accompanying ingredients. The oldest reads the list, leading them to the right sections. When the middle skips ahead and returns with a carton of eggs, the oldest says, Good job. They slide it all onto the back of the checkout conveyer belt, the father pretending not to see, then paying for everything. When they return to the site, he starts a fire and reads the local paper at the picnic table. Inside the trailer, the girls mix the cake's ingredients, bake it in the tiny oven, following the directions adjusted for high elevation. They poke their heads out the door at him and giggle, and the middle has that feeling again. Of the joy filling up and overflowing, of wanting it so bad but knowing it as something that will peak, then float away. It makes her giggles come up fast and nervous, edging out beyond her control.

The cake turns out funny—overcooked in some spots, wet in others. Still they cover it in unctuous frosting, pour on sprinkles, and push in blue-and-white-striped candles, and when they emerge from the trailer, candles lit, the father acts surprised. He says, My little *munchkins*. There must be a moment, the middle will think later—candles lit, the evening sun cutting sharp through the trees—when he feels he is alone. The father's house is not a home. It's the place where he lives. A squat house filled with itchy furniture and cigarette smoke. The girls will not remember the cake as he will, the undeniable adult feeling of getting older. The father wrinkles his nose, says, Daddy's a geezer, and groans and goofs like an old man.

After cake, he says, Spread my ashes here. This place

apart from the rest of the park, as quiet as a vacuum. He's not even sick yet. Won't be for another ten years, but he'll say it when they get home, too. Spread my ashes at the canyon. A refrain, just like everything he says is a refrain. Spread my ashes, and, I saw the Who in a barn in Frankfurt, Illinois, and, There's Hitchcock, there he is, on one of those endless weekend afternoons watching movies at his house, a trick the girls think is particular to him, just as they think every joke is his original own. Hitchcock stepping onto a train, Hitchcock winding a clock. Spread my ashes here, he says, and they will, years later. They'll let some go at the edge of the canyon and some down at its river and some they will put into a campfire in the Rockies and some the middle sister will put into her mouth, a lick of her finger, a dip, and another lick when her sisters aren't looking. The act will feel performative, purely symbolic, but she won't know what else to do. Wanting her actions to mean something more than what she can give to them. Somewhere inside her grief, she will ask herself what is the worst thing she would have done to reverse his sickness, to have provided some momentary relief. She will have heard stories of what mothers have done to soothe their colicky sons and in her mind's eye she will see herself bent over him in his hospital bed. She will feel at once alone in her imagined sacrifice but also closer to her father than she will when she's actually with him. The same way she will imagine a scene in which she and her sisters are kidnapped by a group of faceless men, a dark basement, a locked door, and she will say, Me. Whatever you're going to do to them, only me.

In the evening, they go into their separate spaces. The father into the woods. The girls into the cool, echoey bathroom. They walk to and from the site together, flashlights bouncing along the small, curving path. There are more stars here than at home, the sky messy with them, and the girls are in awe. Whispering in the dark, the middle feels a silent fear they won't find their way back, but just moments later they see their father at the picnic table in front of the fire. The girls go to bed and he stays up. Some hours later, the middle sister wakes. On the foldout bed next to the oven, the older sister is lost inside a mess of blankets, her face barely perceptible within her dark swirl of hair. Hateful and tender, the middle stands above her and a thought, perfectly formed, sprouts within her: It is easier to love you like this. She pulls back the drapes over the window in the door and pads out in socked feet. The father is smoking a cigarette and in his exhale says, Hey, little lady. She sits across from him on a log, and they stare into the fire, the light reflecting off his glasses so his eyes cannot be seen. She wants to crawl into his lap or sit beside him, lean into his torso, but she feels shy with him now. Their talk is spare and quiet, minutes or hours passing, until he lets the red fire dim and smoke.

THE FORK
IN THE RAILS

by ARMONÍA SOMERS

(*Translated by Kit Maude*)

This is a story shared by many but I tell it to all these people lying with me on the grass next to the fork in the rails, where we were left behind. They don't appear to be listening; they don't seem to want anything. Still, I go on because I can't understand why any of them wouldn't get up and shout the same questions I did after my fall. But instead of answering my questions, they asked me some of their own. Questions that were as brutally definitive as this timeless landing.

I MET HIM ONE UNREMARKABLE morning at the train station while the crowd was, as usual, reaffirming its ego by making as much noise as possible. I remember that there was a young child on the platform holding a large bunch of balloons on strings. The boy started to cry, upset that there wasn't enough wind to keep the balloons in the air, and a group of passersby gathered around him and started to blow at them from below, trying to keep them airborne. The man who would later share my compartment and I both joined in the effort, and, as we stood back up again, we caught sight of each other amid the balloons and the child's laughter.

I don't know what it was exactly. Perhaps he and I were exhilarated by the way our eyes had met through all those colors raised aloft on hope alone, but it was a few seconds, an age, before we looked away.

The stranger picked up my suitcase and pulled a rucksack onto his back; you could see the bulky forms of the fruit inside straining against the material. I settled into my seat, struggling with the desires that torment you so when you are young but that you learn to control as you grow older. I did so by turning to the window and focusing on the landscape up ahead.

I remember that the seats opposite us were occupied by

two men carrying large baskets, their oversize heads blocking our view of the mirror in which we would otherwise have been able to look at each other. However, we soon discovered the advantages of a direct line of sight.

Soon, my traveling companion, who was the same age as me but far more experienced in the ways of the world, took my hand and held it between his own. His warm, dry touch plunged me into a vertiginous daze as I compared it with all those soft, damp, or sterile hands I had had to put up with in the past and he took advantage of my apparent acquiescence to bring my fingers to his lips, kissing them neatly and firmly one by one, without a thought for our unseeing audience.

Meanwhile, the train had started to move with that chugging sound everyone loves. I stretched out my legs until they almost touched the baskets in front and closed my eyes in sheer pleasure. The young man asked me in a soft, intimate tone:

"You like that sound, too, don't you?"

"Yes, I like it," I said, on the verge of ecstasy. "It drives me crazy."

"Crazy enough to love me?"

What a question, I thought without answering. I'd let him move too quickly, seeking out my face among the balloons, slipping those kisses directly into my bloodstream, as though my braking mechanism had gone haywire. That would have explained a lot.

The train began to speed up, entering into its customary whistling realm. Now things were passing by the window, a bird in a tree, a house with a garden and residents, a smoky sky, and not much else. For a few brief moments I fell into an unnatural swoon, almost losing consciousness. He seemed to be able to read my thoughts, and, like someone taking a sweet out of their pocket, flashed me his trademark smile. I tried to reciprocate in kind.

"I love your teeth," he said. "They're the sort I look for, the sort that gleam when the light catches them and it's as though they shatter it. Everything always seems so difficult but then, when it goes right, it's so simple..."

He started to kiss me urgently, as though he were saying goodbye, the kind of urgency one feels when they realize that all the kissing they've done before was worthless, just a waste of calories.

"What's in your bag?" I asked breathlessly, trying to distract him from the overly intimate situation in which we found ourselves.

"Some clothes and shaving equipment," he said. "Well," he added slyly, "and some apples. Would you like one?"

"Apples!" I exclaimed, getting into the spirit. "My second favorite thing, after the noise of the train. But right now I just want to share one; a good, clean bite. To prove they're real," I added, showing off both rows of teeth.

After our first heady meal together—I'll never remember whether it was lunch or dinner—I was disappointed to see him checking his watch.

"Damn," he said. "Seven days now, the math is infallible."

"Seven days? We've only just got on the express."

That was when his words must have shaken me out of my mental fug.

"Listen," he explained. "The guys with the baskets changed carriage on the first day. Lots of other people went, too; they were heading somewhere different from where we're going. The guard has come by asking for tickets several times; I've been buying new ones every morning."

"That faceless man, dressed in gray? I think I've seen him on the floor, or clinging to the ceiling like a fly."

My companion began to cackle in a way I'd never seen before. Everyone turned to look at us.

"Yes," he said eventually. "A man as insignificant as the buttons on his jacket. But every time he came by, the dutiful peasant stared so hard at our hands that I had to slip this ring onto your finger while you were asleep."

"I'm going to splash some cold water on my face," I said. "Because I don't just fall asleep like that. It's like a story about the wrong character," I added as I stood up.

"Let's say that first we shared an apple, and then you fell asleep next to me," he said casually, as though it didn't matter at all. "It's normal after a long time traveling. And then it has to happen again and again, until we get to the bottom," he added, nodding toward his mysterious supply of apples.

This was all beginning to feel pretty strange, like some inscrutable test. But mixed in with the delirium was enough objective evidence to convince me it was really happening.

We had grown accustomed to the rhythm of the train. Even the speed, which we could gauge by how fast things flew past the window, now seemed unremarkable. I began to distinguish between day and night, to get annoyed by some of the other passengers, and to notice that some others closed their eyes even though they weren't tired.

One day my man took a pair of winter trousers out of his bag. This signaled the end of my blissful ignorance—it was like a coup de grâce—but it had nothing to do with the cold wind slipping through the gaps in the train.

"Look at this," he said reproachfully, trying to smooth out the material. "My mother folded them nicely and you've ruined them."

I looked at him with a stupid expression that stared back at me from the mirror opposite.

"This is the first time I've ever folded a pair of trousers," I squeaked. "But it's nothing to get angry about."

I was just about to resort to a move I'd almost forgotten was available—bursting into tears—when he put a pair of conciliatory hands to my face.

"Listen," he explained. "You fold a pair of stupid trousers like this, taking them from the bottom and lining up the creases. Then you can fold it twice, or as many times as you like."

Goodness, what a revelation. But I was still sniveling a little, the dampness that results from the undercover insurgency of the common cold. The incident was forgotten as we walked hand in hand along the passage and had dinner outside of our cabin, staring out at the starry night passing by in direct opposition to the course of time. Now I know that I felt as though I was going in the opposite direction from something, something that was taking bites out of us as it went, but it wasn't as painful as it should have been given the size of the bites.

"Would you rather smoke here, or eat our apples in the compartment?" he asked in a now-mature voice, which was growing progressively deeper.

Everyone was stunned by the way we clung like limpets to the actual names of things. To us, though, eating apples meant total love and we indulged in them as though we'd broken into a cider press.

Then one day it happened. I'm going to tell it just as it was, just as it must have happened to so many people. Of course, nobody writes these things down at the time. Then it all comes down around your ears and every last trace is consumed in the embers.

"I'm just going to say it once and for all," he said one night, having come back from a much-anticipated showing of a film. "I'm only interested in documentaries, the ones where real people and things send a direct message. And adventure novels, because then I'm the one doing everything. I'm the protagonist right from the start."

He yawned, kicked off his shoes, turned off the light, and went straight to sleep.

No matter how dark it is, no one wants to just sit there and watch someone sleeping. It was time to take advantage of what light there was to examine our little differences, to take stock while I could, just in case things suddenly came to a head. I thought about the dirty men in the seat opposite whom he chose to talk to because, paradoxically, they kept their hands clean. About his opinion of my hatred of flies and people sneezing in the bakery. The little things, leaping in like grasshoppers through an open window to get in the way. Eventually, they'd grown into obstacles on a collision course, a clash of principles. Eternal loyalty to flies against my sense of disgust. Humanity communing with bread against the microbial explosion of a sneeze. And all the *et ceteras* that are contained within a single *et cetera* as soon as it is uttered.

"You say 'The war is over' as though you're copying out someone else's letter written in their own guts," he had complained, so upset that I realized it would be a good idea never to say those four words again. Yes, but dozing on my shoulder, snoring gently, with a thread of drool dribbling unconsciously from his mouth while a film that had won several awards was being shown in the crowded passage: that was rather more definitive.

When the faceless man came by the next day to sell a new ticket, I spoke without looking at him.

"Wait for him to wake up. Then we'll see who stays on the train and who gets off. I'm not planning on spending the rest of my life here."

Having said this, I felt a suspicious pressure on my solar plexus, but I went on blithely repeating the word *life, life,* beginning to realize the nature of the trap that I had fallen into. And I had no way of knowing how long I'd been stuck there, because the wayward watch had made me lose all sense of time.

Thus began another shapeless day, with the morning shave and brushing of teeth. It was then that I wanted to announce my decision by provocatively taking off my ring, but it wouldn't come off my finger. He stopped his shaving and started to laugh like the little boy when his balloons began rising back up again at that far-off station where we had first met.

"You've gotten fat," he said eventually. "That never happens to my flies. They live on borrowed air and are always alert, even during their most innocent celebrations."

"There are verbal blades sharper than that razor," I mumbled through gritted teeth. "But the time comes for one to explode, to start thinking for oneself, to start to make use of your own brain. The brain that must once have worked."

"Drama," he said, returning to his ablutions. "What harm is there in the fact that even the most challenging neuroses come with the taste of coffee and cream?"

"Well," I went on, swerving around his attacks, "let's have a look at that horrible watch. How long have we been on this damn train? We must be going to Mars, or the moon, like in your adventure novels."

He cleaned his razor and put it away with limitless patience. Then he looked at his watch, fixed his eyes on my own until he had my full attention, and repeated the same old refrain:

"Seven years now. Just the right time for this to be happening. So precise and infallible, God and his wonderful ways…"

I was irritated by his pedantic love of time. I felt like getting rid of him with something powerful, like an irrepressible lawsuit that would put us face to face, a pair of underground boxers.

"Fine," I said harshly. "Don't think I don't know, that I'm oblivious. Our apples, the ones that I thought were just for us when you licked the juice from my lips: I've seen you giving them to other women behind my back through half-open carriage doors. I've even heard you talking about your little affairs in your sleep, saying other names. And there's plenty more that I won't bring up here, we don't need everyone gossiping about our problems. I'm packing my bag and moving to another carriage. It's the right thing to do, I think. The honest thing. Our best years are behind us."

He let me go. *Are you listening? Hey, you, lying in the grass.* But when night fell, the noise of the railway, especially the supremely solitary way in which the bridges shuddered, kept me from getting to sleep. Also, I started to get thirsty and I couldn't find a glass of water. I began to feel cold and I couldn't find any blankets or the light switch. Everything around me had shifted, like on an immigrant's first night in a foreign land. When I heard a gentle knock on the door I stood up, thanking the heavens themselves as they passed by the glass like a black brush and then ceased to exist. Although maybe they continued to exist for those who had nothing else: a poor, insufficient sky for such great solitude.

"See?" he said finally as he helped me move back in. "You unburden yourself a little behind a half-closed door, things are good: there's enough in the rucksack to go around."

After that I learned to laugh at myself. Also, during those frenetic times, we invented the game of throwing objects out of the window. We'd seen that people were overloaded with things. They had to sleep with their legs tucked up against their bodies. Other people couldn't hug each other, because they didn't have enough room. This new appreciation of space ended up reorganizing the chaos. And I suppose now that one momentous day he must have forgotten to wind his watch to ease my worries. "If his years are spent, he lives on inside of us," he said once, when I wondered aloud at how old the boy whose balloons had brought us together would be now. After a chill ran down my spine at his words, I never again sought metaphysical meaning in dangerous nooks or crannies.

Then came the great night. How strange, I've never thought about it before, the moment when a great family of strangers finds themselves cracking the lock together, for all manner of reasons. My feet were freezing. It felt as though the train were slowing down. But you can't mention such things when your tongue is almost rigid. He draped a blanket over my legs, took my hand, kissed each of my fingers just the like the first time, and fell asleep.

That was when it happened. The man without a face sat down in the opposite seat, in the absolute darkness they insisted upon at that time of day. And yet I finally began to make out his features, which I'd never noticed before. Flashing lights from the engine gave me brief glimpses of him, like a country house during an electrical storm.

"You," I said eventually, my teeth chattering, "have been bringing us things for so long. Thank you for everything. But what do you want?"

The fellow looked at me with an inseparable mixture of pity and cruelty. He seemed to have something immense to tell me. But his chance had gone, like someone remembering the name of a forgotten street just as they pass it by and see that the house they're looking for has been demolished.

I held that thought in my brain for as long as I could, hoping that its sad, poetic potential would keep the man away from me. (The man who lived in the demolished house would have called his friend about some secret emergency. His friend wouldn't have come, because he'd forgotten the name of the street, and the house number.) The man, meanwhile, didn't say a word, perhaps mentally going over the details of some imminent chore. (So, I went on thinking, one day, suddenly, he'll remember everything: the name and the number. But only when he passes by and sees that the house has gone.)

"Well," he said eventually, as though he'd been listening to the end of an anecdote, "we're coming up on the fork. And I think it's you, not him, who I should be shoving through the door. Try not to wake him; it would be a stupid gesture, a vulgar scene unworthy of you."

"But I can't break all this off without warning, in the middle of the night. You've seen us together, you saw it right from the beginning…"

He didn't give me any time to make a fuss. I heard the clicking of the points changing for the fork clearly; it passed along the rails straight into my heart, like a different kind of beat. And then came my violent fall into the undergrowth, pushed by the man without a face.

"Hey, where's the station? Where do they sell return tickets? The number, I remember the number of the demolished house!"

That was when I heard it, the train carriages pulling away without me or any of the others:

"What station? What return? What house…?"

MERMAIDS

by NADJA SPIEGELMAN

ALL OF THE MERMAIDS smoked. And most of them were no longer young. Hilda sat astride a corner of her tank, a topography of stretch marks along her wide tail. Olga, who was having hot flashes, was in the water of her own, arms crossed over the rim, bright red hair still dry. It had been a long time since they had had anyone new to talk to.

"You married?" Hilda asked the new recruit. The scrawny girl stood in flip-flops in the sand, twisting her head to look up at them.

"No," the girl said. They had all noted the faded purple

on her left cheek, the red marks on her upper arm, noted them and known she belonged.

The tourists used to come in droves. Little girls with sticky cotton-candy hands blowing spots of fog against the glass, gasping as the mermaids winked at them from upside down. No longer.

"You know it's forever?" Hilda said, taking a last draw on her cigarette and letting the butt fizzle in her tank. It floated there. The girl nodded solemnly. Her eyes were on the only empty tank, long ladder leaning against the side.

"Why?" Olga asked. The other mermaids glared at her, though they'd all wondered, too.

"A dream," the girl said, shrugging. "Since I was a girl." They did not tell her that she was still.

"Then welcome, honey," Hilda said, with a rasping laugh. "Where dreams come true."

They watched in silence as she climbed, bare feet gripping each rung.

RITE OF BAPTISM

by MICHAEL ANDREASEN

OFFICIANT: What name do you give your child?

PARENTS: [Name].

OFFICIANT: And what do you ask of the Church for [name]?

PARENTS: Baptism.

OFFICIANT: You have asked to have your child baptized.
In doing so, you are accepting the responsibility of

guiding [him/her] down the River, through its sluicing corridors and over its gulping rapids. It will be your duty to keep [name]'s head above water, [his/her] pate dry, [his/her] little nostrils clear, and [his/her] little toes unmuddied. Do you clearly understand what you are undertaking?

PARENTS: We do.

OFFICIANT: But do you really?

PARENTS: Totally.

OFFICIANT: Godparents, are you prepared to help [name]'s parents as they guide [him/her] down the River? Are you prepared to keep [name]'s crèche afloat, and to ward off, as much as possible, the many perils of the River, such as the ravenous hippos and crocodiles, the apes with semi-human intelligence, and the creatures that appear to be otters, but are more menacing than otters, as evidenced by their tendency to bite? And, if necessary, are you prepared to pull the body of the nearly drowned, otter-bitten [name] from the baleful current of the River and perform CPR, keeping in mind that, when performing CPR on an infant, one should use only two or three fingers to apply chest compressions at a rate of approximately one hundred compressions per minute?

GODPARENTS: We are.

OFFICIANT: [Name], the Church welcomes you with great joy and claims you in the name of the Lord of the River. I now invite your parents to place you in your crèche, which they have fashioned out of a collection of pliable synthetic twigs and briars from the craft bin, meant to represent, in its own crude way, the crèche of Our Lord, fashioned by his own doubtlessly loving but almost adorably naive mother and father out of actual twigs and briars collected from the banks of the River.

(PARENTS place CHILD in crèche.)

OFFICIANT: We now ask [name]'s parents to place the crèche into the Baptismal Canal, which stretches the length of the Church, representing the River into which Our Lord was once placed by the same almost certainly loving but again—it must be said—rather dim parents, but also representing the same River into which we all

arrive, be it in a crèche, or lashed to a log, or tied to a
bundle of smooth river stones, the ballast of which we
might struggle against our entire lives, forever aching
and gasping for breath. I also invite [name]'s godparents
to place into the crèche a sleeve of saltine crackers, as
a reminder of the crackers placed in the crèche of Our
Lord by his parents, and as a representation of the minor
affordances and occasional kindnesses that we might
receive on our journey down the River.

*(PARENTS place crèche in Baptismal Canal. GODPARENTS place
sleeve of saltines in crèche.)*

OFFICIANT: [Name], as you travel down the first few bends
of the Baptismal Canal, I invite your brothers and sisters, your cousins, and all of the children gathered here
today to place their hands in the water of the canal and
splash you a little bit, just a little bit, to represent the
small torments that one encounters while navigating the
River; the whirl of its eddies, the snag of its drooping
branches, the mocking of its waterfowl. I would also
ask some of the children to submerge their arms up to
the elbows and make small, serpentine motions—yes,
just like that—to represent the vipers and eels of the

River, which wait just below the surface, looking for an unattended limb or a twiddling finger to latch onto and drag under. Parents and Godparents, do you understand the predatory nature of the River's many shallow lurkers?

PARENTS AND GODPARENTS: We do.

(*ACOLYTES* *distribute water pistols filled with imitation ape urine to older members of congregation.*)

OFFICIANT: Now, as the Baptismal Canal winds its way between pews and folding chairs, I invite the older members of our community to look upon [name] disapprovingly, as the apes with semi-human intelligence once looked upon Our Lord from their treetops above the River, where they sneered simian sneers and took turns urinating into his crèche, jealous, perhaps, of the sleeve of saltines, or the untroubled ease of his passage. As we bring to bear these plastic water pistols filled with imitation ape urine and squirt [name] as Our Lord was squirted, we recall those times when we were urinated upon, figuratively speaking, by the many sneering apes of the world, and how this wasn't so bad in the long run. How we survived being urinated upon, realizing, as [name] inevitably will, that being urinated upon is part of being on the River. Parents and Godparents, do you recall being figuratively urinated upon by your own version of the apes, whatever that might be?

PARENTS AND GODPARENTS: We sure do.

OFFICIANT: And did you survive it?

PARENTS AND GODPARENTS: Ultimately, yes, we did.

OFFICIANT: [Name], as you float down the River in a small pool of imitation ape urine, know that the dampness is only temporary, that the smell of ape urine fades, that the insults of the apes are but one moment on the River. Remember that the River is long, and wide, and gets worse.

(*CONGREGATION meditates on this. OFFICIANT and ACOLYTES remove their vestments and don hard hats and reflective vests. ACOLYTES begin operating whirring blades.*)

OFFICIANT: As [name] now floats silently down the Baptismal Canal, past the emergency exit and the wicker shrines erected to Our Lady of Baffled Wonder, we recall

Our Lord's encounter with the Sawmill, activating the whirring blades and lighting the trash fires to remind us of the industrial perils of the River. We also point the PA system directly at [name] as [he/she] bobs between the miniature cranes and smokestacks, playing a recording of sawmill sounds at maximum volume to remind us of how loud the actual Sawmill must have been, how it must have rustled the water and shaken Our Lord's infant resolve.

(PA system plays sawmill sounds at full hork. ACOLYTES *direct whirring blades alarmingly close to crèche.)*

OFFICIANT: (bellowing over PA) [Name], as your eyes water at the smoke and smell of burning garbage, recall the tears Our Lord must have shed as he looked upon the Sawmill, with its smoking chimneys and rainbow-slick water. We now sprinkle sawdust into your crèche as a reminder that not every breath on the river is a clean lungful. As you wince at the sawdust in your eyes, or the whirring blades passing within inches of your face, recall how Our Lord must have winced at the sight of this dull and tainted stretch of the river, and at the crippled and disfigured workmen, who surely puzzled over him, saying—

(ACOLYTES each slip one arm from its sleeve to suggest maiming.)

ACOLYTES: We are puzzled. We are puzzled. We are puzzled by this child. Who is this child? Who would willingly float a child down this dull and tainted stretch of river? Look at what working in this Sawmill along the river has done to us. Count our missing fingers, our subtracted limbs. Observe the grossness oozing from the drainage pipe, which gathers on the surface of the water like soup skin. Breathe this horrible air. What manner of parents would set a child upon this course? How almost adorably naive they must have been to do such a thing!

OFFICIANT: Parents and Godparents, do you realize the industrial perils to which you have exposed [name] simply by bringing [him/her] here and setting [him/her] upon the course of the river?

PARENTS AND GODPARENTS: We do.

OFFICIANT: Speak up, please.

PARENTS AND GODPARENTS: Sorry. Yes, we do.

(*CONGREGATION meditates on this. PA system is turned off.* OFFI-
CIANT *and* ACOLYTES *remove reflective vests and hard hats.* ACO-
LYTE *posing as* SECRET ENEMY, *masked and wearing turtle shell,
approaches Baptismal Canal.*)

OFFICIANT: [Name], as you leave the Sawmill, drifting
farther down the Baptismal Canal, out of the Church
proper and into the hallway near the restrooms, we ask
that you keep in mind that not all perils of the River
are easily recognizable. Recall now how Our Lord
encountered the Spiteful Turtle, his Secret Enemy,
who pretended at first to be his pal, paddling alongside him and singing the ridiculous songs of the river
turtles, only to later capsize his crèche for no apparent
reason.

(*SECRET ENEMY caresses CHILD's chin with forefinger in transpar-
ently false act of fondness and security.*)

SECRET ENEMY: [Singing]
Loo-de-loo, loo-de-loll, river turtles are so small
Loo-de-lim, loo-de-leek, river turtles feel so weak
Loo-de-loo, loo-de-lie, river turtles can't say why
Loo-de-lim, loo-de-lutz, river turtles hate your guts

(SECRET ENEMY rocks crèche, first soothingly, then stormily, then hatefully. Crèche takes on water. CHILD should cry anxious and/ or terrified cries between gasps for air. PARENTS AND GODPARENTS should regret everything.)

OFFICIANT: Parents and Godparents, do you regret everything you have done to [name] in bringing [him/her] here today and leaving [him/her] at the mercy of strangers and confusing, perilous rituals?

PARENTS AND GODPARENTS: We do. We are up to our ears in regret.

OFFICIANT: And do you shudder to realize that, through the gatehouse and the barbican, near the entrance to the parking lot, the Baptismal Canal will empty out into the rushing torrent of the honest-to-god River, depositing [name] into the very real perils that this ritual has heretofore only simulated?

PARENTS AND GODPARENTS: We do. Oh god, we do. We are literally shuddering.

(Crèche follows Baptismal Canal out church door, through

gatehouse and barbican, into raging storm outside. Sharp-shooters on parapets overlooking Baptismal Canal paint crèche with laser sights until CHILD *is covered in a quivering red pox.* CONGREGATION *dons rain slickers and ascends stairs to parapets overlooking Canal, rubber-belted Inclined Conveyor, and honest-to-god River beyond. Rain falls as it always has. Thunder cascades across a gray world, intimating a general lack of sanctuary in this or any other place.* CONGREGATION *meditates on this.)*

OFFICIANT: [Name], you are outside the walls and battlements of the Church, and have been targeted by those with the power to destroy you, just as Our Lord of the River was targeted by those who found his teachings reckless, misguided, and needlessly cruel. But what else was he to learn on his infant journey? What is the chief lesson of the River, if not needless cruelty? For example, look at you now, [name]. Your crèche is rain-soaked, and sawdust-soaked, and ape-urine-soaked. You are alone, desperate, panicked. What can you do? Parents and Godparents, what can you offer [name]?

PARENTS AND GODPARENTS: We have given the child a sleeve of saltines. What more would you have us do?

OFFICIANT: Assembled brothers and sisters, is there anything you can do for [name]?

CONGREGATION: From this parapet, we can but watch in dumb horror.

OFFICIANT: [Name]'s Secret Enemy, how close are you to [name]?

SECRET ENEMY: Even atop these battlements, I am so close. Close enough to smell ape urine. Close enough to smell [name]'s own name. I am always just a few bends behind you, [name], for I am driven by a wild jealousy that even I don't fully understand.

(Crèche approaches Inclined Conveyor.)

OFFICIANT: [Name], know that it was here, when all seemed lost, that Our Lord of the River chose to become a Famous Celebrity.

(Crèche enters Inclined Conveyor, begins to ascend.)

OFFICIANT: Why did he choose to become a Famous

Celebrity? How did he manage it? What does a celebrity even look like? We cannot say. The world is so much darker, and the celebrities who once littered our skies are more distant from us now than they ever were. We cannot make you a Famous Celebrity, little [name]. We do not know the secret. We cannot even tell you where to begin, except to tell you to begin at the River. But we can raise you heavenward for a brief moment before giving you to the River, that you might know what it is to see the world shrink beneath you, as Our Lord did when he ascended the gilded ranks of fame and fortune and left this doomed world behind.

(Crèche ascends.)

CONGREGATION: We are smaller. We are smaller. We are like ants.

OFFICIANT: Why do we tell [name] this story, and why in this way? How else might we tell it?

CONGREGATION: How? How?

(Crèche ascends.)

OFFICIANT: Here's how: one day a man and a woman, for reasons they never bothered to explain to anybody, put a baby into a river, wherein it listened poorly, learned poorly, and made mostly poor decisions until it died. But there's nothing to be gleaned from that account, no way to make it meaningful. It's a sad, empty story. It needs a better hero. Plus danger and excitement. Mystery and ritual. Hope spitting in the dumb donkey face of an inexplicable and indiscriminate evil.

(Crèche ascends.)

OFFICIANT: And look around you, [name]. As you approach the apex of the Inclined Conveyor, look at this roiling maelstrom, these wind-warped trees, these angry roadkill-lined streets ripe with faunal decay. We must have meaning in a world like this, [name]. As you teeter at the Inclined Conveyor's precipice, look to the River below.

CONGREGATION: Look! Look!

OFFICIANT: It is a swallowing River, [name].

CONGREGATION: Loo-de-lim, loo-de-leek!

OFFICIANT: A devouring River.

CONGREGATION: Loo-de-loo, loo-de-lie!

OFFICIANT: Feel it dragging you forward, [name], pulling you in, like the baited hook at the end of the—

CONGREGATION: WHEEEEEEEEE!!!!!

(Crèche slides down what remains of Baptismal Canal into River, landing with a cannonball-esque sploosh. Along River, apes with semi-human intelligence should already be sneering, Sawmill furnaces already smoking, sort-of otters already bobbing in dagger-toothed flotillas. Crèche should surface. Crèche usually surfaces.)

OFFICIANT: Brothers and sisters, the Rite of Baptism is complete. I now invite the Parents and Godparents to leave the safety of the battlements and run breathlessly toward [name]'s point of impact. Trust that our sharp-shooters will do their best to cover you while you attempt to rescue [name] from the River. As you do, remember that, figuratively speaking, there is no rescuing [name] from the River, just as there is no rescuing anyone, which makes the lack of rescuing bearable, and beautiful, and forgivable. Amen.

CONGREGATION: Amen.

(PARENTS AND GODPARENTS should descend battlements, exit gatehouse and barbican, rush to River's edge. PARENTS AND GODPARENTS should arrive sooner than they actually do. Storm should howl. PARENTS should howl. River should course with a deep, unsolvable howling. CONGREGATION meditates on this, descends battlements, returns to sanctuary. Hymns are hummed. Slickers are held tight. Little is said. All is forgiven.)

THIS
EVERYTHING

by EMMA HOOPER

OH DO YOU HEAR that oh listen oh oh.
      Stop
      Listen.
Do you hear that?
Such a thing, such a sound such music
      Music!
Is everything
Isn't it
Light and goodness and warmth and wind and

God.
That's God
Isn't it.
Music is God
Isn't it.

Outside the window a street boy—or girl, he couldn't really tell, hair short and body thin—was playing a flute, a simple flute, not too well, but not too bad. And inside the window Joseph was sitting up, straight up, in bed. He wanted to call his mother, wanted her to hear this, to hear it, too, but also didn't want to say a word to make a sound and interrupt this, this

Light
And goodness
And warmth
And wind
And everything
This everything.

So he stayed silent until she came in herself, to see why he wasn't up yet, why he wasn't down at breakfast, and he whispered to her, Do you hear that oh listen oh.

And she walked over to the window and looked down and saw the street girl—or boy—and the flute and said, Oh, yes, I hear it.

And she walked over and sat on the side of his bed and put a hand on the head of her boy, body of a man, mind of a boy, her boy, and said, like she did every morning,

Yes, Joseph, it is beautiful, isn't it?

Even though it wasn't, really.

And then she used that hand to wipe away his tears and lead him down toward breakfast.

We are lucky, said Joseph, on the stairs, so tall he needed to bend to fit, so broad his mother had to walk behind, aren't we? To be so close to God?

Yes, said his mother. And that the chicken decided to lay again so we can have eggs for breakfast. We are lucky and the chicken is lucky.

His mother was good.

His mother was she was always good she was she was good But

She didn't hear it. Not like him.

The music played and she closed the window she walked

away she wanted breakfast, she wanted him to stop, she wanted him to stop, to come, to breakfast, she didn't know he didn't need food, he was full, he was full up with listening. His mother was good but she wasn't full like him, she wasn't full up.

She was tired.

Sometimes she said she was tired. And sometimes she would stop and listen. But her feet would always stay on the floor, on the ground, on the cold cold hard hard floor. How could you stay on the cold cold hard hard when something like that was trying so hard to lift you? Filling you, pulling you, up, up, up, all you had to do was let it and you'd be lighter than birds and you'd fly.

Joseph ate his breakfast anyway, ate all of it, and his mother smiled and said, There, that's better, isn't it?

They were walking into town one day. Walking to get milk because their cow had died last winter and they had eaten her and didn't have another one. They were walking on cobbles that tripped Joseph's feet if he didn't watch them every step and sometimes even if he did. He held his mother's hand. He carried the basket for her. He tried not to drop it, and tried not to cry when he did. People looked at them because that's what people did.

They were walking the church way, because he had asked to. Because he cried if they didn't, because sometimes there was singing that came out of there, out of those doors. Sometimes singing and sometimes organ and sometimes, sometimes, both, sometimes both.

Please, Joseph, his mother had said. We are in a hurry today. It is much longer that way. We will go that way tomorrow.

No no no, said Joseph. He sat down on the cobbles and closed his eyes and opened his mouth. There might be no singing tomorrow. There might be singing today but not tomorrow. No no no no. It was important, it was so important to go today. He banged the basket up and down, up and down on the cobbles and little brown bits came loose, came off. People ignored him because that's what people did.

Shhh, shhh, said his mother. Okay, okay.

So they were walking the church way. The basket had holes in it. Joseph carried it carefully, so carefully.

*   *   *

Joseph heard it before his mother, of course. It was already spread out, from his ears down, in warm and gold, down his arms, his heart, his guts, when his mother said, There, there you go, Joey. There you go. They walked closer and it got louder, spread down the big muscles across the tops of his legs, his knees. And closer until they were walking past the door, right past the church door, open a crack, the morning vespers leaking out the cracks around the hinges and through the space where the wood met the dirt of the street, and it spread down into Joseph's feet and, like it always did, it lifted him up, right up.

Oh, oh, oh.

Not far, an inch or two, just enough to be up, to be away from the ground. The cold, the hard. Up and yellow and warm. Barely noticeable, really. But up, away, just enough.

Oh, oh, oh, he said.

Yes, yes, said his mother. Shhh, shhh. And, holding his hand, she walked a little more quickly, away from the door, the sound.

People ignored them, because that's what they did.

*   *   *

A priest came around the corner, from the back of the church, from where the latrines were. He was visiting. He was from the big city, the real city, of Bari. He was old and visiting and from Bari so he could go use the latrines whenever he wanted, even during vespers. He came around the corner and saw Joseph. Big as a bull, one hand in his mother's, one hand tight around a basket handle, both feet clear off the ground.

Oh, he said.

Shhh, Joseph's mother was saying.

Oh, said Joseph. Oh, oh.

Excuse me, please, said the priest, now walking level with them. With Joseph's mother, anyway. Excuse me, but what is the name of your son?

The first cathedral they took him to was in Bari. Joseph had never been anywhere so crowded, with so many smells. His mother traveled all the way there with him in the cart, sitting across from two priests, both thin and serious. It's a miracle, said one, the elder.

It's terribly holy or terribly unholy, said the other.

We don't know which.

It's very hot, said Joseph. It's very hot in here.

I know, said his mother, I know, I know.

His mother cried when they arrived and Joseph said, It's okay, it's okay. The cart turned around with her still in it, headed back home.

Joseph walked with the two priests toward the biggest church he had ever seen. So many walls, so many walls, he said. Inside it was totally silent.

They changed his clothes. They gave him bread, which he ate, and wine, which he did not drink. They had him wash his face and body and when he didn't do it well enough they did it for him.

Then took him to the Cardinal. Okay, they said. Show him. Show him what you can do.

And Joseph, who still had the basket in one hand, stood there in front of the Cardinal, whose cassock was red as red as red as chicken's blood, and Joseph did not drop the basket. He stood and he held on and he did not drop the basket for a minute, for two, for five.

Um, said the Cardinal.

Well, said the old priest, he…

Joseph, said the other priest, the young one, show him.

I'm showing him, said Joseph.

You're not doing anything.

I'm not dropping anything.

What? said the old priest.

Joseph, said the young priest. Show him the miracle. Show him your flying.

Flying?

Your flying. You, flying.

Oh, said Joseph. I can't.

You can't? said both priests.

Um, said the Cardinal.

It's quiet. Quiet, quiet, quiet, said Joseph.

Um, said the young priest.

It's too quiet, said Joseph.

Joseph, please, said the old priest.

Too quiet, said Joseph. Too quiet too quiet too quiet. He said it loud. He said it louder and louder and louder.

Um, said the Cardinal.

You need noise? said the old priest.

No, said Joseph, no, no, no, no.

Oh for heaven's—said the young priest.

Music, said Joseph. Music.

Music? asked the old priest.

Music? asked the Cardinal.

The old priest left the room, went to the pipe organ, and started playing. And even though the organ was in another part of the cathedral altogether, it was louder than everything except God, which was the point. Joseph closed his eyes. And the music shone

And it shone

   And shone

   And shone

   And shone.

And Joseph's feet were two inches off the marble tiles. His basket was on the floor. Well, said the Cardinal. Well, well.

They showed Joseph to his room, offered him more bread, this time with cheese, which he ate, and more wine, which he did not drink. They left him with a bible he could not read and a candle and some water and some more wine, just in case, and went back to the Cardinal's rooms, where everyone was gathered. Everyone in black, everyone serious, everyone excited.

What do you do with a miracle, once you've found it? Once you've got it?

They couldn't decide.

We could kill him, said one monk, and see if he dies.

And if he doesn't die when we kill him then we'll know it is God and not the Devil with him.

But what if the Devil protects him from dying?

Or what if he dies? Normal, not like a devil, no smoke or anything, just normal, dead, and then we've killed him?

I liked his mother...

Does he have any other miracles?

Another miracle would be helpful,

Would be a clue.

I don't think he has any more miracles...

We could feed him stones.

Yes! Stones!

Stones?

And see if they turn into bread in his mouth,

Or berries,

Or snakes.

Feed him snakes?

No, see if the stones turn to snakes...

That's not a bad idea, though, feeding him snakes.

Where would we get snakes?

I have an aunt—

There was a sound. They stopped. They turned toward the door, toward the sound of heavy feet at the door. It was Joseph. His new clothes were soiled, already. He had followed the voices, the only sound in the quiet, quiet cathedral, to find them.

I'm afraid, he said.

They waited.

He waited.

For a second, for a minute, no one said anything. Joseph had the basket in one hand. It had the bible and the candle in it. He had put the bible and the candle in it. He liked the white and the black. The black and the white.

Well, there's our other miracle, said the old priest, finally.

Other miracle?

Yes. Another miracle. Look, the candle and the bible. The basket is full of holes, and yet neither falls out. The man is an idiot and yet he carries with him The Way and The Light. It's a miracle, we can surely call that a miracle, which means two miracles, total, one of which, this one, is definitely not a Devil's trick, what with the Bible, and the candle, so that settles it. No need for snakes, no need for killing.

I'm not sure—

I'm afraid, said Joseph, again. I'm afraid of snakes.

It's okay, said the old priest. There are no snakes here. It's okay, it's okay.

They decided against the snakes, the rocks, the killing. They took the weeping Mary statue out of one of the alcoves and draped white cloth from one sconce across to another and down the back inner wall. Joseph was to stand here, just in front of the white cloth, during certain set hours. A monk had drawn a circle in chalk on the stone alcove floor so Joseph would know where to stay. During certain set hours, the public could come and stand before him, not too close, not touching the circle, and the old priest would play the organ, one of his most full and shaking pieces, and

Oh

Oh

Oh

Joseph would, always, close his eyes

Oh

And the gold warm, the gold good the

Oh
  Oh
  Oh

Would spread out and down and

Oh,

His feet would lift. He would be lifted. The music would lift him up and off. Not far, not high, but enough. Enough to be off. Off the cold hard floor that everyone else, everyone watching, stood on. The floor dirty with them. The floor cold and hard and shared and not enough, not enough to hold him, to hold the gold warm the gold good, oh, no, no, yes, yes, good there is good, there is good there is God and up he would go, up, just a bit, gold and warm and music and God and oh.

They had him in bare feet to maximize the effect.

There was a stool just off to the side, for when he wasn't working. He could sit there and eat bread and cheese. He could sit there and look at pictures in the Bible they gave him, the new one, with pictures, or rearrange the candle and the Bible, the old one, in his basket, so that the black, the white, sat just right next to each other, and so that the candle wouldn't roll away.

And the monks and the priests and the Cardinal stood a little ways off, and watched, and saw all the people, every day more people, drawn to the miracle, people awed by the awesomeness of it all, God, life, the cathedral, the white cloth, and they felt fairly sure, almost totally sure, that they were doing the right thing, the best thing.

And when Joseph couldn't sleep, back in his room, he ran his hands up and down the stubble of his cheeks and thought about the chicken at home and hoped she was laying and hoped his mother had eggs. Eggs and no snakes.

More people came. Every day more. They pressed in close, toes right up to the chalk of the circle. They breathed heavy and wet across it. Still, Joseph closed his eyes and let the music in and shut everything, everyone else, out and rose up, up.

And more people came, and more, toes and breath and eyes all looking, watching, ears not really listening, not really caring about the music, just eyes watching and still Joseph shut them out and rose up, up.

And then, one day, someone touched Joseph.

It was a woman. A medium-aged woman, who had a child at home. A girl with blue-pox fever, whose whole body was crying in sweat with it, whose face was shut, turned off, for two days already when the woman left home, on foot, to come here, to find the miracle, to find help. Her husband had already died of it, two weeks ago. Her sons, too. The girl was left with an aunt. The woman reached out. The woman touched Joseph.

And Joseph fell.

Everyone gasped.

And the floor was cold, was hard where Joseph hit.

Okay, said the Cardinal. No touching. That has to be a rule.

The others agreed. They put up a sign.

The people weren't happy. What's the point, they said, if we can't touch the miracle? If we can't be healed?

Be healed by witness, said the young priest, who was on Joseph-guarding duty. Be healed by the presence of the miracle of God.

But there was a man whose leg had been trampled by a horse, a man whose living was made running messages and packages from house to house, who wasn't good for anything else, a man who needed his leg back, needed a miracle.

And there was a man who didn't love, didn't want, the woman his family was having him marry. Who didn't love, didn't want any woman. Who knew this but also knew that if anyone else knew he would be killed and, worse, his father would cry, would cry both before and after the killing.

And there was a girl whose kitten had lost all her fur and one eye.

And there was a woman who gave birth to sleeping children who wouldn't wake, again and again.

And there was

And there was

And there was

And they shouted their stories at Joseph, and they reached out toward him, and they shouted against the music, over it.

The young priest put a pew in the way, lengthwise between the crowds and himself and Joseph. He pushed them back, away, with as little force as possible, given the circumstances, Please, he said, please, stay back, stay quiet, please.

And Joseph fell. Again and again.

He backed into the farthest bit of his circle; he lifted the white cloth up and over his head, he hid behind it, rose up behind it, like a ghost. When he fell he tangled in it like a seagull in a net.

Once he fell and tangled and landed on his face and his nose hit first and blood, red and red and red, like chicken blood, sprayed out onto the white cloth. The pilgrims tumbled over each other to reach out to it, to touch it. Holy man, holy blood, healing man, healing blood.

It's too much, said the young priest.

I thought that was the point, said a monk. The more people affected by the miracle, the better. The more people who witness the wonder—

He's falling, said the young priest. What kind of message is that to send? God lifts, then drops, his children?

The Cardinal sighed.

Maybe if we had a rope, said the monk. Or ropes…

It's too much, said the old priest.

I'm afraid, said Joseph. He was on his stool, in the corner. He had brought it in himself.

It's too much, said the Bishop, who had come down just to deal with this. Who was in a seat taller and redder than anyone else's.

So they moved him. There were too many people in Bari. It was a capital, it was a port; people came from everywhere, every day people in and out and in and out, it was overwhelming, it was too much. They moved him to the cathedral in Lecce, smaller, inland.

Before they did, the last evening before they did, the old priest took Joseph out to see the sea. He had never seen the sea before.

Blue,

    Huge,

    Moving and moving and moving.

My mother, said Joseph.

Yes? said the old priest.

Bigger than the entire inside of him.

Remember my mother, said Joseph. I, I...

I'm sure she remembers you, said the old priest.

The water bigger than the entire inside of him.

Everything, everything,

Blue, blue.

Joseph walked toward it, toes getting wet, and the old priest stopped him and helped him take off his sandals and his hose, helped him lift up his tunic, away from the water, helped him walk into it. Joseph stepped over the waves as they rolled past, like a child's jump rope. I want home, said Joseph. It was November. The cold of the water was acute. Joseph walked out and out and out into it.

It will be better, where we're going, said the old priest, guiding Joseph around, back toward the shore, both their tunics dark and wet. It will be.

My mother, said Joseph.

*   *   *

The cathedral in Lecce was smaller. It was brand-new, didn't have any miracles of its own yet. The Archbishop met them at the doors. Welcome, Friar Joseph! he said, arms open. Welcome! Welcome! We are so glad to have you. We are so glad.

Friar? whispered the old priest to the young priest, one on either side of their lumbering, limping miracle, helping him up the stairs.

Just go with it, whispered the young priest.

Joseph clutched his basket and said, Blue, please? Blue cloth?

So they draped blue cloth around his alcove this time. Even though it wasn't Advent. It was close to Advent, anyway, and it was what Joseph wanted. At dinner they had him sit with everyone else, nuns and monks and priests and archbishop all together, and gave him tomatoes, along with the bread and cheese and wine. Joseph ate all of his and then all of the ones surreptitiously rolled down the table to him by the Archbishop. Joseph didn't drink his wine.

*   *   *

The organ wasn't finished yet, so they had to make do with a small choir. They did a trial run after dinner, Joseph in his new, blue alcove, the choir just a little bit away from him, in their stalls. They cleared their throats, found their notes and,

Oh,

It worked. The Archbishop hugged himself, grinned.

The next morning there was a queue outside the cathedral doors. It snaked down the steps and across the square and out along the road, past the shoemaker's, even, all the way to the silversmith's. A young girl walked up and down selling fruit to the people waiting. A young boy was offering bespoke portraits of people with the new Holy Friar or the cathedral or both. By the time the 6 a.m. bells rang and they opened up the doors, the line had stretched past the silversmith's to the cooper's, and on and out to where the streets gave way to brush and pebbles, to where you could feel the salt of the sea.

They poured in through the now-opened doors. They pressed up against Joseph's blue cloth. They reached out for him.

*　　*　　*

There were two nuns, one on either side of the alcove, holding hands across it. Please, they said. Please, sir, please, ma'am. Joseph turned away, faced the cloth. The choir started singing and he closed his eyes and rose up and half-said half-sung,

Swimming,

Joseph swimming.

Even though he'd never been swimming in his life. Even though he had been to the sea just that once.

The crowds continued on and in, even when they had to stop to give Joseph and the nuns breaks. Even when it was time for mass, the point at which, normally, all the curious visitors would leave. This time they stayed. They all lined up again, this time for communion, and the cathedral, still small, still new, ran out of bread, out of wine, before even half of them had taken it.

What about the emergency supply? whispered the serving priest to an altar boy.

That was the emergency supply, said the altar boy. That's it.

Oh dear, said the priest. Oh dear.

Is the bakery still open? asked the altar boy.

We can't, said the priest... Can we?

All week the nuns held hands firmly across the alcove so that their wrists had to be bandaged, had to be reinforced against the people always, always pressing against them. All week the crowds grew and grew again, just like in Bari, only this time in a smaller space, so it was even harder for Joseph to hear, to breathe. All week the altar boy slung his plainclothes cloak over his vestment and ran to the bakery, buying every last bit of bread, running loaves and rolls back to the cathedral, again and again.

And the Archbishop watched and was unsure how to feel.

Joseph started to hide under the cloth again. The crowds started breaking through, past the nuns, and the baker one morning refused to sell any more bread to the altar boy.

I can't keep turning away all my regular customers, she said. There's never any bread left, never anything left for them.

And, under the heavier blue cloth, Joseph could barely hear anything, could barely breathe. Couldn't fly.

*   *   *

There was a meeting. The Archbishop rubbed his temples. The nuns held out their bruised wrists, wore slings. I was wrong, said the old priest. I'm sorry, I was wrong.

But we can't ignore a miracle! said the young priest. We can't hide it away!

Nobody likes me anymore, said the altar boy.

Okay, said the Archbishop. Okay.

Okay, said the old priest, Here's an idea.

He asked Joseph, that evening, that last evening, if he wanted to go back to see the sea again before going away, before going home.

I've seen it, said Joseph.

You're sure? said the old priest.

Joseph didn't reply. He was folding and rolling the blue cloth as small as he could and stuffing it into his basket. The nuns had said he could keep it.

A laborer in the vineyards was the first to see the cart coming, to see Joseph, asleep between two priests, drooped down onto the older of the two. The laborer put down his shearing knife, buried it a little in an out-of-the-way place so as to be safe and left a marker of two crossed vine leaves so as to be able to find it again, and took off running, back to the village, back to the home of Joseph's mother.

She was mending. The needle and the linen both fell onto the floor as she stood, as she followed the laborer, back out to the road. They ran, they both ran.

She was the crowd there to meet her son and the crowd was her.

They gave her a plaque to put on the door of their home:

HERE LIVES FRIAR JOSEPH
MIRACLE OF GOD
WONDER OF WONDERS

Which the neighbors ignored, as they'd always ignored that door. Which faded in the sun so that the letters and the wood behind them were all one color, almost smooth.

* * *

The laborer went back to working in the vineyards, just like always, alongside all the other workers from the village. And when pilgrims came, lost, searching, looking for the miracle, the laborers would be the first to see them. They would stop them on the road, on the outskirts, and give them grapes to eat and wine to drink and would listen to their stories, their troubles. Then they would shake their heads and say, No, not here, I'm afraid, not here. This is a quiet village, a nothing village. They would turn them around and send them off in other directions, to wander toward other villages, other hope.

And some days the child played the flute outside Joseph's window.

And some days Joseph and his mother walked to the market past the church.

And Joseph, in the tunic his mother made him, in his tunic of bright blue cloth, closed his eyes and rose up, up.

And people ignored him, because that's what they did.

And the chicken laid.
She laid
and laid
and laid.

EVICTION

A STORY FROM DETROIT

story by JEFFREY WILSON

art by ARMIN OZDIC

KENNY BRINKLEY AND SANDI COMBS, PICTURED BELOW, WERE LIFE LONG DETROITERS. MR. BRINKLEY PLAYED SAXOPHONE IN THE RENOWNED MOTORTOWN REVUE, WHICH SUPPORTED TOURING MOTOWN ARTISTS IN THE '60S. ON THESE TOURS HE PLAYED WITH LEGENDS SUCH AS STEVIE WONDER, THE TEMPTATIONS, AND THE SUPREMES.

MR. BRINKLEY INHERITED HIS HOME FROM HIS AUNT—A FORMER CHRYSLER AUTOWORKER WHO HAD MIGRATED WITH THE FAMILY FROM ARKANSAS IN THE EARLY PART OF THE TWENTIETH CENTURY. KENNY AND HIS PARTNER, SANDI COMBS, LIVED IN THE HOME THAT HAD BEEN IN HIS FAMILY FOR NEARLY SIXTY-FIVE YEARS. THE MORTGAGE WAS PAID IN FULL.

678

IN 2002, HOWEVER, THE COUPLE FELL ON HARD TIMES, WITH KENNY UNDERGOING MAJOR HEART SURGERY AND SANDI LOSING HER POSITION AT COLLEGE FOR THE CREATIVE STUDIES. WITH LIMITED RESOURCES, THE COUPLE FELL BEHIND ON THEIR PROPERTY TAXES, ULTIMATELY LOSING THEIR HOME IN TAX AUCTION IN 2009. THE FOLLOWING IS BASED ON SEVERAL INTERVIEWS WITH SANDI.

SC-I THOUGHT EVERYTHING WAS FINE. WE'D BEEN PAYING FOR FOUR YEARS, UNTIL THIS DAY IN OCTOBER WHEN I CAME OUT AND FOUND MY CAR ON BLOCKS. SO I HAD TO GO TO THE POLICE STATION TO MAKE THE REPORT.

I COME BACK AND THERE IS A WHITE GUY IN A LITTLE SPORTS CAR SITTING ON THE OTHER SIDE OF THE STREET, STARING AT OUR HOUSE.

AT FIRST I THOUGHT, WHATEVER, BUT THEN I GOT TO THE FRONT DOOR AND I TURNED AROUND AND WENT BACK OUT THERE.

CAN I HELP YOU WITH SOMETHING?

DO YOU LIVE IN THAT HOUSE?

YEAH, I DO. WHY?

ARE YOU AWARE THAT IT'S ON THE AUCTION BLOCK? THE ONE THAT STARTS MONDAY.

SC-THIS WAS THE FRIDAY BEFORE.

NO... NO, IT'S NOT.

YEAH, IT IS, AND I'M GONNA BID ON IT.

HEY, SANDI. HOW YOU DOING?

WOULD YOU MIND MOVING THE VAN SO WE CAN GET THIS OTHER TREE DOWN, THE BIG ONE?

SC–HE SAYS, AS IF WE'RE VERY GOOD FRIENDS... THEY HAD ALREADY CUT DOWN THE SMALL ONE.

WHEN HE SAID THAT TO ME, I WAS JUST, YOU KNOW... I WAS IN SHOCK. AND I LOOKED AT HIM AND I SAID, "DO YOU KNOW WHAT?"

I SAID, "THIS TIME YOU'VE CROSSED THE LINE."

I WENT BACK INTO THE HOUSE AND KENNY RAN DOWN THE STAIRS.

CALL THE POLICE!!

KENNY RAN TO MOVE HIS VAN...

SC–BUT HE DIDN'T MOVE T SO THEY COULD CUT THE TREE.

INSTEAD, HE PULLED IT RIGHT UP SO THEY COULDN'T EVEN GET NEAR IT.

I WAS GOING UP THE STAIRS TO CALL THE POLICE AND I GOT TO THE LANDING. I SCREAMED OUT, AND EXCUSE MY FRENCH, BUT I SAID...

OH MY GOD, THEY CUT DOWN OUR FUCKING TREE.

I HAVE NEVER SCREAMED IN MY LIFE, EVER. I'M A QUIET SPIRIT. BUT IT JUST CAME OUT OF ME, YOU KNOW.

AT THAT MOMENT I HAD SOME DISCOMFORT IN MY CHEST. I WOULDN'T REALLY CALL IT CHEST PAIN. IT WASN'T THAT BAD. IT WAS LIKE A TIGHTNESS. LIKE MAYBE WHEN YOU RUN TOO FAR OR WALK... YOU KNOW... WHATEVER.

I DID A FEW THINGS TO CALM DOWN AND PROMISED MY FRIEND I'D GET IT CHECKED OUT.

LATER THAT DAY IN THE EMERGENCY ROOM...

SC—MY HEART WAS FUNCTIONING AT 10 PERCENT BUT THERE WAS NO BLOCKAGE.

SO THIS THING, IT'S... IT'S CONSIDERED HEART FAILURE AND IT'S CALLED TAKOTSUBO CARDIOMYOPATHY [BROKEN-HEART SYNDROME]. THAT'S THE DOCTOR WHO DISCOVERED IT.

AND IT'S SOMETHING THAT HAPPENS WHEN YOU GET SO CRAZILY STRESSED THAT IT CAUSES, UH, MUSCLES AND VESSELS IN YOUR HEART TO SPASM UP AND MIMIC A HEART ATTACK.

THEY SAID IF I HADN'T GONE IN THERE, I WOULD HAVE DIED IN MY SLEEP THAT NIGHT.

AFTER THAT THERE WAS NOTHING WE COULD DO, REALLY, TO GET THE HOUSE BACK. THE JUDGE SIGNED THE EVICTION ORDER. WE COULDN'T WIN AND I DIDN'T WANT ANYONE GOING TO JAIL. I COULDN'T LIVE WITH THAT.

678

ALSO, I WOULD HAVE ENDED UP IN THE HOSPITAL AGAIN, AND KENNY, TOO, FROM THE STRESS.

SC—I KNOW DETROIT NEEDED TO GET BETTER, BUT I WISH THEY WOULD'VE CHOSEN A DIFFERENT MODEL.

SHIP OUT ALL THE DETROITERS. SHIP IN NEW, YOUNG PEOPLE.

WE'RE GOING TO KICK YOU AND STEAL YOUR HOMES FROM YOU. AND JUST GO AWAY. THAT'S NOT RIGHT. THAT... THAT'S WHY KENNY AND I ARE ANGRY, THAT'S WHY WE'RE LEAVING.

BECAUSE DETROIT, MORE OR LESS, HAS BECOME A PROSTITUTE AND THAT'S NOT THE KIND OF PLACE WE WANT TO LIVE.

DEAR SANDI,

I WANTED TO SEND MY CONDOLENCES. I DIDN'T GET TO KNOW KENNY THAT WELL BUT MY IMPRESSION WAS HE WAS A COOL, LAID-BACK GUY. WOULD'VE BEEN GREAT TO TALK MORE ABOUT MUSIC WITH HIM.

GREETINGS, JEFF,

KENNY'S HEALTH HAD BEEN DECLINING FOR A LONG TIME. THE ONLY PLACE HE WENT WAS TO THE DOC OR HOSPITAL AFTER WE MOVED OUT. WHEN THEY TOOK HIS HOME, IT WAS THE STRAW THAT BROKE THE CAMEL'S BACK.

1933-2017.

STAY BRAVE
MY HERCULES

by ERNIE WANG

THERE'S A TUG ON my skirt. I look down.

"Hi there, young fella," I say.

"Hercules," he says.

I nod.

"I have a question," he says.

"Go on then, young man."

"Hercules," he says, "how do I become strong like you?"

I look at his parents. They beam at their son and smile like they already know.

We're at the corner of Frontierland and Fantasyland. From a distance, I hear screams at the top of Splash Mountain and calliope music from the riverboat making its way downstream. The smells of buttered popcorn and fried churros wafting through the muggy afternoon air remind me that I'm hungry and that I'll be done with this shift soon.

In the far corner, I see Buzz and Woody ham it up for a large Chinese tour group. Cameras click, and the tourists point and shout furiously at them in Chinese. Buzz and Woody take it in stride and swivel randomly and wave enthusiastically and do this jiggy kind of dance. Today, Zac is Buzz. He's a good dude. He sees me, and without turning from the tourists, he lowers his arm and flips me the middle finger.

I kneel down and clasp the kid's hands. He stands straight and puffs out his chest. I no longer have to think back to the script. I got this shit on lock.

All of Disney's eighteen Herculeses have nicknames for each other; mine is Babyface Hercules. There's also Douchebag Hercules, Nascar Hercules, the high-school twins Juicehead Hercules and Jailbait Hercules, Born-Again Hercules, and everybody's favorite: Grandpa Hercules. Grandpa Hercules is literally a grandpa, and between shifts he brings out photos of his granddaughters in the break room, and we tell him they're beautiful, because we love him. Then one of the Jasmines or Snow Whites helps him reapply his makeup, because he needs a shit-ton.

I've been Hercules ever since I dropped out of college to be with Jay. I would've come back even if he wasn't sick. But the night he called and matter-of-factly explained that it had spread to his lymph nodes and his testicles and brain, I immediately packed a backpack and left the Michigan snow and drove straight back to Florida.

Jay is thirty years older than me. He had warned me when we first met that something like this might happen. Bodies break down over time, he had said.

On the drive back, I replayed his last words on the phone: *I am statistically unlikely to make it to the end of the year, but these standard deviations are large, as you might expect, Jeremy.* Jay always talks like that. He's an actuary, which surprises nobody.

When I pulled into his driveway that morning in yet another torrential Orlando rainstorm, my fuel tank empty and my eyes bleary and my breath reeking of gas-station coffee, he walked out onto the driveway, his glasses fogged and dripping, his robe pressing into his gaunt frame as it absorbed the rain. He looked at me as if he was struggling for words, and then he said, "You just drove a little over twelve hundred miles, which by my calculations puts your average speed at—" I flung myself onto him and kissed him.

"Not fast enough," I said as I pulled him back into the house.

"I'm starving. Let's grub," I said later as we lay in his bed. "And I'm done with this long-distance shit," I said.

"And I told my parents I'm moving in with you, and that you're not doing well." He just kind of shook his head and looked sad.

The first thing I did after I moved in with Jay was look for a job. Aladdin and Gaston and Donald Duck train at my gym, and one day we were all talking by the water fountain, and they said they might be able to help. Things kind of snowballed, and the next thing I knew, I was at Disney employment headquarters getting my head measured and my chest waxed under the watchful, glowering scrutiny of the casting director.

I got over myself and threw all my chips into this job. I mean, it's not awful, and at night, after Jay falls asleep, I hop online and look for other jobs, like I promised him I'd do. I get to the park an hour before my shift and they tell me where I need to be at and at what time and anything I need to be aware of. Then I get in line with the other cast members for makeup. I go to the locker room and change into costume. The casting director sometimes examines me—she calls it quality control—and checks me off on her clipboard. Then I'm out the door, squinting under the bright Disney sun. For the next three hours, I smile and hug and flex, and the best part is that I get to drop wisdom bombs on adoring crowds, even though my answers are limited to what's on script. Be strong and be brave, I say. Listen to your parents. They're not half-bad.

During orientation, the casting director handed me a thick binder filled with scripts to memorize so I'd know how to stay in character for every conceivable situation. Every catastrophe here is called a situation, and every single one is covered. If lightning strikes and fries a sixth-grade class, there's a section on what Hercules would do. When a soccer mom tries to kiss me on my lips, I'm supposed to pretend to play hard-to-get and then try to distract her by shoving my muscles in her face. Hercules can be such a tease. Then when her husband tries to pick a fight with me, I'm supposed to pretend that we're actually play-fighting, and then I'm supposed to run and get out of there. Hercules can be a bitch. When a kid's being a jackass and asks a dumb question—this part I actually like—I'm supposed to twist his question into one that's more family-friendly, and then from there I'll give one of my stock answers. In the end, it's all about staying on script and running and evading. I am a born natural at that.

The boy and his parents stare at me expectantly.

"Hercules," the boy repeats, "how do I become strong like you?"

I'm hungry and it's my break soon and the scent of those churros is slaying me, but this kid is adorable, so I squeeze his hands and gaze into his wide eyes.

"Young man, what's your name?"

He takes a deep breath and shouts, "Garen."

"Young Garen, I want you to be strong, I want you to be brave, and I want you to listen to your parents. Do you understand?"

Garen swivels and looks at his parents, who look this close to combusting with pride. They reach for each other's hands and nod and mouth the words *I understand, Hercules* at him.

Garen focuses his attention back toward me. He puffs his chest out again, and he shouts:

"Dad wears Mom's dresses and makeup like you do."

When he sees me with my mouth agape, he attempts to clarify.

"But only when Mom's not home," he says.

I know the absolute worst thing I can do in this moment is to look at Garen's parents, but that's what I do. Their hands are clasped, and their smiles remain plastered, but nothing registers in their eyes. It's like four vapid orbs gatewaying into an abyss. Then she shoves away his hand and turns to look at him, and it's like I can already see her about to say *Honey, is that true?* and I can already imagine him struggling to come up with some way to respond, and then I'm like: Nah this fool is so boned. And in this moment, the only thing running through my mind is, I'll be damned, that binder doesn't cover everything after all.

"They don't pay us enough for this shit," Zac says. Zac and I are slumped in our chairs in the break room. We're still in costume.

In the far corner, Annabelle is having lunch with her daughter. In the past, as Ariel, Annabelle was legendary for how she connected with the kids. There would be a line of children with their parents snaking around the corner, patiently waiting to hug her and tell her about school and their pets. She would smile with delight and say, "Tell me more." Then Annabelle had her daughter. When she returned from maternity leave, she had put on a little weight. They gave her an ultimatum: take a new job as a fully covered Mickey or leave. Her Mickey headpiece sits on the table as her daughter cries and says she doesn't like to be left in employee child care. "I'm so sorry, sweetie," Annabelle says. She looks exhausted.

"So what did you say to that train-wreck family?" Zac asks.

I shrug.

Garen's mom had marched toward us and was about to yank Garen away when I stood and gently held her hand.

"Ma'am," I said quietly. She tried to shake my hand off. Her back and shoulders were as rigid as a springboard.

"Just let us go," she said, and her shoulders slumped, and I saw tears begin to well around her squinting eyes.

I nodded. "Can I just say something real quick to Garen?" I asked. She hesitated, and then she tightly nodded.

I knelt down and grabbed Garen's hands once again. He looked confused and as if he might cry, too. I leaned forward and spoke directly into his ear.

"Young man," I said, and he whispered a tiny *yes* back.

"Hercules wants you to know," I said, "that no matter what happens, your dad and mom love you very much, okay?" He nodded. "So I want you to be brave, and I want you to be strong, and I want you to listen to everything they tell you, okay?" He nodded again. "And now," I whispered, "Hercules wants you to go give your mom and dad a big hug. Can you do that for Hercules?" He nodded one last time, and he ran to his mom and hugged her tight, and he ran to his dad, who had been standing unsurely in the background. Then they were gone, and my shift was about over, so I stood and walked back to the break room.

I think for a moment. "I guess I stayed on script," I tell Zac. He stares. "I mean the script's not half-bad," I say, and he nods and loses interest.

Jay looks up from his spreadsheets when I come home that night. His company lets him work from home, so most nights I find him surrounded by reams of paper. He doesn't let the cancer stop him from putting in a full workday, so he's meticulous about tracking his hours.

"How was your day?" he asks.

"Total shit show," I say. "This woman found out her

husband is a cross-dresser, and their son is probably going to blame himself for the next ten years."

"So just another Disney day?" he says.

"Yep. How was yours?"

He takes off his glasses and rubs his eyes before he reaches for a stack of papers and pointedly lifts one.

"Jeremy," he says, "we need to talk inheritance and insurance. I've run some initial calculations, and the projections indicate…"

I tune out when he begins to use big words, but he gets more animated as he picks up steam on his findings, and he's sexy as fuck as he incessantly taps his paper with his pen, but I can't sit still, so I strip off my shirt and straddle him.

He stops talking.

"Ah," he says.

"Let's talk about your impending death some other time," I say.

Later, I step out of the shower and find Jay curled up on the sofa. His glasses, off-kilter, are hooked onto one ear and hanging on his forehead over wisps of his fine hair. He snores lightly. I stare at his face. When he's awake, he always looks as if he's worried about something, probably because he is. Worried about me, probably. He likely has months left, and the only thing he seems to have on his mind is whether I'll be okay after he's gone. It's only when he's asleep that he ly looks relaxed. He snorts, and traces of a thin smile begin to form. I wonder what he's dreaming about, and that makes me smile.

I was back home with Jay for summer break when we first learned about the cancer. By then, we had been together for two years. The prognosis was bright then, and Jay was adamant that I return to college.

"I'll be cured before you come back," he said.

That night, needing to get out of the house, we went to P.F. Chang's.

"Are we celebrating anything special tonight?" our server asked.

"Just our health," Jay said, gently.

"That's very sweet," the server said, smiling. She studied us, and she said, "Well, you two look as healthy as—"

"It's my birthday," I cut her off. Her mouth curved into an O, and she said she'd give us a minute to look at the menu.

Jay turned and gave me his look.

"What? Health doesn't get you free cake at P.F. Chang's," I said.

"I suppose that's true," he said.

We were subdued for most of the dinner. It was toward the end, after dessert, that I could no longer hold back.

"What if things go wrong?" I blurted out. I was reeling from too many apple martinis.

"Jeremy," he said, "do you realize, statistically, how many standard deviations off we need to be to see the treatment fail?"

I said nothing.

"It's a little under three," he said. "Expressed numerically, that equates to—"

"Okay. Okay."

He reached for my hand and nodded.

"I'm going to be fine, Jeremy. You have to trust me, and you have to trust in the numbers."

I relented. In the darkened room, the candle flickered over his creases and reflected tiny orange flames in both lenses of his glasses. He's all lit up in fire, I thought. And I believed.

But I should never have left him.

Everybody's in a shitty mood at the park today. This happens sometimes. Some days, with no reasonable explanation, foul moods spread and take over entire sections of the park like a contagion. By midmorning, under the already-wilting sun, tempers flare within families and in groups of middle school friends, Tomorrowland's Space Mountain dome standing glumly in the backdrop.

This includes Cody, the eight-year-old bald-headed Make-A-Wish kid who's sitting in his wheelchair with his arms crossed. He glares as his parents stand helplessly to his side and as the swath of media photographers fumble with the cameras draped around their necks and do not take photos.

Cody's mom approaches him and places her hand on his frail shoulder.

"Honey," she says, "is there anything we can do to make you happy?"

"I want to go home," he says, and the Make-A-Wish and Disney public relations people wince in unison.

"But sweetie," she says, "isn't this what you wanted to do more than anything in the world? What changed?"

"Disneyland sucks," he shouts, and I see two photographers quietly pack their cameras back into their cases.

Dad is starting to unravel, and I see him approach Cody with his fists clenched. Before I realize what I'm doing, I find myself standing between Cody and his dad, my face lit up in smiles. I motion subtly at his dad before I kneel down and face Cody.

"Hi there, young man. Your name is Cody, right?"

Cody stares at my biceps with wide eyes. My physique generally has that effect on most boys who regularly worship Marvel superheroes, and I can imagine, tragically, that the effect is greater on a kid as sick as Cody. He nods and looks into my eyes shyly.

"Young man," I say, "I hear you on your discomforts. It's too hot and it's too crowded and everybody's in a bad mood." He nods emphatically. "So tell me," I say, "if you could do anything right now, what would it be?"

His face brightens.

"Video games," he says. I nod in complete agreement. I say, "Hercules loves video games. What's your favorite?" and he shouts, "*Minecraft*," and I silently sigh in relief. That's like the one game I have some knowledge of.

"That's Hercules's favorite game," I say, and he looks as though he might jump out of his wheelchair and hug me. "What are you working on right now?" I ask, and Cody smiles and closes his eyes for several moments, as though he had transported himself out of Disney and into his Minecraft world. When he opens his eyes, they are shining.

"I found a way that I can fly forever," he says.

I say, "Hercules wants to hear *all* about this." The photographers take their cameras back out of their cases, and as the cameramen begin to record from a distance, Cody explains to me in a feverish pitch and with two animated hands the mechanics and items he acquires before he sprints and dives off a cliff and launches himself higher and higher into an infinite horizon—eventually so high, in fact, he explains, that the game stops rendering his image, and he disappears entirely from the screen.

"That is very high," I agree. "But Cody," I say, "if you fly beyond the horizon and disappear, won't you miss your parents?"

"It's just a game, Hercules."

"Touché."

"Hercules?"

"Yes, Cody."

"I'm dying, you know," he says. From the corner of my eyes, I sneak a peek at Cody's parents. They stare intently at their son.

"I know," I say.

"Hercules?"

"Yes, Cody."

"Will you come to my home and play *Minecraft* with me?"

I say nothing.

"So we can fly forever?" he says. I look into his eyes, and I can see that he is bracing for the inevitable no.

"I have an even better idea," I tell him as I begin to smile. He looks up. "Peter Pan's Flight is a short walk from here. Have you been on the ride?" He shakes his head. "Hercules promises you," I say, "that riding that ride feels just like flying. How about we take that flight together, just you and me?" He considers this for a moment before he says a quiet *okay*. I turn to his parents for permission, but they already look like they might throttle me with gratitude, so I stand and take Cody's hand as his mom pushes his wheelchair. Behind us, the photographers and media and public relations team quietly follow, and the crowd ahead splits to make room when they see the procession. But I have eyes and ears and heart for only Cody—script be damned—and he has me eating out of his hands as he patiently explains master-level tips on how to rule over the *Minecraft* domain.

A photo of me kneeling and clasping a smiling Cody's hands makes the front page of the local newspaper the next morning, along with the caption "Local Hero Captures the

Hearts of Boy and Disney Community." Over breakfast, Jay lowers the paper and raises his eyebrows.

"You sure work hard for nine dollars an hour," he says.

"They should promote me to management," I say crossly. I couldn't sleep last night.

"Or at least to playing Gaston. Now, that's a real man," Jay says as he dodges the Cheerio I flick at him. He returns to the paper, and I get ready to leave for work.

The Orlando roads are slick with rain this morning, and the traffic is heavy. I've always wondered why they chose to build the Happiest Place on Earth in practically the Wettest City in the Country. I like it when it rains, though.

I stare past the windshield wipers, sweeping frenetically to keep my vision unobscured. Outside is a sea of gray. With every gust of wind, sheets of rain shimmer. Trees shudder.

I hear the approaching wail of sirens. I pull over and stare at the ambulance as it passes by and then turns at the intersection, in the opposite direction from home. I remain parked by the curb. The sirens fade until I hear only the rain pelting the roof of the car and the furious beating of my heart. I rest my eyes and feel the heat radiate through my closed eyelids.

Yesterday, on Peter Pan's Flight, while waving a very temporary goodbye to Cody's parents and the media folk, I helped Cody step on board the suspended galleon that served as our flying ship. We settled into our seats and launched high into a dark London night. We flew over Tower Bridge and Big Ben before rising to clouds of wispy white fluff swaying under giant whirring fans made invisible behind the cloak of night sky. Below, a sea of tiny golden lights—villages of homes shining kerosene lanterns—twinkled and pulsed, as if the constellations lay not above us but below.

I looked at Cody. His face was spellbound as we glided and swooped over mountain peaks and into the heart of Neverland. At one point, our galleon dramatically lifted high into the sky to escape the wrath of an enormous crocodile. Cody whooped and wrapped his arms around me. I squeezed his shoulder and pointed down at the crocodile, who now held Captain Hook in the clutches of his jaws.

As the galleon emerged through the exit that led to the disembarking zone and to Cody's parents welcoming us back, Cody sighed and rested his head on my shoulder.

"How'd that feel, Cody?" I said. "Was that just like flying or what?"

He sighed again and embraced me and said, "That was way better than *Minecraft*." I squeezed him tight before I stood and helped him off the galleon and into his waiting wheelchair.

After insisting to Cody's parents that it was not a big deal and posing for a final round of photos, I said my goodbyes and jogged back to my post in Tomorrowland. As I navigated between throngs of people making their way to their next attraction, I imagined that it had been Jay and me flying on the galleon. Jay, being Jay, would peer over the ledge at the city below, and he'd squint and point out, "The placement of Big Ben seems off. It should be over *there*." I'd tell him to shut up and enjoy the ride. He would remain silent for a moment, and then he'd look up toward the ceiling and say, "The engineering in this facility is really quite remarkable, if you stop and consider—"

"Shut *up*," I'd say again.

I'd close my eyes and shiver when the cold air blew over my ears. In the distance, I'd hear Peter Pan and Hook's swords whirl and clang in battle as the Darling kids cheered and whistled. Jay would turn to me and pause and cock his head, and he'd say, "Is everything okay, Jeremy?" And I'd grip the ledge so hard that pain would shoot up my wrists, but he wouldn't see that, and I'd smile and say, "Yeah, just hungry. Let's get a turkey leg after this." And for the rest of the ride we would remain quiet, our galleon propelling us above a dark ocean and gliding toward the exit, where sunlight would peek in from around the corner and the cast members, bored shitless, would remind us to watch our step on our way out.

TOWNSVILLE

by NATHANIEL MINTON

I

O N A COOL OCTOBER evening Spencer Maugh walked a mile to Darrow's Orchard and entered the little shop where Clive Darrow worked for his father selling cider, pies, and jerky from a local hunter. Spencer, who'd known the Darrow family all his life, pulled out a revolver and he held up Clive to the tune of eighteen dollars and seventy-three cents.

"That's all I got, Spencer," Clive told him.

"How about that? In that bag." Spencer pointed his revolver at a greasy paper bag on the counter behind Clive.

"Just a sandwich, that's all."

"What kind?"

"Pastrami."

"You got cheese on that or anything?"

"Just mustard. On rye."

Spencer tucked his bottom lip between his teeth and placed a bullet between Clive's ears so deep even the surgeon couldn't remove it. Then he grabbed up a half gallon of cider, pocketed his eighteen and change, sat down at the picnic table out front, and ate Clive's sandwich. It was a little dry for his taste, but the cider helped it along and eventually he walked home and told his parents what he'd done.

He told them maybe he was living in a dream.

"Listen," his father said to him, "when your neighbor's dog comes for your chickens, you got to shoot that dog in the gut so he'll run home and bleed out there and you don't have to clean up the mess. You understand?"

Spencer nodded, but he didn't mean it.

"What you did to that man, there wasn't any value in it, or justice."

Spencer's mother brought some coffee and the three of them sat around the kitchen table for a while until she said, "Well, I guess I'll call the sheriff now." And she did. The sheriff came and got Spencer and took him down to the county jail, where he waited, reading back issues of *National Geographic*, for the day his peers would judge him.

He sat in the jail, learning about the death of the sun while Clive's funeral proceeded at the West Hill Cemetery, and Clive's father, Carlton, eulogized his only son with an oath to kill Spencer. Carlton was an apple grower who had married his eighth-grade sweetheart. He cut his own palm with a pruning hatchet, spilling his blood upon the coffin of his son. He cried out to the Lord. "Lord," he cried, "take my blood, so that my son may once again live through your almighty vengeance, that all our children may overcome the specter of chaos, that all our wives and mothers might bear the precious fluid of our ancestry." Clive's mother poured soft tears upon the earth and the funeral party wept and the collective seepage of their anguish filled Carlton's swollen heart.

In the fog of night, Carlton approached the county jail from the river with a Colt .45 and a sawed-off Remington. He hunched close to the ground as he crossed the newly cropped cornfields of the prison farms, and he listened for the muffled cracks of the guard's feet on the frost-dried stalks. He was not a particularly fit man. He was not a man who had spent time hunting, or in the military, or planning for post apocalyptic survival, but he was a determined man, the kind of man who needs to accomplish something specific and terrible in the limited time before he realizes what he has done. It was a brave thing he needed to do, and in his bravery he abandoned his surreptitiousness and announced himself at the gate where two deputies stood guard.

"I'm here for the man who killed my son," he said.

"That you, Carlton?" a deputy called out. He shined a light in Carlton's face.

"It's me."

"Visiting hours are over. You'll need to come back tomorrow. No exceptions."

Carlton nodded. He took out the Remington and waved it dangerously.

Shots were fired. Exceptions were made.

Climbing over the locked gate was easy for a man with a purpose, but his hands began to shake when he reached the other side. He closed the eyes of the deputies and said a short prayer over each of their bodies. Carlton prayed for their souls to go unpunished for his sins, and he prayed for forgiveness, and he prayed for their families. He prayed that their deaths had been righteous casualties of his purpose but he cried as the soles of his boots squished through brain matter to the front door, because he no longer walked with justice.

The sheriff met him at the door, and he had his gun out, and he said, "Carlton, this isn't something you need to do.

This is a thing that I, as a sworn officer of the American legal system, have under control. You need to lay down your arms. You need to realize the futility of your actions. You need to think of your family, and, for the love of God, Carlton, you need to think of my children."

Carlton had some respect for the sheriff, so he shot him in the gut with the .45, and as the man bled out on the front steps he took the keys and allowed himself entry to the jail. He walked past five empty cells before he reached Spencer. He pointed the barrel of the .45 through the bars and asked Spencer if he had any final words.

"As a matter of fact, I do," Spencer said. "I really feel I should…"

But Carlton didn't have the time for a long explanation about morality or justice, and he certainly didn't have time to listen to a forced apology from his son's killer. He had time for very few things, but he did have time to interrupt Spencer with a bullet and he had time to remove the security tapes from the jail and dispatch any remaining witnesses with an assurance usually reserved for the Almighty.

II

The surgeon did his best for Spencer. He plucked the shot from his heart with tidy hands, and he sutured each wound with delicate haste, and he really tried to save the convict's life with a jolt of electricity and a tarnished fleam because this was his oath, and because he believed if he saved this man on this momentous day, his wife would once again find him sexually attractive, and while that fantasy served as stronger motivation than his base need for food and shelter, his skills and ambition were little match for the forces of lead and blood and entropy that dictate the stanchions of a human life span. In the end, he failed to sustain Spencer's heart, and watched instead as the immortal spirit of a murderer traveled to another realm. His efforts, however, did not go unnoticed by the Darrows and the Maughs, who knew that the size of the earth is but a fraction of that of the sun, and that the seminal dynamics of heat and liquid that ignite the universe and give order to chaos are of little recompense to a heart broken or the dereliction of the sacred oath sworn by the surgeon.

The following morning the surgeon told his wife he would live forever. She shifted from heels into sensible shoes and told him to make breakfast. So he made some pancakes and served them with butter and syrup and half a grapefruit each.

"I understand it was a difficult night for you," she said. "I understand you're out there trying to save lives, but that doesn't make things any easier for me."

"I'm sorry," the surgeon said. "I'm doing the best I can. I'm doing my job, what I do best."

"But... Spencer? We all wanted him dead. Do you know how people will look at me?"

"He died." The surgeon said. "That should be the end of it."

She shook her head and slapped him so hard that the golden braid of her wedding band opened a small cut beneath his left eye. He dabbed at the blood with a paper napkin and the phone rang.

"It's for you," she said, without picking up. She handed him the receiver.

He said his name. He said yes, and no, and yes again, and then he hung up.

"I'm going to the hospital," the surgeon said. "Somebody stabbed Carlton Darrow in the throat."

"Who?"

"They didn't say."

"But we know who did it, don't we? There's less than a thousand people in this town, so we can't pretend we don't know it was Spencer's father. Right?"

"Yes," he said. "We probably can't."

"So what's being done about it?"

"Again, they didn't say."

"With all our policemen getting buried tomorrow, I doubt anybody's doing a damn thing about any of this death?"

"That's very likely," the surgeon said. "But we all need to remain calm and wait for help to arrive."

After the surgeon left for the hospital, his wife sat on the porch drinking iced tea and injecting rat poison into the three grapefruits they hadn't eaten yet. When she was ready, she put them in a gift bag with pink tissue paper and brought the package over to Spencer's parents with a smile and a note that said, "Sorry for you're loss." They thanked her, and she hugged them, and she went home, turned off all the lights in the house, and waited.

By the end of the week much of Spencer's extended family was dead, as were Frank and Jans from the paper mill, who did yard work for the Maughs and lost their lives as obstacles to a gunfight. An escaped attack dog ran down Theodore Poule and his wife, Barbara. Peter and Drew Mekner tried and failed to protect Drew's wife, Evelyn Darrow, a distant cousin of Clive's and an even further removed cousin of Spencer's, whose uncle Bart took their lives with a length of baling twine and a roll of duct tape. It was Bart's wife, Kelly, who mistakenly killed their neighbor while shooting at Sarah Mekner, who killed Bart, and it was Sarah's boyfriend who put the surgeon's wife in a coma with a .22 slug to her brain.

Her name was Marie, and the circumstances of her condition were more than one man could be expected to bear. He was a man of science and a man of faith, and both were tested in the days that followed. In one week, he performed surgery on nineteen victims of the feud and lost only three patients. He slept each night in a chair beside her bed. He knew she could hear him, because when he talked her heart rate changed, and he knew she loved him by the way her nervous system presented increased skin conductivity on the polygraph sensors he attached to her forearm.

He was not a brain surgeon, but he couldn't have helped her if he had been. There was no pressure in her skull, no bursting veins or aneurisms, nothing that could be repaired with a physical intervention. Instead there was nothing, not even sleep, because she didn't dream, and didn't have thoughts at all. She was simply alive, and there were no plugs to pull.

So he talked to her. He said, "When I was nine years old, my father took me to the hospital and had me circumcised so the kids at camp would stop making fun of me. I don't know if that helps," the surgeon said. "But it's what happened, and I'm going to keep talking, because I can tell by your vitals that the sound of my voice calms you, and if you wake up I might be able to understand how this happened to you."

He rubbed her feet and turned her so she wouldn't get bedsores, and he bathed her with peppermint soap and a sponge. He left the room only to stitch up the holes and cuts of gunshots and knives and also to monitor the inpatients after the nurse was killed by the headless deputy's first cousin, who blamed her for not being able to reassemble the deputy's brain and reattach it to his vital organs. The surgeon went to her funeral, and while he was there he saved one life and lost two, which both ended instantly when the bomb hidden in the coffin vaporized the attendees' hearts mid-beat. The minister died that day, too, and some felt it was only a matter of time before God himself started meting out vigilante justice in the town.

The surgeon stopped going to funerals. He moved into the hospital, put up a bed in his office, and waited for the only living left to stumble through his front door. Maybe this was the reason he became a doctor.

"I want to tell you something—about my sister. I never told you the whole story," the surgeon said to his wife. "The facts are simple and easy to understand. You know our parents left when I was eleven and Julie was fourteen, and they left because Julie was either too loud or not loud enough, and after they left people at school were always wondering how we got enough to eat, but our parents didn't take the root cellar, or the car. The thing you need to understand about Julie is, she believed DNA was from outer space and she needed to have her hand held when she crossed the street. She lived in her own world. At the time I believed it was a very special world, but I stayed out of it because it frightened me. Sometimes I think their fear of Julie's world was why our parents left. Let me say something about Julie's world. In her world there were a lot of babies. I knew this because I heard the goo-goo noises she made when I was trying to fall asleep, and I knew she was talking to the babies who lived in her world. I have to admit I don't know much about babies, and when you wake up, and if you want to have some, I'm going to need your help taking care of them. I think they need a special kind of attention that I don't know how to give and I have no idea how to feed a baby. They need a lot of things, don't they? I mean, I'm sure the babies in Julie's world got everything they needed, I wasn't sure a real baby was something I could help with, so I worried every single time she brought a boy home.

"When she was fifteen, she brought a boy home for Thanksgiving and she said he worked at the paper mill and that was how he'd lost his arm. He sat in the family room and rocked back and forth in our rocking chair while I sat on the edge of the stairs grinding my teeth. I didn't think we should have people in the house while our parents were away, because something could be broken or stolen. I was really protective of our belongings, especially if it was something we might need, like the clock or radio, or something else we could sell when we needed some money. So this boy she brought home, Scott Shepherd, was a particularly mean bruiser, with curly red hair that was matted like a dog's. He'd once kicked me in the shin, before he knew I was Julie's brother.

"I remember Julie was making turnip pie. She peeled the turnips, cut them into cubes, boiled them. She rolled out dough on the marble breadboard that was set into the counter. She put the crust in a tempered-glass pie pan, she crimped the edges with her fingers, and she set the crust aside. She seasoned the turnips. She mashed them so they were not too mashed. She made a really good turnip pie back then.

"While she cleaned up the kitchen, Scott strutted around the house saying things like 'Nice lamp' and 'Where'd you get that Audubon print?' or 'What are all the tools for?' But mostly he talked about how he liked to break rules.

"I don't have any pictures of Julie, but her other problem, aside from her living in her own little world, was that she was a very pretty girl.

"They started laughing in the kitchen about something stupid he'd done in the woods with some friends, I don't remember what exactly, it isn't important... but all of a sudden he stopped laughing and she stopped laughing too, and they stared at me.

"And this one-armed guy pointed at me and said, 'What's with the cretin?'

"I remember trying to hold very still, trying to keep everything under control, but I started shaking and I couldn't stop, and then I started yelling at him about how Julie was crazy and lived in her own world and he needed to get the hellfuck out of our house, and I really wanted to kick him in the shin. I actually stepped toward him, and they both looked at me and started laughing again.

"So I backed away. Went up to my room and started thinking of ways to poison the guy, stuff like grinding up rhubarb leaves and extracting toxins from them because my father had told me they were poisonous. I had a chemistry set, so I probably could have done it, but eventually I fell asleep.

"When I woke up it was to the sound of Julie's world, like the sound of her babies crying. There must have been hundreds, because their wails were muffled, smothered under one another. I took my time going down the stairs. I thought maybe that was why my parents had left, because of the noise.

"Of course, there weren't any real babies, but Julie was crying and there was a significant amount of blood. It looked like Scott Shepherd was still breathing, but he was bleeding, and he was unconscious. There was a wet rattling sound coming from his mouth. His shirt and pants and a big part of the floor were soaked red. Julie was unharmed, and I knew that was going to be a problem with the police.

"I remember telling her—I laid it out—I said, 'Jules, when the police come they are going to see that you attacked that man, and that you were unprovoked, and that is because there is no evidence, and so we need there to be some evidence, and that means you need to be visibly hurt. You need to have his skin under your fingernails.' I was really clear about it but I wasn't sure if she'd heard me, because she kept crying that baby-wail. I put my hand on her head, and I said her name real quiet a few times. After a few minutes she wiped her face on her sleeve, sucked in her tears, and went into the kitchen. She was careful not to step in the blood, and when she came back she handed me the rolling pin. And it was okay, she didn't cry."

Maria was perfectly still, her vitals steady, not a blip on the EEG when he told her how he prepared the crime scene and sat by Scott Shepherd, checking his pulse and waiting until there wasn't one before calling the police. The surgeon and his sister were separated after that, given to foster parents and moved around the country, until they lost touch completely, but it was that night when Julie was brought to the hospital, broken and and blind in one eye, that he decided to become a doctor. Everything was so clean in the hospital, and they took such good care of her, and the last time he saw her, before the final separation, her limp was barely noticeable.

When Maria died, the surgeon went into town. He made his way among the abandoned homes and shops, the charred frames of former dwellings, and the wails of those who remained. The general store stood firm, though, and he bought himself some new T-shirts and a pair of blue jeans. He got a new car radio, a case of beer, a pistol, a potted rubber tree, a flashlight, a can of condensed milk, a lawn mower, a pair of sunglasses, a hot plate, a book on dowsing, a baby carriage, a rolling pin, a roll of toilet paper, a bottle of shampoo, a kitchen towel, a pair of driving gloves, a television, a Monopoly set, a tube of toothpaste, a nine-volt battery, a closet organizer, and ten gallons of gasoline in a big red can.

He brought his purchases back to the hospital and stacked them in Maria's room. Her body had swollen in the coma and more so in death. Her face was pale and puffy, her hands inflated into white blobs, her arms and legs and feet bloated like she had drowned, soaking up saline solution and filling the balloon of her skin with the leakage from her damaged veins and the slurry of her decomposing flesh.

He packed a small black bag with the gun, the T-shirts, the gloves, and the sunglasses, and he poured gasoline on everything else. He put the Monopoly game on the hot plate, turned it up to high, and left work for the last time. He left his car in the lot and walked down Weimer Road with the sun in his face. He walked upwind and was untouched in any way by the smoke and the fire and the smell of death.

III

The hunter came back to town after living in the wilderness for five weeks of hunting bucks, quail, moose, and pheasant. He did this each fall and spring and he butchered, smoked, dried, and cured the meats, hauling them home in a horse-drawn wagon. He usually sold some of the meat to local stores, but he also had a small plywood shack by the scenic overlook where passing motorists would buy his jerky, and he advertised with a spray-painted cardboard sign that read MEAT, just as he had for thirty years.

He had made the transition from wilderness to world sixty times before, and every time he was startled by the noise and bustle of the town. Cars were an offense to his ear, and the streetlights seared his eyes. This time was different.

He was met with a silence and a stillness that touched all but the wind. He was met by a blackened heap of rubble where the hospital once stood, by the burned-out shells of abandoned cars, by a thousand broken windows, by bullet shells clinking against his wagon wheels, by the soot of destruction, and by the familiar stench of rotting meat.

He was met by the surgeon, who stood motionless outside the white clapboard hulk of the town hall. A trickle of blood leaked from the front doors and dripped down the flagstone steps and seeped into the street, joining a shallow pool beneath the surgeon's feet. His T-shirt was red and brown and black with layers of bloodstains. His torn and frayed pants revealed scars and bruises on his legs beneath.

The hunter stopped his wagon next to the surgeon, who looked up at the man's gray, bearded face. The surgeon shielded his eyes from a sun that wasn't there. He swallowed hard three times before he spoke.

"Nobody is left," he said. "Everybody died or moved away from here." He had the pistol tucked into his waistband, and he cupped the butt with his palm as he talked.

His actions did not go unnoticed by the hunter, for the hunter was an acute observer of small movements.

"You need a ride somewhere?" the hunter asked.

The surgeon looked like he didn't understand the question. He chewed on his lip, and after a while he started saying, "No, no, no," over and over again before pulling out the pistol and firing in the hunter's general direction. "I wasn't trying to hit you," the surgeon said. "But I thought you might fire back. That was literally the last bullet in town until you got here."

He kicked the wagon. He spat and shouted, "You have to understand, they killed my wife." He said, "Are you still offering the ride?"

The hunter extended a hand and helped the surgeon up into the wagon. As he rose, the surgeon thrust a blade below the hunter's chin, killing him. The hunter was part of the town, and if he hadn't been, the surgeon wouldn't have stabbed him. If the surgeon had had something wise to say, he would have said it then. If he had needed anything, he would have taken it. If he had been civilized in the least, he would have done something besides loosen the reins, cluck his tongue at the horse, and ride a burning wagon through hell as the apple blossoms filled the air with the crisp sweetness of pollination and the wheels of darkness rolled across the earth.

ORDINARY
CIRCUMSTANCES

by HADLEY MOORE

MY KID LIKES GOING to the doctor. I can't explain it. She greets him like he's Santa Claus, and she's sitting there shivering in her yellow socks and her kitten underpants and a paper gown with clowns on it. The doctor—I like him; he was my pediatrician—is this old guy with a bow tie and suspenders. He's got one hell of a head of silver hair. His hairline hasn't moved in decades (mine's been moving since I was twenty-two; now I'm forty), and I contemplate it as he talks to my daughter.

"Lillian, how are you feeling? I'm very glad to see you."

"I'm glad to see you, too," she says. She grins.

He sits on his rolling stool and peers at her, and she looks down at him from her perch on the exam table.

"She's had a cough," I say, and they ignore me.

Lil coughs, and he brings his stethoscope to his ears. "Let's see what we can hear."

She corrects him. "Let's *hear* what we can hear."

He tips an imaginary hat to her and winks, then slips the metal disc under the top of her paper gown. He turns his head my way and listens. He's not looking at me. He's concentrating. He moves the metal disc and listens some more.

Lillian is fine. She's had a cough for two days, is all. She's seven and healthy, though small. This is a well-child visit, and she'll get a flu shot and have a nice chat with her friend Dr. Phillips.

He moves his metal disc again, and my kid leans forward.

"Lillian," the doctor whispers, "don't hold your breath."

She giggles and looks at me and I wink, too, and then she turns serious and remembers to breathe for several seconds.

Everybody's quiet, and Lil says, "Are you listening to my heart now?"

The doctor says yes.

She's quiet again.

"Breathe, Lillian," he says.

"Can you hear God?" she asks him. "In my heart?"

"Lil—" I start. This kind of stuff comes from her mother. I can just hear her. *God is in your heart, Lillian.*

But Dr. Phillips interrupts. "Well," he says, and looks at me. I shrug.

"Not literally," he tells her. He takes off the stethoscope. "Do you know what that means, *literally?*"

She shakes her head.

"It means that what I hear with my ears is your heart beating and your lungs breathing. So I don't hear God the way I hear your insides, or the way you hear me now."

It's a pretty good answer. I'd have been tempted just to tell her no.

He keeps going. "But here in the middle of your chest, where your heart is—" He taps his own chest, and he taps Lil's. "Sometimes it seems to people that they feel happiness there, or love. Or they put their hands over their hearts when they hear the national anthem, because they want to show it's important. Do you know the national anthem?"

She nods. It's news to me.

Dr. Phillips puts his hand over his heart, and Lillian does, too. My tiny daughter—last time we were here she was in the thirtieth percentile for height and weight—she puts her tiny hand on her tiny chest and turns to me, and I put my hand on my chest, too, and it's like we're all going to break out in "Oh say can you see?"

"So if people say God is in their hearts, what they mean is they have a special feeling and it seems like it comes from right here." He holds his hand there a moment before placing it on his knee, and Lillian and I drop our hands, too.

"Okay," she says. "I can feel it."

"Great," the doctor answers, and he gets on with it. He looks in her eyes and ears and nose, and taps her knees and does all the usual stuff, and when he takes out his chart and compares her numbers we learn she's inched up to the thirty-fifth percentile.

"That's wonderful, Lillian. You're growing," Dr. Phillips tells her. "You're not a large child, but you're a healthy one." She grins and grins, and he shakes her hand and shakes mine—"A lovely daughter you have, Jeremy"—and bows on his way out, and when the nurse comes in to do the flu shot, Lil wants me to note that she is very brave and it doesn't even hurt that much.

When we leave she takes my hand. "You're a wiseacre," she tells me. "You're a real weisenheimer."

"You're a knucklehead," I answer.

"You're a knucklehead *and* a bonehead. And a weisen-heimer."

Weisenheimer is her favorite.

"You're a ninnyhammer," I say.

"You're a scallywag."

We go on like that, and I take her back to school. When she gets out of the car, she shouts, "You're a nincompoop!" and I blow her a kiss.

"Lillian's fine," I tell my wife later, over the phone. "Tiny, but not as tiny."

"That's great," May says. "I thought so. She seems more robust."

"She'll still be a runt."

"Maybe she's a late bloomer."

I doubt it. Lil did things early—teethe, walk, talk—and May's people and my people are not impressive physical specimens.

I listen to May breathing. Maybe I can't even really hear her, but I know she's there, breathing. She's at her parents' restaurant, and what I for sure do hear is a lot of clatter and shouting. It's dinnertime, and I resist asking my wife whether she's coming to our house after.

But I throw her a bone. "Lil asked the doctor if he could hear God while he was listening to her heart."

"Ohhhh," May says. "That is so sweet. What did he say?"

What the doctor said reminds me now of *Yes, Virginia, there is a Santa Claus*. "He said not literally but sort of, if you feel it."

It's a terrible answer, and May is quiet.

"Lil said she feels it."

My wife exhales. "I love that," she says. But I'm not sure how to respond right away so she says, "I know you don't love it."

"Honey, I'm just telling you."

We both hear how weird that sounds, me calling her honey, and it makes me sad that it sounds so weird.

May comes around sometimes. She brings us fried rice and vegetables from the restaurant, or sweet-and-sour chicken, or moo shu pork. Lillian has two twin beds in her room, and when May sleeps there I can barely sleep at all. I lie in our bed and feel like I'm being electrocuted. I don't really know what it's like to be electrocuted, but I'm pretty sure it's exactly like lying in a queen-size bed down the hall from your wife, who hasn't let you touch her in months. Just try telling me electrocution isn't like that.

I married the only Chinese woman in northern Michigan.

That's not really true. It's just a stupid thing I like to say. There are two other Asian kids in Lil's school, actually, and two black kids (one's biracial, like her), and a handful of Latino kids, and some Native Americans. Mostly they're white, but she's not the only one who isn't.

Lillian appears to take our new precarious living situation in stride. She's happy to see May when she comes but doesn't ask what the hell is going on when she doesn't. And she visits her grandparents like normal and lives in the same house with me and goes to school and seems just fine. But I fear this can't last. Plus, May's gotten religion and I'm a jerk for being skeptical, especially since it started when her cousin's kid was dying of leukemia.

Kids aren't supposed to die of leukemia anymore. You hear cure rates like 60, 70 percent and you think, Well, that covers this kid, then. But Albert ended up in that smaller percent for reasons that are incomprehensible. Besides the cancer he was healthy, which sounds nuts. Oh, he's got a strong heart and lungs? That's just terrific, but when the cancer gets him it's going to stop his top-notch organs, too.

May and her cousin are pretty tight, and when Albert was diagnosed her cousin somehow got tangled up with this cuckoo Christian witch doctor who talked about "energy" and the light of Christ and giving Jesus your burden, which was harmless in the sense that she didn't suggest stopping treatment or anything, but listening to this woman added up to a lot of wasted time and wasted *energy*. I didn't meet her, but I heard about her because May fell for it, too.

When Albert died, almost a year ago, May told Lillian he'd gone to heaven. Lillian asked me if that was true, so I told her, and here I quote myself, "Yep."

I couldn't say, "No, Lil. Your cousin's nothing anymore. He's meat now, and he's going into the ground," but neither could I muster any enthusiasm for heaven. "Yep" was good enough for Lillian, though. It wasn't good enough for May.

And that's when our marriage started to trickle away. I couldn't comfort my wife in the way she wanted. She says I was (am) disdainful of her faith. But it's not so much disdain as bewilderment.

Before Albert died, May believed in God in an offhand way. God was a comforting idea. She's second-generation, but her parents came here as kids, so they're all used to the American ambivalent/secular approach to religious holidays. We'd acknowledge Jesus at Christmas and Easter, but the main show was the trees and the eggs and the magical gift-givers.

And she'd do prayers with Lil: "Now I lay me down to sleep," and Lillian would go along in her tiny singsong voice, "If I should die before I wake, I pray the Lord my soul to take."

May would do prayers, we'd read a couple of stories, and Lil and I would exchange a few old-timey insults:

"You're a slugabed."

"You're a jackanapes."

"You're a clodhopper."

"You're a weisenheimer."

Then we'd turn out the light, and several nights a week I'd seduce my wife in our big queen-size bed. That was back when prayers were more like nursery rhymes and God was a comforting idea and none of us had ever been to a ten-year-old's funeral.

Besides May's newly fervent belief and unpredictable habitation, she is a solid person and a good mother. She sees Lillian a lot. She comes here and takes her to the restaurant and her parents' house and even my parents' house. She shows up for school things and helps at the restaurant even while working thirty hours as a dental hygienist. But sometimes I come home and find her doing laundry or weeding in the front, and that stuff just kills me.

The fact that May is still invested in our household does seem encouraging. Her paychecks go into our joint account, and she hasn't mentioned separate accounts or getting her own place (she stays at her parents', I assume, when she isn't in Lillian's extra bed) or divorce.

I love May. Jesus Christ, what am I supposed to do with that? I can't turn it off, and that is the cruelty of desire. By desire I don't mean just sex. I mean longing, like *soul-longing*, if that's not ridiculous. I do all the usual things—take care of Lil, go to work, keep the house from falling apart—but for months it's like I've been screaming. There are two parallel Jeremys: one carries on and the other one can't stop screaming. That's probably how Albert's parents feel, too.

It was Dr. Phillips who sent Albert to the children's hospital in Grand Rapids, where they diagnosed him. What a job. I wonder why he's still doing it. He must be seventy.

When Lil had strep throat six months ago, he said to me, "Ah, Jeremy, I've thought about your family every day since young Albert died." I bet if I asked him how many of his patients have died as children he'd be able to tell me right off. But when you go into pediatrics, I suppose you know what you're signing up for.

So anyway, for reasons having to do with wanting to please May and wanting to keep her on the phone, I tell her about Lillian feeling God in her heart, even though it worries me some. What the heck does Lil think she feels?

After May and I recover from how weird it is when I call her "honey," she says she'll come by that evening, but it's Friday so she might be late at the restaurant. I have that familiar jubilant feeling followed immediately by that familiar despairing feeling, and that's pretty much my life these days. Double Jeremys: screaming and getting on with it.

It's six o'clock and I go find Lil in her room and suggest we go to the beach. In September it's still nice up here. You might not want to swim, but I'll sit on the sand and watch Lake Michigan and let Lil run around any day. We even go in winter, with hats and coats. It's crazy how dangerous the lake is. Summer and winter people go out on piers when they shouldn't. They get blown off and bash their heads on rocks and drown.

At the beach Lil wants to play on the monkey bars and swings close to the parking lot. I let her do that for ten minutes or so, then hustle her down toward the water. Lake Michigan: how to explain it? The first time I saw the Atlantic Ocean, I said, "It looks like the Great Lakes." People who've never been here don't get it. They pay more attention to the word "lakes" than the word "great," and they picture a reedy, shallow pond. Some of the lakeshore is rocky, but here there's approximately one million yards of white sand from the parking lot to the water. It's beautiful. I could look at it forever.

At the shore Lillian digs in the sand and shrieks when the surf grabs her. By the time she tells me she's hungry it's dusky and she's soaked through and shivering. I make her stand still and tolerate a brisk brushing-off of wet sand, which is mostly fruitless, and we head home. I don't mention May, but when we get to the house the lights are on, and when I open the door there's that warm, rice-y smell. I think of May's parents' food as one of the major sensory accompaniments of our marriage.

"Mama!" Lil squeals when the door opens. "Noodles!"

She wriggles out of her wet, sandy pants in the entryway, and I toss them over the porch railing before shutting the door behind us. May comes out of the kitchen, wiping her hands on her jeans. Lil runs to her.

"Oh, you're so cold!" my wife says. "Let's get you in the bath." She looks at me. "Jeremy, you could put the food in the oven to keep it warm."

Every last thing she says to me, I hope to hear encouragement in it. But I'm not supposed to question her coming and going while she—I don't even know what. Decides whether to leave for good, I guess. So I wait for her. I sit in our house drinking a beer and warming our dinner while she bathes our kid, and I wait for her.

When they come back to the kitchen, Lillian's in a fluffy yellow nightgown that makes her look like a black-capped duckling, and she's flushed and dewy from the bath. We grin at each other as though a warmed-up meal of Chinese food after trips to the doctor and the beach is the most delightful thing. Which it is.

It's all familiar to her, this house, the food, the beach, Dr. Phillips—what happens when he dies?—May and me. Sometimes in my desperation I forget that if May leaves me for real it will hurt Lil, too.

I have this thought that's both comforting and disturbing. If May leaves I'll feel like killing myself but I won't do it, because I have Lillian. And not killing myself will benefit other people, too: my parents, and May's parents, I suppose, and the people who work for me. But nobody needs me the way Lil does, so without her I might seriously be tempted to walk into Lake Michigan.

We have this small table in our kitchen with one side pushed against the wall, so there's room for just three chairs. A couple of years ago, before Albert was diagnosed, we were thinking of having another kid, but now my focus is on preventing attrition. Three of us seems perfect. May and I are only children, too.

After May gets the food she sits and clasps her hands and so does Lillian. I put mine in my lap to wait for them.

"Dear lord," my wife starts, "thank you for this food." She gives thanks for our health and for God's loving embrace of cousin Albert in heaven.

Maybe you could have just left him here, God, I think. This is the kind of thing that makes me impatient with May's new Christian devotion. Albert died and it sucks, and it isn't part of some plan, because what a shitty plan that would be. So great job, God, taking care of him in heaven, but that would be plan B. Actually, that's plan Z.

May wraps it up, and Lillian ends with her usual "And thank you, God, for our happy family. A-men!"

You hear that, May? Our happy family. A-men!

"Tell Mom about Dr. Phillips today, Lil."

"I'm growing!"

"That's wonderful. I knew you were."

"Me, too," Lillian says. "I knew it."

I smile and catch May's eye, and I want to wink but it seems too flirty. She smiles back, though.

So dinner is fine, and predictable at this point. May and I are courteous, familiar if not friendly, and Lil chatters and seems thrilled to have us both here.

When she gets tired she reaches for me. May says she'll clean up and I carry Lil to the bathroom, coax her to brush her teeth, and carry her to bed. I lie down with her, on top of the covers, squishing myself against the wall. Fatherhood is this lovely, ordinary thing, and sometimes I feel like I want to sort of rest in it, snuggle up to it, like I'm snuggling with Lillian now. I used to feel that way about marriage too.

May and I cannot be said to have exciting lives, but I liked to tell her we had an epic love story in ordinary circumstances. It became a thing: one of us would say, "Epic love story," and the other would answer, "Ordinary circumstances." It was one of the first things I said to her after Lillian was born.

When I wake up my arm is violently asleep, still pressed to the wall. I sit and scoot to the end of Lil's bed and lift my dead arm into my lap with my other arm. Lying in the second twin bed, perpendicular to Lillian's, is my wife. This is the first time in months we've slept in the same room.

I can make out the contrast of her black hair on the white pillow, so I stare at that. What will she say if she wakes? My arm is prickling back to life, and I wonder how long I'd have to cut off the circulation to do real damage. Probably a long time, but it's weird and scary, all the easy ways to injure yourself, cuts and burns, stopping blood flow, falling off the pier. Getting cancer. Walking into the lake.

It's maybe creepy, staring at May, and the fact that looking at my wife might be creepy starts to piss me off, which is dangerous. When I get angry she seems further away.

I don't want to be creepy, so I get up and head to the bathroom, where the clock says 3:33. I consider all kinds of crazy things for the middle of the night: taking a walk, making coffee, getting online for no good reason. I should go back to sleep, but I decide to take a shower first. It's a comfortable place to cry and not as lonely as our bed.

In the morning—real morning, not 3 a.m.—Lil wakes me up.

"Get up, ya milquetoast."

She's leaning on my chest in her yellow nightgown, a cheerful morning duck.

"Mom's making breakfast."

I can smell it.

I pull on some pants. It seems—I don't know, presumptuous?—to walk around in my underwear in front of May.

There's coffee and scrambled eggs and pancakes, made by my wife, here in our house. Ordinary circumstances.

She's showered and dressed. She keeps some clothes in Lil's closet. Sometimes I go in there and look at them. There are clothes in our bedroom closet still, too, but I guess those she's abandoned.

After breakfast Lil scampers off, and May and I sit at the table with our coffee cups, not looking at each other. I swear I start to blush. My face and neck get hot and I put my coffee down, and May says, "I talked to Julie yesterday."

Julie is her cousin, Albert's mom.

"They want to have a little service, like a celebration of life."

Today is September 26. Albert died October 3 last year. This year he would have been a sixth grader.

"I thought a celebration of life was a funeral."

"I don't know. Something, then. A ritual."

And just like that we're both irritated. The way we've been with each other over this almost-year has evolved. Or devolved. First there was a lot of careful discussion about religion and why May didn't always stay here, and then a lulled period of painstaking courtesy, and now that is changing to include flares of frustration. Maybe where we're headed next is open hostility.

"Something with the family, an observance. Just—to say we still love him and... that we're okay. And he's okay."

She says this like a challenge, but the truth is I don't think Albert's not okay. Death isn't the worst thing. I just don't think he's anything anymore. I can't help it. I can't talk myself into belief.

"Also, Julie's pregnant."

"Wow."

"Right?"

I hope May is thinking about what I'm thinking about: Julie and Carl having sex. Not in a gross way, but the fact of it. Albert's parents had sex, and we're just Albert's mom's cousin and her husband. I wish May and I were a comfort to each other, and it hits me that if she still loved me it would be too hard for her to stay away. She would feel electrocuted the way I do.

Or maybe not. If she didn't love me she would get the hell out of here. Millions of times I've thought, *I can't stand this any longer.* And then I stand it some more.

"Will you come? To Albert's—whatever?"

"Of course."

"I should go. I told my parents I'd help with lunch."

"I'll clean up."

"I want to come get Lillian later."

I nod.

And she's off.

May and I met eleven years ago. She's four years younger, so we were never in high school together, and then I went to college and she cooked at the restaurant and did the dental hygiene thing at the community college.

This is a small city, but there was no reason for us to be in each other's orbit until her car started making a weird knocking sound. I got a BA in philosophy, but I also know about cars, so I came back here and worked with my dad and got certified, and a few years after that we started phasing him out so I could take over his shop.

I'm not a big guy, but I've been told I'm good-looking, baldness and all, and I think I cut some kind of figure for May when she came in, panicked about her car. She probably expected an older, fat guy. She probably expected my dad. But it was me who came out from the back, breathless and holding a wrench. You know, it's a type. She noticed.

And I noticed. May is a small woman, but she has a steeliness, too. That day her eyes were kind of wild, and she looked so serious. It was the seriousness I noted first. There was a second of recognition between us, with sex bound up in it, then a second of embarrassment, and then I asked what I could do for her.

That was the start of our epic love story.

The knocking turned out to be the end of her engine, and I helped her sell the car for parts and pick out a new car. To say thank you, she opened the restaurant one Sunday evening, when they were normally closed. She cooked for me, no one else there, and later I went home with her, to this apartment she had on top of a storefront downtown.

For a year we went to the beach in all seasons and ate Chinese food and had a lot of sex, and then I asked her father for her hand. I felt weird about it, like, Can't she make her own decisions? But he loved it. He was so excited I feared he'd tell her before I could, so I went right to her apartment and when she opened the door I said, "Marry me." We raced to her bedroom and only after did I remember the ring. She still wears it, and her wedding ring, too. But they seem incidental.

This can't be all about God and Albert, though I might never know. If she finds her way back to me, I will swallow my curiosity. I will swallow it every day like some huge, dry pill.

Albert's funeral was at the beach, on a cold, sunny day. It was windy, and the minister had this crummy wireless microphone. Lillian wore her winter coat and hat, and halfway through she climbed into my lap. She put her lips to my ear and asked, "What is he saying?"

I moved my lips to her ear. "He's saying we all loved Albert very much."

She laid her cheek on my shoulder, then lifted her head again. "What else?"

I didn't know. There was wind and a drone of word-like sounds, and from some yards away the surf, which didn't help, but before I could come up with a gentle and believable answer, Lil said, "Mommy's crying."

I looked at my wife. She had a handkerchief over her nose and mouth, pinned there with a gloved hand, and her torso bobbed in an odd way that took me a second to recognize as sobbing. Her parents were on one side of her, and Lillian and I were on the other, but there was something contained and private about her grief that I was both afraid to disturb and afraid to let her get lost in. It seemed—honestly, and as sad as the situation was—out of all proportion.

Holding Lil, I moved into her chair and let my shoulder touch May's. Lil put her hand out and I eased her into May's lap, where she stayed only a few seconds before climbing back into mine. She tucked herself into my chest, and I pressed my shoulder against my wife's. For the rest of the service I felt her sobs.

She didn't look at us until it was done, when she managed a tiny smile for Lil. She took her hand, and we walked from the beach to our car with the other mourners, the minister and Julie and Carl in the lead, then their parents, then the rest of us in heads-down procession. To the cars, to the cemetery, in the blinding cold and chilling sun—that was how it felt, sensory information muddled—to drop Albert's cremains in a hole. *Cremains.* The minister actually said that when we were gathered at the gravesite.

I saw a crematorium once, in Spokane, Washington. It was in a neighborhood, not a great neighborhood, but an okay one. You could see the wavy exhaust coming out the top of the building. Imagine looking at that every day. After a body is cremated they have to pulverize the bones. I hadn't known that.

So their son's bones were pulverized, and Julie and Carl

had managed to have sex at least once these past months. But they must have a sense they're walking through the same fire. May feels like she's on her own.

She's left me here at our kitchen table, but invited me to Albert's thing. And I'll see her later because she wants to get Lil. All these increments of encouragement and discouragement. I can't stand them. And then I do.

I get up to stick my head in Lil's doorway, and she and May are on the floor, my wife brushing my daughter's hair. They don't register my presence so I leave them to it.

I'm back in the kitchen when I hear May leave, shutting the front door. Lil races in, her hair in a neat braid that won't last, to announce, "Mom says we'll go to the beach later."

Such an indeterminate pronoun, *we*.

"And then maybe you can help Grandpa whack down that old tree," Lil says.

She means cut down a dead branch hanging over the roof at May's parents' house. First relief, then jubilation, then anger, in super-fast succession. Jesus Christ, May: *talk to me.*

She meets us at the beach after lunch, and we sit on the sand with our arms around our knees. Our bodies don't touch, but our body heat does, like we're in each other's atmosphere.

Lillian's running around, in and out of the water, on her knees and back up and scooping sand into her pail and dumping it.

"Albert's service?" May says. "It'll be next Saturday."

I nod.

"At the grave site. People will say a few prayers and maybe we'll have a song and—" She lifts her hands and clasps her knees again. "Then we'll get ice cream."

She turns to me. "Do you want to come?"

"Yes, yes. I do."

"It will be religious."

"I understand."

Lil waves to us and we wave back and watch her take a running leap at a mound of sand.

"How far along is Julie?" I ask.

"Three months."

"Wow."

"She said they planned it, even."

"Good for them."

"I don't believe God took Albert. I don't know if you think I do."

I look at her, but she stares straight ahead.

This could be an opening, or a shutting down. "May, I—I don't know. I guess I did."

"I don't believe that."

"Tell me, then. What you do believe."

She looks at me. I hold my breath, and into this space she's opened—I'll choose to believe it's an opening—I say, "I love you."

"I know."

Then she dips her head, and I can't see but I sense her tears. I leave her alone with them for a minute, and I say, "May, tell me." I'm afraid it sounds like *Tell me* "*I love you*," a command, but she understands me and says, "I don't think God makes bad things happen, but that he's there when they do. Do you remember what the minister said at the funeral?"

How did she decipher a word of it?

"About how God meets us in our sorrow? And rests with us there?"

It's very pretty, and I can see the appeal.

"That's what I believe. I'd hoped you would hear it and understand, like it might be more convincing from someone else."

"I'm sorry. He was difficult to hear." It sounds so lame, and what I want to say is that I wish she would let me meet her in her sorrow and rest with her there. I would hold her forever.

"May, I am sorry," I say, and she is watching our daughter, and the lake beyond.

*   *   *

The night before Albert's thing, May comes over, and we make lasagna. We'd told Lillian about the service. I explained that we would get together with cousin Julie and Carl and everybody to say goodbye to Albert once more, to which she responded, "But we already did that." So May said that it would make Julie and Carl feel not so sad to have the family all come to where Albert was buried and say they love him and thank God for taking care of him now, since it had been one year, and that seemed to make more sense to Lil.

The lasagna is autumnal and sort of festive, and we'll have ice cream after the service tomorrow, and we ate pierogies after Albert's funeral, and is there any starker display of mortality than all this fueling? We are so inefficient and weak.

I wake in the middle of the night and get up to walk past Lillian's room. May's not there. The bathroom is empty, and I open the door to the garage and see her car is still parked there. She's not in the kitchen, and when I go by the living room she says, "Jeremy."

I back up and stop. She's in the chair by the far corner window.

"I can't sleep," she says.

"Can I get you anything?"

"No."

I'm in just my underpants. There's only a bit of moon filtering through a big spruce tree, but I feel lit up.

"Can I—" I start to say again. What? Can I get us some wine? Can I rub her feet? Can I hold her?

"Julie's upset with me."

I can't move. I don't want to spook her. "She's upset? Why?"

"I didn't act happy enough when she told me she was pregnant, but I'd been thinking about Albert's anniversary. I was shocked. I started crying."

"Oh, May."

"Our moms were there and I pulled it together, but yesterday she told me—she actually said this—that she's been handling Albert's death better than I have and I should see a therapist. Jeremy"—my name again, happy jolt—"do you think I should?"

"Do you want to? Would it help you?"

"How do I know?"

"Our insurance covers it." I say this for two reasons: to tell her she can try it and we'll be out only the co-pay, and to emphasize that the insurance is *ours*, because we're married, like the house is ours and Lillian is ours. It's calculated but not insincere.

"She also said that I'm treating you badly."

There's no correct response to this, and I exhale.

"I'm sorry," she says.

"May—"

"And I'm jealous. That is the truth. I am jealous of Julie, who lost her first child. What is the matter with me?"

There is no wailing when she says this. It is still just her solemn voice from the dark corner. She gets up and comes toward me, and in hopeful confusion I put my hand out. I'm cold and I have to pee, but she seems unfazed that I'm nearly naked.

"I should go to bed." She looks at me, and my hand drifts down. "Jeremy, I'm sorry."

In the morning I feel wrecked. I think May does, too. When my eye catches hers my heart, already skittery from coffee and lack of sleep, goes galloping off. After breakfast I claim a headache and get back into bed.

But I am showered and dressed by 12:30, and helping Lil on with her tights. May comes out of the bathroom in a navy blue dress she knows I love, but I only glance at her in the doorway of our daughter's room.

"Come on, Lil, don't bunch up your toes."

It's a cold, drizzly day. It rained all morning and could start again. At the cemetery I imagine May's people making their appraisals: we came together, we're holding Lil's hands, we look like a family today. Her parents have been polite and gentle this past year, and they don't look at me anymore so much as peer and squint, like they're looking *for* something. Who knows what May tells them.

The dopey minister is here, and so is that woman Julie got mixed up with when Albert was in the hospital, the Christian witch doctor. I know it's her. She's got that earth-mother-of-the-universe look: flowy purple dress, salt-and-pepper braid winding around her head, and a gigantic brass cross around her neck. The chain takes a steep dive off her bosom, and the cross *thwap*s her stomach as she walks toward us—*thwap*, *thwap*, *thwap*.

"May, here you are with your lovely family."

The earth mother takes both of May's hands, and Lil turns to me.

"This must be Lillian."

I hoist Lil up and she regards the woman from her perch on my hip.

"And Jeremy, it's wonderful to meet you."

"Nice to meet you."

"This is Margaret," May says.

Lillian turns in my arms and whispers, "You're a weisenheimer."

"Shh," I say and pat her back.

"I've prayed with Julie and Carl," Margaret says. She looks at me. "I used to be a nun."

"That's interesting." Actually, it kind of is.

Back to May. "They are holding up. But how are you, dear? Should we take a moment?"

May says yes and looks at me and I nod. I can handle her family without her.

Lillian and I make the rounds. She hugs her grandparents, and they peer and squint. May's dad shakes my hand and claps my shoulder. Her mom hugs me and says, "Oh, Jeremy, I'm so glad you're here. I am *so* glad."

We say hi to cousins and friends, and I keep an eye on May and Margaret, off under a tree, heads bowed. I also keep an eye on Julie and Carl. Good old Julie, my defender. She's not looking very pregnant yet, but she rests a hand above her belly. They're standing by the gravestone. I feel shy about approaching them, but I do it. Lil gives them hugs, and we all look down. It's hard not to.

ALBERT YUAN BARTELSKI, 2004–2014, BELOVED SON AND GRANDSON, NEPHEW, COUSIN, AND FRIEND

The minister inserts himself, and Lil and I step away.

"Where's Albert?" she asks.

"Lillian, honey, you know this." I suppress a flare of irritation. "Albert's not here. He died."

She looks around. "I know."

May joins us, and I see the minister and Margaret conferring with Julie and Carl. I wish Dr. Phillips were here, and Albert's oncologists from Grand Rapids.

"Why wasn't Margaret at the funeral?" I ask May.

"She had another funeral. For her aunt."

"You didn't tell me she was a nun."

"Yes, I did."

The minister raises his hand, and people stop talking and gather around Julie and Carl. Margaret and the minister stand behind the gravestone, and the rest of us face them.

"Friends," the minister starts. He wears a regular suit and tie and a big white sash over his shoulders. "We are here to remember the life of Albert Yuan Bartelski." He clears his throat. "Let us pray." He clears his throat again. "Our Father," he says, and people chime in.

I look down at Lil. She's studying an insect on her shoe. I take her hand. On the other side of her May has closed her eyes and crossed her arms, and she leans so far forward I'm afraid she'll crash into Carl. But the prayer ends and she stands up straight and takes Lillian's other hand.

Margaret leads us in the twenty-third psalm, the one about the valley of the shadow of death. Then there's a mumbling verse of "What a Friend We Have in Jesus," fifteen or so people, a cappella.

There are more prayers, and I wonder what it would be like to put my arm around my wife, meet her in her sorrow and rest with her there. Everyone would notice.

The minister finishes by holding up his palm. "May the Lord bless you and keep you."

It's like a tiny church service. It's fine. It's what I expected.

Afterward, there's some milling about and hugging and crying, but it's cold and I want a cup of coffee. Lil and I wait for May, who's talking to Julie. Maybe they're making up. Maybe Julie's talking about me.

Margaret startles me while I watch my wife, and in her face I can see what my face must betray, because she doesn't say anything at first, just gives me a sad, closed-lipped smile.

"Jeremy," she says.

"Hello."

"I asked May if I might talk to you."

"Okay." My heart starts going.

"I know things have been difficult." She looks at Lillian.

"Lil, go hang out with Grandma for a few minutes." I point her toward May's mom, and she trots over.

I look at Margaret. *Who is this woman?*

"Jeremy, I realize I might be overstepping, but I want to

tell you I believe May is trying. We don't know sometimes why we have the emotional responses we do. It can be a real mystery." Her speech sounds rehearsed, and when I don't answer she carries on. "And just like you are a mechanic who diagnoses the problems people have with their cars, I like to think of myself as a mechanic of the human spirit." She throws up her hands. "But before you roll your eyes—"

I'd already started.

"Before you roll your eyes, I'll tell you that sometimes I can't figure it out."

I just keep looking at her.

"I can't explain everything going on with May, but I know she's hurting."

No shit.

"I didn't tell her what I was going to say to you. But I think that part of what's fueling this standoff in your marriage is that she's so deep in she doesn't know how to stop."

I want to hate Margaret and stalk off, but I am riveted. "It should be easy," I say, but I know it's not true.

"I don't think so."

"What should I do?" I ask this to challenge her and, honestly, to see if she might know.

She shakes her head. "There is no real answer. All I can tell you is that it seems this isn't necessarily the end."

I would like to respond that her hedging is small comfort, but the truth is it is something, so I ask Margaret, this stranger, "Does May want another baby?"

She looks away and puts her hands on her hips, and I explain to her profile, "She said she is jealous of Julie."

Margaret is quiet for countable seconds. I count them and make it to seven before she says, "Children cannot save you," and looks back at me.

"I know."

But even if this is not the answer, it might still happen to be true, and implied is that May wants another kid *with me*, right?

"The question is not so simple. Define 'want.'" Margaret is irritated, but I don't care. "I suppose the answer is 'yes and no.' Or 'yes and wait.' Do you understand me?"

It's something I say to Lillian. Do not touch the stove when people are cooking. *Do you understand me?*

We stare at each other.

"Jeremy, my point is not that this is irrelevant, but I advise a great deal of patience."

How many more years of patience, Margaret? I look over her shoulder at May, and Margaret turns around and looks, too.

"Thank you," I say.

She turns back to me. After a pause she says, "You're welcome. But I mean it. There is no easy answer."

"I understand."

She sighs and takes my hands. "I wish you peace."

"Thanks."

She squeezes and lets my hands go and gives me a nod that is almost a bow. Then she turns and walks away and I am left with this hopeful scrap of corroboration, but it is no answer and will not be easy.

I find May's parents and ask them to take Lillian to the ice cream place. I let May drift my way. "Lil's going with your folks," I tell her, and she raises her eyebrows but says okay.

We walk to the car and get in, and she is silent when I veer from the ice cream route and end up at the beach. Since it's the only useful bit of intel I've had in a year, I come right out and ask my wife, "Do you want another kid?"

I don't expect her to answer immediately, but she does: "It's a strange thing to want right now, I realize."

My heart reasserts itself. It is not faster so much as bigger, too big. The lake is huge before us, gray with whitecaps and disappearing on one side into nearby cliffs, and on the other into faraway ones, and in front of us into the horizon. Some people need mountains, some people need prairies, some people need cities, and I need this lake.

"Did Margaret tell you that?" May asks.

"You did, May. Last night. You said you were jealous of Julie."

"That isn't all I meant."

"Tell me."

"And my point was I feel guilty about it, Jeremy."

"But can't you support Julie and also be happy?" I lower my voice. "We could have another baby."

She shakes her head. "Please, can we not do this now? People will wonder where we are."

"I want you," I say, and it is a sound like *Help* or *Water*.

May doesn't look at me when she says, "I am jealous of Julie because she has her marriage, and because Carl believes in God. And, yes, now she is pregnant again, and I am jealous of that, too."

There is only our breath and the waves' soughing, muted by the car. And there is also my heart.

"I want to go," she says. "We're supposed to be having ice cream."

"But tell me why it's so terrible that I don't believe what you believe."

"You know that's not all it is. You're disdainful. I embarrass you."

"No."

"Yes. I really think so."

Now she looks at me, so serious, and it might be that my life is over. I remind myself I have Lillian to keep me from walking into Lake Michigan.

"I am sorry," I say. "I don't know what to do."

She turns away. "What did Margaret tell you?"

"Nothing. Just that I should be patient and this is not—not necessarily the end."

"Hmm," she says. It's not even a word. It could mean anything. "I don't know if it's good or bad that she talked to you."

"How did you and Julie meet her, anyway?" I'm grasping, and I can hear the shrill echo of my voice.

May inhales. "I honestly think I explained this. She was a hospital chaplain. Which means she drove here this morning from Grand Rapids."

"That was nice of her." It was, more than two hours each way.

"May," I say, gently, gently. "What do we do?" I look at her, and she is clenching and unclenching her jaw.

"What do we do?" I whisper it this time.

"Sometimes wanting something is inconvenient, Jeremy. Another baby—" She stops and sighs, and I want to say, *I love you*. I want to say, *Epic love story*.

This is not (necessarily) the end. Be patient, patient.

I lean toward my wife and touch my mouth to her shoulder, not a kiss. She doesn't flinch, and when I straighten up she sighs again, which could be nothing. It could just be her breathing.

CANÍBAL THE
REAL DEAL

by XAVIER NAVARRO AQUINO

PAQO STARTED ACTING OUT more the day we knew Papi was dying. Didn't seem like any news, nothing that couldn't be handled or even channeled. But when Doctora Grecia read the script to us, confirming all of Ma's doomsday scenarios, Paqo became insatiable. He had just moved back in after his job in construction didn't pan out. He bounced around employers for half a decade after dropping school. Now he was back and mooching hard. Ma let him get away with murder after the official news of Papi broke. Had him coming in late, skipping on wiping down the table, as was his designated chore, or trimming the engorged branches from the *almendra* tree. All part of the conditions he agreed to. And he even managed to sneak Rosa in a few times to *meter mano*, as he would say. Would do her right above me, the bunk bed swaying and her letting out soft grunts like held coughs. It was Ma's biggest rule and Paqo became a prized and happy repeat offender. No stopping him. They were recently made up, some lovers' quarrel he never did clarify, so they acted on the lost time, compensating for some failed romance with our house falling apart right before our eyes. My theory for his exploits was the guilt about Papi. Rosa gave out her *canto* just to give Paqo some guidance.

Zero accountability when it came to Paqo's *locura*. No monitoring or satellite-probing Ma could've done to keep up. And he made sure of it, too. He'd throw the money he'd started collecting from cockfights onto the table, declaring to us, *"Victory!"* Maybe to throw Ma off his scent. *"There you have it,"* he would say. *"No need to worry"* was his new anthem. I thought about whether that meant he wanted to take Papi's role after he croaked, the de facto man of the house. Yet every time he went into one of his trances, Ma rolled her draping shirtsleeves over her thin arms and tossed all those singles

CANÍBAL THE REAL DEAL

right back at him. *"Get a real job. Don't bring this dirt into my house."* She emphasized *my* with that drawn frustration only addicts know. Papi tapped out of every one of those fights. As if he'd given up on us. The chemo was wearing him hard. The Ignacio I knew would've barked right back at Paqo.

Our barrio started catching drift of Paqo's new hobby, his shiny new pride and joy. The white rooster he bought from Don Chao, an Asian-looking man said to have arrived in Puerto Rico after the Korean War. Papi handed his service over to Uncle Sam, too. Many guys did back then. It was their golden ticket. But Chao never really spoke about how or why he chose to exile himself on our green rock. Paqo claimed he was fleeing, said the old guy had failed at opening fast-food noodles or some crap like that. So he got started on raising underweight roosters. I warned Paqo that Chao's rooster was faking the funk. After he bought the bird, Paqo raced him on a treadmill to "improve his speed." Tried injecting him with hormones and I reminded him that they weren't dogs. That you weren't supposed to train them like our buddies used to do to pits.

"What do you know?"

"You need another rooster to help build their aggression."

"Idiota. These things fight on instinct."

"Paqo. In order to train…"

"I don't have any more money, *bicho*." He stopped working on the bird and combed his stringy hair back. "I'll draw a face of another *gallo* on a pillow. That'll get him going."

"Yeah, sure. And remember to add the spurs to pillow cock. It'll make it more challenging for your *gallina*."

"Back off, Yamil."

Paqo carved out a den just down the rocky hill from our home. Managed to scrap together old rusted sheet metal and plywood for the cage. There, Paqo conducted his grand design. He creamed baby oil under the scales of his bird. Truth was, Paqo didn't know much about *gallos* or how to train them. He emphasized his labor with a face of cold determination, his large shoulders bent over the bird, lathering his glowing white feathers with Vicks. He then stuffed tablets of fish oil and Glucosamine down the cock's throat.

"He'll choke, Paqo!" I made to stop him before a pill was shoved into his beak.

"Easy, *mano*. I punctured the pill with my nail. The oil empties right out."

"How is that stuff supposed to help?"

"It'll make him strong."

"Those cocktails are going to kill him."

"*Cállate*." Paqo kept rubbing the talons. "Check it, an old tip Chao told me. Good for him to wash down the nutrients."

Paqo put the bird on the table and took out a can of Swanson chicken broth. He rummaged through the metal barrel where he kept all his equipment and teased out a blue plastic bowl.

"Paqo! *Qué carajo?*" I ran up to him and made to yank the can opener from his tight fingers.

"Yamil. *Relax.*" He shoved me back and the rooster began to hop up in the air, his feathers sluggishly splayed open and his skeletal body grazing the cage's rotting wood. "This is the secret. *Un truco chino.*"

Paqo poured the broth into the bowl and made to swipe at the bird's neck. He stretched his beak toward the bowl, but then hesitated.

"He's not going to drink that shit. That could be his cousin," I said. Paqo kept trying to move the bird to the blue bowl but the little cock fought him. He slipped away from Paqo's grip and started strutting in circles. Paqo lunged at him again and straddled the inflated bird. He forced open his beak and began to pour the broth slowly down his throat.

"That's real fucked, Paqo."

"*Cállate, cabrón.* I know what I'm doing. Chao's not wrong about these things."

I let out a chuckle before picking up some of the long white feathers let loose by Paqo's bird.

"Have you thought of a name?"

He finished pouring the broth down the rooster's throat. The bird shrugged.

"El Caníbal?" he said. "It flows, right?"

"Sure..."

Paqo kept working me after that. Said Caníbal would need me to look after him. And if I played along, he would help me get it in with one of Rosa's friends. Stupid, really. Paqo wanted that damn thing so bad but as soon as the shine wore off the feathers he was skipping out on the rooster's meals. I had to be the one making sure that cock was getting his food. I had to be the rope between Paqo and our home. I had to be the one. Even if there were no guarantees in reeling him in. At least for Ma and Papi, as long as he was still a thorn in my side, maybe he'd manage a way back to them.

Paqo then told me he wanted Caníbal ready for a fight, and I was suckered into becoming the dipshit's personal trainer. Not one *carajo* given by Paqo. Paqo el Rey. He started commanding more with his finger as he went off prowling with Rosa, leaving me to clean up his mess. I told him I'd get him back. Told him to keep on the lookout, his day was coming.

Papi tried tracking down Caníbal's cage. He attempted to spy his way to the location. Paqo, however, knew about his extensive Noticentro-like investigation. Maybe it was Ma's new obsession with Perry Mason that had Papi all inquisitive. Whatever it was, Paqo would deny any wrong-doing. Then, whenever he had enough energy to tail Paqo or me, we came up with the brilliant idea of exhausting him into submission. Would walk around the block just enough to tire him out. Didn't take much either. About two rounds down a few of the sloping hills and Papi was wheezing at a distance. After a while, he just threw in the towel. His weaknesses grew and Paqo fancied himself cut by Jesus. He began to taste blood in the water.

I prepped Caníbal hard. Paqo got it in his head that he might actually win. Started flaunting his success to Rosa, saying he was gonna make bank. She stumbled her way down the rocky hill to the secret den Paqo stitched together. As soon as she appeared, Paqo sashayed and waltzed up to her to the tune of his offbeat whistling.

"We gonna win, Rosa, yes, Rosa, yes. We gonna win one, two, three, one two three. One. Two. Three," he sang. They stumbled together until she brushed him off.

"You really think this is making a living, Paqo? How's your dad doing?"

He stopped trotting as those words hung over us.

"This will work. And it'll cover the health bills."

"That money won't even cover a month's trips *en el carro público*. You'll be back walking and asking me for *pon* soon enough."

"Then it'll cover something, Rosa!"

He puffed his chest out. His face was red, and his shaggy hair hung over his high cheekbones. Paqo never censored their fights or disagreements around me. It was one of the few things he continued to do consistently.

"Let's weigh him, Paqo," I finally said, hoping it would distract them from each other.

"*Vamo' allá*," he said and turned to dig into the barrel where the scale was crammed. He placed it on the ground, tapped the end, and weighed himself. Then he grabbed Caníbal from his cage. Rosa sneered. Caníbal started fidgeting in Paqo's grip and tried freeing himself from his clasping arms.

"*Increíble*," Rosa whispered under her breath.

"*Cállate*!" Paqo struggled. "Yamil, grab this thing's feet or something. He's cutting into me."

I squeezed Caníbal's feet together. His talons were as sharp as glass. Paqo's forearm was scraped. The talons sank into my palms as I continued to squeeze them together.

"Easy, Yamil. Don't pull down. You'll tip the scale." We both looked down at the numbers.

"What's the difference?" I said. Paqo stared at the red

digits below him. He started mumbling to himself. He shoved Caníbal into my arms, bent over to grab the scale, and shook it. Then he repeated the entire weighing process.

"This is impossible. There is no way," he said.

"What's the difference?"

"The difference is three fucking pounds." He grabbed Caníbal's neck and tossed him into his cage, the cock clucking as he bounced off the cage walls.

"Have you been feeding it, Yamil? Have you been running it?"

"What difference does it make if I run it? The damn thing isn't doing a marathon."

"You were supposed to follow the fucking directions!"

"That's probably why it didn't gain a damn pound. Running a chicken..."

"You were supposed to follow directions!"

I stopped and turned to walk away.

"Don't leave, *mamón*. We have work to do."

"This isn't my bird, Paqo!"

He rummaged through the cask and picked out one of the cans of chicken broth.

"They are all here. You haven't been feeding him the proper diet."

Rosa started chuckling loudly when she saw the Swanson

can. Paqo was floored by the noise. His eyes bulged out of his damn skull—motherfucker looked like he was hyped on speed. He juggled the can with one hand. Then he tossed it at my head. The can split the side of my scalp, just above my ear. I fell to the ground and heard bells. I felt the density of the metal push through my scalp and exit out the other side of my head. The can dropped dead on the ground and tumbled into a shrub.

"You're next, Rosa, *si no te cállas.*"

I curled up in the dirt and swiped at the small pebbles on the ground, clutching what I could. I unleashed torrents in Paqo's direction, hoping to land something as a consolation prize. I didn't cry, but tears fell out of my eyes. I could hear Paqo pounding his fist on the table.

"Paqo! *Ya!*" Rosa tried helping me up but I wanted to stay on the ground. I kept my weight dropped. Didn't let her find leverage. She eventually gave up trying and melted right next to me. She applied pressure to the side of my head with her black shirt, the blood drizzling down my ear.

Paqo didn't acknowledge what he had done. He returned to that cask and fished out another can of chicken broth, pouring it into the blue plastic bowl. He took out the white Caníbal, grabbed him by the wings, and forced the broth down his throat. His eyes were dull like cinder blocks. The trees and bamboos snapped against each other, their sounds biting into the silence of the air.

We left him there. Rosa and I stumbled our way up the stony side of the hill. She kept pressure on my head and cradled my weight on the side of her shoulder. The moon was visible even though the sun was still casting its final strong rays over the swaths of green mountain. Some things never last. In more ways than one. I kept questioning Rosa's commitment to Paqo. But looking back, it probably was more legit to say she was determined to outlast her commitment. I wanted to feel sorry for her because I knew she was wedged between that commitment and walking away. Ma always preached to us that dry grass is fragile, that it could easily go up in smoke, and Paqo's anger was a glint thirsty for air.

When we reached the house, Ma and Papi weren't home. Figured Papi was at his chemo ritual. Trying to vomit the mutation away. The radiation scared out not only the bad cells having a fiesta but also any willpower and strength needed to heal him. Papi trembled when he walked after therapy. Doctora Grecia prescribed a wheelchair, but he wasn't having it. At the very least he wanted to keep some appearance of iron will.

I landed on the couch like a rock. Rosa moved into the kitchen and started pouring hot water into a large gray stockpot and took out some meat from our rusted fridge.

She set it on the counter to defrost. She grabbed a packet of frozen green peas.

"Here." She handed the bag to me. "For the swelling."

"I can't just put this on. What about the gash? I need *puntos*, Rosa. Think we should go to the hospital."

"I'm not taking you there, Yamil." She turned away and headed to the kitchen. She started opening the cabinets and inspecting the rows of Goya cans, as if looking for the perfect one. "You're gonna have to live with that. What is wrong with you, Yamil? Why do you have to fight *con él*?"

"What is wrong with *me*? Are you fucking kidding me? The guy's gotten all crazy. Chicken and treadmills and all."

"*Lo estabas cucando*. If you wouldn't have dared him to—"

"I'm not daring anyone!" I stood from the couch, still pressing the peas to my head. "This is how he is now. You haven't been around. Only to *chingar* late at night. So don't come around here trying to tell me what I should or should not be doing."

Rosa stopped fidgeting though the cupboards. The soft yellow light from the kitchen flickered as she turned to me. She glided out of that space and moved to *retar* me.

Just then the front door shook and then opened. Ma walked in. The creeping night was let in with her as she pushed an empty wheelchair on through.

"*Hola*, Rosa," she said without lifting her head. "Yamil. *Ayuda a tu papá.* He's lying down in the backseat." I walked toward her and she stopped to look at me. It was only a second. She scanned me and my nice cut and didn't say anything else. Her face was plastered stiff.

I opened the backseat of our Buick Estate. Papi was curled in the fetal position, a heavy wool blanket draped over his emaciated limbs. I moved him upright and tried picking him up like a baby.

"*Ni te lo creas.* I can walk," he said. He smelled terrible. The sweat had caked under his armpits and his breath gave off that tonsil-stone stench. His lips were lacerated in different places with dried blood. He complained often about his dry mouth. He had black ulcers dotting the edges of his jaw and bruises all over his veins from where they'd probed him. He had a scar running down his chest where they'd found it. He'd complained of heart pains before going into the hospital years ago. Doctors said not to worry. Said it was just routine testing. But the labs picked up on the aggressive mutation. He was a beautiful mess. A canvas depicting the full spectrum of brown tone. A skinned impressionist painting that was dying.

He trembled to his feet and leaned against the car door before inching his way to the house. No comment on the gash on my head. I knew he saw it. Glanced at it before continuing on his way. I don't think he wanted to admit that things around him were slipping. Because I was certain he knew Paqo was to blame.

He stumbled a bit. I ran up to him to offer my shoulder but he insisted.

"You're going to fall down, Pa," I said to him in a matter-of-fact way.

"Keep bugging me and you're going to get it from me. And you will be the one on the ground," he snapped back.

"Let him help you, Ignacio," Ma interjected.

"*Cállense todos.*" He waddled through the door, leaning on every piece of dusted furniture.

Rosa stood petrified in the kitchen as Papi made it to his leather recliner and sat down. He let out a deep and long sigh before closing his sunken eyes.

"Where is your brother, Yamil?" Ma said.

"No idea, Ma. Last I checked he was trolling Ocean Park."

"Right…" She pushed the wheelchair into the empty hallway closet. The pale walls of the hallway were decorated with our family pictures in frames of dark varnished wood. Those dead eyes of relatives absently indicting us as we lied. The dozen crosses hung in perfect equilibrium, searing their sharp Ts into our tongues.

"Where is Paqo, Rosa?"

Rosa tried shaking her head convincingly. Shaking away that lie that hung over both of us. Ma knew we were both full of shit.

"Well, whenever you see him, tell him I want to speak with him. *Ya se acabó este jueguito*." There wasn't a trace of anger in her voice. Ma was never the one to yell or bark at us when we fucked up. That was Papi's area of expertise. He learned it through caning. Still had the old scars splattered across his dark shins. Abuelo's handiwork.

Rosa and I got back to cooking. She worked on boiling the water and *sazonando* it with Ma's homemade *sofrito*. I cut up the yuca, the chef knife popping against the cutting board like a gavel in a courtroom every time I pressed it through the stubborn root. Ma disappeared into her cave. Papi was knocked out on his recliner with the TV on as ambient noise.

After we tossed all the prep into the boiling *sancocho*, we joined Pa. I figured we'd try keeping him company even if he wasn't conscious to appreciate it. We dumbed away to Noticentro's nightly reel: the 452nd murder of the year and counting, the water shortage and rationing that was threatened, the upcoming election. Filiberto Ojeda was still at large, too. Wanda Cordero always tried her best to slant the truth when she reported the news. I caught on to her tell: her left eye would scrunch up whenever she spewed her biased opinion. Her coanchor would sigh and nod every time. He never disagreed outright, but you could see he never approved of a word she spat out. Ojeda, *"el criminal."* Ojeda, *"el maliante."* Funny thing was we're talking about an old geezer. A man in his sixties. Ma was full Yankee about anything that involved politics. Papi leaned on the other side of the colonial debate: *revolución* crazy. Had he been paying attention, he would've probably thrown a *medalla* at our crap-ass TV. Sung us a spectacle. Paraded around the O.G. baby blue flag. Gone all Boricua rah-rah until he wore himself to sleep. It all flashed before us as Papi let out delicate snores through the surgical mask Doctora Grecia gave him.

"Who would you vote for?" Rosa nudged me.

"None of the above."

"Why?"

"Because they are all playing the same game."

"Wouldn't you want to see Sila win? About time we had a woman as governor."

"I'll vote by scratching out my ballot."

She released two blunt *tsk-tsk*s and flipped her long, curly black hair into my face.

"Don't be angry that your *fupista* nonsense can't make the cut. You know Berríos is," she moved her lips to my ear, "full of *pura mierda*."

"Rosa." I pushed her away. "If Papi hears you he's gonna send you packing."

"Whatever, Yamil. I'm going to vote for Sila."

"Good for fucking you. Why don't you go home and write about it?"

"You're such an ass, Yamil." She got up. "Don't let Paqo's bull infect you. You'll end up the same."

She went back into the kitchen. It was Rosa's combo hit she liked to occasionally deliver: the seek-and-destroy, the slap-and-leave. I jumped off the couch and walked up to her.

"You should try to slap the stupid out of him, Rosa. He listens to you. He's gonna get into trouble with this scheme of his. And Ma is already up to her eyeballs with Pa."

The pot steamed over and foamed at its mouth. Rosa uncovered it and let out the hot cloud, the warmth of the *sancocho* attacked our taste buds. The steam touched my forehead and it ate into the thick gash like rubbing alcohol. I winced.

We served the stew into four bowls. I made to take a fifth bowl out of our wooden cabinet and Rosa commanded me to leave it. "Paqo can get what's left on his own," she proclaimed. I placed one of the filled soup bowls on a white ceramic plate and took it to Ma.

She was in her bedroom teasing her eyebrows. There was

a faint yellow glow in the room. The light shining out of the porcelain temple jar lamp was dim. Ma looked as though she was struggling to pluck at those rogue hairs above her pencil-thin brows. The small oval mirror she used to study herself was on the nightstand. She sat on the bed hunched toward its tiny face. The old bedsheets in her room were worn and dusty, as if they hadn't been washed since Ma and Papi became regulars at hospitals. I stubbed my toe against the door, and the plate I held trembled in my grip.

"Where is he, Yamil?" She didn't turn to me or notice how I almost dove face-first into her stew. I steadied myself and sat down next to her on the bed. She kept wrestling with the stubborn hairs in the middle of her brows.

"I brought you some *sancocho*. Rosa made it."

"Did you give some to your father?"

"He's asleep. I didn't want to wake him."

"Where is Paqo?"

"I brought you *sancocho*. Do you want it?" I was pissed by her persistence. Even though she knew I wouldn't rat him out, it never stopped her from trying.

"Leave it there."

I kept thinking I couldn't get out of there quick enough. But she stopped me as I neared the door.

"You and your brother are killing your father," she said,

her voice unfazed by the bitter words she dangled over my head. I wanted to snap, to curse her. Wanted to take the hot soup and slam it against the wall.

Rosa left at midnight, just as the signal from the TV went out. The electricity shortly followed. Papi didn't want to be taken to his room with Ma. Felt it necessary to keep watch from his recliner, waiting on Paqo to slither by him and be ready with the snare pole. I was nodding off in the darkness of my bedroom. A thin ray from the moon reflected on Paqo's pull-up bar. He had drilled it into the door frame when we were kids. I remembered him stomping in after school when I was just twelve. He was finishing up high school. Those were his prime days. Dude never wore a shirt and would always prop himself on the bar and muscle out a rep of fifty as a warm-up. He'd wink at me after every heave. The girls would swoon over his apple-sized biceps. His body had its own gravitational orbit, his muscles inflated and his abs like strong cobblestones. And he had taken major advantage of the attention. Told me it was the natural thing to do, that whatever Rosa found out about his *sucias*, she would have to understand. I knew that he would become spoiled goods to Rosa if she caught wind that he was still pounding away rabbit-style all these years later. Still! Even after she granted him that royal pardon.

There wouldn't be a long enough Hallmark card or Luis
Fonsi *balada* to eclipse another transgression. Not a single
lyric from "Perdóname" could save his ass now, but I knew
I'd end up being the messenger even still, the one relaying
those types of lyrics to her on behalf of his sorry ass. He
thought Rosa was easier to persuade if I was the brunt of
anger. "Hold on," I would say. "I'm not your safeguard,"
or "Leave me the hell out of it." He'd exploit our history
shamelessly to patch it up, then get back to work *cueriando*.

The front door creaked open and I could make out
mumbling in the living room. I shook myself awake and
went to the low voices. Papi was pointing his finger at
Paqo. He leaned against the couch with one hand while
the other conducted the choir. Paqo's face was crinkled
and pruned; he wore a soft, veiled grin and seemed to
have difficulty standing straight. He was drunk. The
smell of Bacardi wafted in the air and moved over all of
us with the delicacy of a pregnant rain cloud. I slipped
out of the hallway so they could see me. Paqo was known
to go on tirades when *borracho*. Wished he would elect
to quell his ire if an argument got too hot. But Papi
wasn't letting up.

"You need to clean house and get the hell out," he forced
himself to say. His magic wand nudged Paqo's chest. "We

aren't going to keep having this happen. There is no drinking in this house."

"I'll leave when I'm damn well ready, *viejo*." He slurred his words and tried pushing past Pa, but Papi elbowed him back against the front door.

"Get out."

Paqo jumped up and stuck his forehead against Pa.

"Don't push it, *mamón. Ya tú no mandas.*"

"Get out!" Papi pushed him against the glass accent table. Paqo tackled him. The weight of Paqo in full bloom and Papi's dead body echoed throughout our home as they hit the floor. Papi struck a weak hit on the side of Paqo's head but it didn't have any effect. Paqo slugged Papi's ribs, then pressed his forearm against Papi's neck. It was over. Papi flailed like a fish out of water as Paqo's dark-red face hovered over his body.

"Don't even try it!" he shouted at Papi.

"Paqo!" Ma jumped into the scene and smacked him across the face, knocking him off.

"Don't come around here! Get out!" Ma shouted. Paqo sat up and traced out the two of them with his eyes as if trying to memorize their features. Papi was winded and clawing at Ma. He started crying and Ma cradled him against her breasts.

*   *   *

You could imagine what happened next. Paqo disappeared for a week after that night. I kept returning to Caníbal's cage, feeding him and hoping to run into Paqo. Caníbal got more and more anxious. His white feathers were displaced and ragged. His thin crown was blotched with dirt. He wasn't gaining weight. Still a pathetic three pounds. I even took up the stupid broth ritual Paqo believed in so furiously. Wasn't sure if Paqo was still going to go through with fighting Caníbal the following month. The prepping alone was going to be tedious. Getting Caníbal used to being shaven. I couldn't imagine doing all of it by myself. Even if they were going to set him in the low weight class of three, three was being generous. He felt so hollow when you cradled him. He would get creamed in a fight. All his aggression was built on Paqo being there, being present and egging him on.

Ma didn't speak his name. And Papi was practically comatose. He didn't move from the bed. Ma would spoon-feed him his soups and often he would spit it out. She would wait patiently until he wet his lips with his tongue, puckered his mouth, and attempted to sip at the broth again. I caught all this by peeking into their bedroom. I knew Ma knew. And Papi knew. I was watching closely. But they stopped hiding how bad Papi was getting after that night.

He fainted a couple of times after Paqo's desertion. All I could do was watch it happen.

Ma cooked him *jamonilla* and eggs and he tumbled out of his chair and onto the floor. She rushed to him and had him sit back up. She commanded me to bring her the rubbing alcohol. I nodded and shot to the medicine cabinet. She rubbed it over his neck and had him whiff some.

"Should we take him back to San Pablo?" I asked, trying to find anything to feel useful about.

"It's going to happen. No need to worry, Yamil." She rubbed some of that clear elixir on his bald head. It became routine to see things in that way: Papi struggling to keep pace, Ma picking up after him.

One day when I went out of the front door and checked for mail, there was a letter pinned against the lowered flag. It was Paqo's writing, a cursive as legible as smeared ink. He asked me to meet him at Caníbal's tomorrow. The tone wasn't urgent, almost like it was an expected eventuality. But I needed to breathe because had he been watching from behind the *almendra* tree, I would've charged at him. Would've smacked his head against the asphalt and watched the blood run down the back of his head, as indifferent as he had been when he cold-cocked me with the metal Swanson can.

The following night I snuck out once Ma and Papi called

the day early. Papi had just gotten back from another batch of chemo and went to bed. They spared me a couple of twenties tucked under the candlesticks on the kitchen table. They were going to be away most of the week and figured it should hold me over until I started work bagging at Mr. Special. I was hooked up with a few starting shifts out of pity. When word got around that Paqo had rumbled with Pa, the manager felt sorry, took it upon himself to assuage his pity. I was left spare keys to the Estate, too. It started seeming like I had won the lottery. All thanks to Paqo's stupidity. But the rules were simple. Ma warned it was only for emergencies. They were receiving pro bono rides to Papi's appointments from Tía Camila. The whole family lot began creeping out of the woodwork, offering their penance. I ended up receiving most of the "good fortune." Papi spent 90 percent of his time delirious and Ma was too preoccupied to bask in all the half-assed perks people offered.

When I arrived at Paqo's secret spot, dude didn't even turn around to greet me, just kept shaving Caníbal's thighs. He pulled out a nail file from his back pocket and began sanding away at the bird's spur claw. He had asked me to clip it weeks ago to leave room for the plastic spur they tape on the fighting roosters. Seeing him prep Caníbal like that could only mean the obvious: he was going through with the fight.

"Not even going to apologize, are you?"

He sanded Caníbal harder, swiping away and blowing on the dust that collected on his yellow feet.

"Caníbal's fight is this Friday. I need your help at Arena Gallística. Need some paperwork filled out."

"You got two hands that work."

"I need you to take care of the paperwork while I speak with a friend about an arrangement." He finished sanding Caníbal's feet. He combed back some of the ruffled white feathers, then pushed him back into the cage. There were dozens of moths and cockroaches crashing into the kerosene lantern that hung over a stray branch.

"You're not planning a *truco* again, are you? They don't mess around down there. If you fuck with your word with those people, they're gonna fuck you up, Paqo."

"I have a friend..."

"I can't believe this, *mano*. You are really out of it. First Pa. Now this? Keep it up and we gonna find your skinny ass in a *cuneta*."

"Okay, stop the bitching. I know what I'm doing. *No me crecí la barba ayer*, Yamil. It's just a small... adjustment I'm paying a guy to do. Nothing more. It's a big cash-out. Told

them Caníbal will fight three pounds above his weight class."
He started smirking. As if he'd gotten a five-finger discount
on Snickers. He slammed his palms against the table. "And
they took the bait. I heard many were going to put in high
stakes to see our beautiful Caníbal 'lose.' Little do they know
he is more than a runt cock. It's gonna be too easy."

"I don't want any part in it." I turned to leave but Paqo
sprinted up to me and tugged me back to him.

"Look. Trust me. It's gonna be good. This money is going
to help Ma with some of the bills. Pa will be grateful."

"Don't."

"It's better than anything you're doing, *mamón*."

"Cabrón, I got a job. All thanks to your *estupidéz*. But
because of your little annoying self, they don't even care."

I pushed him off me and started making my way up
the slope.

"Then I guess you should be thanking me. You're
beholden to me. Careful, Yamil. Or you'll end up in more
debt than Ma."

"Fucker." I bent over to pick up a stone from the ground.
I shot it toward Paqo, but I missed miserably. The stone
crashed into Caníbal's cage. He jumped and smacked his
little body against the wiry roof. He clucked, then started
bouncing and crowing.

"I swear to you, Yamil." Paqo lunged at me, speared his hand forward and tugged at my shirt, tethering me toward him like Scorpion. "You hurt that bird…"

"Get off me." I started climbing back up the dark hill.

"You should learn how to aim, *papito*. I'll teach you when your balls drop."

I flipped him off, hoping the kerosene's rays shone just enough light on me for him to notice.

"I expect to see you there, Mr. Benítez," he shouted at me. "Three thirty p.m. sharp. Don't be late. Fight is at four forty-five."

I had every intention of bailing, I tell you. Really wanted him to suffocate in his mess. But for some reason I was invested. He had mind-fucked me enough for me to feel as though Caníbal was also mine. I raised him and fed him and spoke with him when Paqo decided to go MIA. By then, I knew that no matter how crappy Paqo was becoming, short of murder, I would follow him.

Fight day came upon me quickly. By the time I made it to Caníbal's den, Paqo had already taken off. He left another illegible note saying to meet him at the arena. I trekked with the rhythms of our barrio's winding hills. The forest clouded the sun. The crickets and *coquís* dusted the air with their soundtrack.

Arena Gallística was an old cement hexagon. The turn-stile gates were guarded by security checking entrants' bags. Most of the tall trees surrounding it moved with the gusts of wind and the wood snapped as their branches crashed against each other, their shadows crawled on Arena's roof, their bark spread over like a man in stilts. Demonic looking things. The popularity of these events was on a who-you-know basis. Word got out through newspapers, sure. But it was usually the regulars who came flocking. This time, however, people were lined up to see the main act.

I made it to the check-in counter and began filling out the paperwork Paqo had asked me to do. The desk wobbled as I wrote Caníbal's details and checked all the necessary boxes. After that, I waited for Paqo. I wasn't sure where he was but I couldn't go to the tunnel where they kept the fighters. You needed a badge.

Paqo finally appeared from the crowd. He was tightly wound. He wore a dark blue button-down shirt and a loose tie lassoed over his head, his shirt tucked into black dress pants. The only blemish in his outfit was his shoes, old Chucks stained by years of trolling, brown scratches on their fronts that had become part of the design.

"Where's Caníbal? You get him primed?"

"He's waiting his turn." His eyes were bouncing from person

to person, barely making contact. A large man who looked like Otilio Bizcocho Warrington came up to us and bear-hugged Paqo. He then shook his hand repeatedly and grinned.

"I can't wait, *mijo*. I'm looking forward to this one. You're the talk of the town today," the man said. He pointed his finger at him. On the surface it seemed playful enough, but in his eyes there was a look that screamed, *I'll break you if you cross me*. He had arms as large as logs, and his head had a dark, bald finish like a biker's helmet.

In these cockfighting events, there weren't any written wagers. What you bet was verbal. I could see Paqo was nervous. *Don't break your word*. I repeated this to myself, hoping Paqo would get the message. *Don't break your word.*

The buzz alarm sounded through black intercoms. It was Caníbal's turn. We made it through the entrance of the hexagon. Large banners dressed the chipped cement pillars. The floor was pliant and hollow, almost fragile, like linoleum. When we entered the main corridor where the oval rink was, all the men gathered and sat down on foam cushions that buffered their asses from the cement bleachers. It was as if we were going to witness gladiators slugging it out; coliseum bravado at its finest.

Paqo and I sat in the front row, as was expected of us. He bumped my shoulder.

"We got this, Yamilito." He pointed in the direction of the tunnel where they cart the two contesting roosters into the oval rink. "Our white king's gonna appear soon. Just you wait."

I leaned into Paqo's ear and whispered to him, "What did you do, *mano*? You did something."

He pushed his face back and pulled a crumpled brown paper bag from his pocket. He passed it to me discreetly. I unraveled the mess. In it there was an assortment of sharp metal spurs no larger than fingernail clippings. Metal. There was a thin layer of white nail polish painted on them to distract from the initial glance. You'd have to do a triple take and run your fingers down them in order to catch it. I crumpled the bag and scanned my surroundings in fear that someone might have caught a glimpse of those white-edged claws. It was a dirty move. Paqo knew it. He must've paid the prep guy who taped the roosters to replace the legal plastic spurs. He knew he'd get away with it, too. The owners usually managed their cocks when the fight started.

"How much did you pledge, Paqo?" I said to him in anger. He sat there proud of this moment. He wore this smugness that felt contagious. "How much?"

"Three K."

"Are you out of your damn mind, *mano*? To who the fuck?"

A second alarm sounded and the ushers carted in the two competing roosters. Paqo started clapping and whistling.

"Our boy's looking regal!" The white feathers on Caníbal were stainless, the crown above his head polished and trimmed. Paqo was ecstatic. The intercom gave the two-minute warning in case there were any final lingering wagers. Caníbal sat there in the plexiglass cage unfazed by all the yammering.

Bizcocho's lookalike walloped next to Paqo and threw him a confident wink. Paqo nodded. He jumped over the rink and took Caníbal from his plexiglass cage. We were given the thirty-second warning. Paqo cradled the bird. He pressed his lips against the rooster's crown. He prayed. And then he let him go and the fight began.

Paqo and others surrounded the rink. They hollered and pounded the barrier. Men were screaming and chanting while Paqo was silent. Caníbal hadn't moved. His opponent hopped in the air and lashed at him, the rust-colored feathers around his neck flared. Caníbal was snoozing. His eyes were shut and he sat there looking as though he were warming an egg. Bizcocho burst into a hysterical fit. His fat stomach heaved air and he started coughing. Paqo turned to us and his face was pale. His eyes pleaded with me to fix it.

"This is just perfect. You really did a good job there, *flaco*," Bizcocho man barked at Paqo. Every person in the crowd burst into laughter as Caníbal's crown feathers were slowly chipped away by the rooster's kicks, Caníbal's eyes cut open and specks of blood started dotting his white body.

It took him almost two minutes to register that he was supposed to be fighting. He speared his beak forward rather than striking at his foe with his spurs. He waddled around in circles, missing every blow. He clucked after every hop. He was thrust back against the barrier of the oval. When he did manage to engage the rooster with a traditional attack, he opened his wings but couldn't get much air, almost as if the metal spurs weighed his skinny body down. Their wings snapped against each other and sounded like clattering dominoes.

We knew Caníbal wouldn't last much longer. His blood was being syphoned by the plastic spurs of the rooster. Paqo stomped over to the Bizcocho lookalike and shook his head.

"Deal's off," he said and grabbed my hand to leave.

"Wait wait wait." The man stood up and blocked our path with his large arms. "You owe me something."

Caníbal was screeching behind us. He crowed. The rival rooster continued to peck at one of his eyes until it burst. Caníbal limped a bit before the rival body slammed him and knocked him out. The blood continued to spill from Caníbal's neck.

"We are leaving," Paqo said and pushed through. He held my hand and tugged me as he started power walking out of the arena and into the cool night air. Paqo's gait grew longer. His arms felt like Jell-O.

The light posts started disappearing. Each individual strobe of light that outlined the road evaporated in the anxiety of darkness, each empty gap of light blurred into longer trims of night until it was black.

They ambushed us, Bizcocho and his men. It almost felt like we got away. In the deepness of *el campo*, you start to get comfortable when the artificial light stops shining. The men filed out of their white minivan. I elbowed Paqo and we both took off sprinting. One of the men caught my shirt by the collar as I shot by him. Another hooked Paqo by the tie and yanked him to the ground. I was tossed out of the scuffle. They barraged Paqo with kicks. They landed. Every one of them. His face began to swell.

Bizcocho commanded his crew to stop.

"Take this dead thing with you. I don't want it." He smacked Paqo across the face with Caníbal's droopy red body. "Don't you even think about showing up around the arena. Or these parts. From now on, *yo soy tu dueño*. You hear?"

The men moved quickly, reminding me of mountain

roaches, quick to confront and quick to leave. Caníbal lay next to Paqo. I helped Paqo up the hill using my body as a rigid pole. He nudged at me to scoop up Caníbal. I did. I dragged him along with one hand. Used the other to propel Paqo and keep him level. He applied pressure but his knees buckled, his heaviness straining my arm.

"Try putting some weight on your legs. You're damn heavy."

"I can't."

"You have to try."

Paqo loosened his hold on me and walked on his own for a few feet before stumbling. I swooped under him and grabbed him again.

"I can't."

When we got to the ledge of the hill, you could see the dark shadows of the mountain in the night sky, each mound lit with specks of houses. Paqo told me he didn't want to go home. Asked if I could help him get to Caníbal's den.

We stumbled up the rocky bed to the den and the kerosene light. I lit it. Paqo took Caníbal's body and spread it across the table. He untaped the spurs. I petted the back of his head as he worked on cleaning Caníbal's red body. He dug around the barrel in search of a knife. He tipped the tube over and kicked it. He ran out into the clearing where you could see the empty ocean. He started yelling at the darkness. Later, he hung Caníbal's body by his neck on a tree branch.

Paqo went all in this time around. Disappearing act 2.0. The guy was gone, and this time, I wasn't sure if he was coming back. I had been working at Mr. Special for almost two weeks, bagging and helping old men and women on welfare ring up their vegetables. Had them a few times burst into fits of anger because *la tarjeta de familia* wouldn't cover their Depends. I would drift off and think about him. No Paqo in sight.

I was coming home on a Friday. Ma had left me a note at work that she and Papi were returning from the hospital after spending a full week there for Papi's treatment. Papi was mending better. Doctora Grecia expressed optimism and gave a better outlook. Tía Camila was especially Jehová; started reciting tongues, you'd think in Latin. Ma reserved her opinion and told me over the phone in a defeated voice, *"Vamos a ver."*

The sun cooked the asphalt and a haze rose out of the ground. I drove the Estate into the driveway. The house was quiet. I turned the key and pushed my way through. There was soft whimpering in the background. Ma was sitting in Papi's recliner, calcified to the leather. Her eyes were stone.

"Ma? What's up? Where is Pa?" I shook her but she looked through me in the direction of my room. I stepped softly. The picture of me in a bathing suit, crying as my brother tossed sand on my head, was slanted. The crosses lining the cement seemed muffled, unable to emit their religious radiance.

I could make out Pa. He was crying. His thin body and bald head were curled up next to Paqo. Paqo was splayed on the floor, his body tangled in a gray bedsheet, his hands trying to stroke Papi's neck. The metal pull-up bar was on the floor, the wood from the door frame chipped and scattered. I came up to them and scanned their features. Paqo's neck was swollen and marked in a deep purple and his eyes were red. He was out of it. He mumbled as Papi rocked him back and forth. The gray sheet that constricted him like a soft snake was tied at the end like a noose. He swiped his hands in the air, trying to shoo me away, telling me, *"To' esta bien."*

"Yamil, everything's fine."

LAURA ADAMCZYK was born and raised and still lives in Illinois. Her fiction has won awards from the Union League Civic & Arts Foundation and the Dzanc Books/Disquiet International Literary Program and has appeared in the *Chicago Reader, Guernica, Hobart, Salt Hill, Vol. 1 Brooklyn*, and elsewhere. FSG Originals will publish her short-story collection in 2018.

MICHAEL ANDREASEN's fiction has appeared in the *New Yorker, Tin House, Zoetrope, Quarterly West*, and elsewhere. His first book, *The Sea Beast Takes a Lover*, will be available in February 2018. He lives in Southern California.

NICK ARVIN is an engineer living in Denver. His third novel, *Mad Boy*, will be published by Europa Editions in 2018.

RAJEEV BALASUBRAMANYAM is the author of the novels *In* *Beautiful Disguises, The Dreamer*, and *Starstruck*. His awards include the Betty Trask Prize and the Clarissa Luard Prize for the best British writer under thirty-five. He writes for *VICE*, the *New Statesman*, the *Economist*, the *Washington Post, London Review of Books*, and others.

IACOPO BARISON was born in 1988. He graduated with a degree in Cinema from the University of Torino. His short stories and articles have appeared in many different magazines; he also writes on *minima&moralia*. His first novel, *Stalin + Bianca,* has been translated into Spanish and soon will become a movie.

AMY BERKOWITZ is the author of *Tender Points*, the host of the Amy's Kitchen Organics reading series, and the editor of Mondo Bummer Books. Her work has been honored with residencies at Alley Cat Books and Gallery and the Kimmel Harding Nelson Center for the Arts.

PATTY YUMI COTTRELL is the author of *Sorry to Disrupt the Peace* (McSweeney's, 2017). She lives in New York City.

CHRIS DENNIS holds an MFA in Fiction from Washington University in St. Louis, where he also received a postgraduate fellowship. His work has appeared in *Granta*, *West Branch*, and *New Stories From The Midwest*.

MERRILL FEITELL's first book, *Here Beneath Low-Flying Planes*, won the Iowa Short Fiction Award. She lives near the edge of Los Angeles and is at work on a novel, stories, and a series of multimedia essays.

EMMA HOOPER is an author, musician, and academic. She lives in England but comes home to Canada to cross-country ski whenever she can. (emmahooper.ca)

JESSE JACOBS works from his home in Hamilton, Ontario. A selection of his work can be viewed at jessejacobs.ca. His books can be found at koyama-press.com.

ETGAR KERET is an Israeli writer known for his short stories, graphic novels, and scriptwriting for film and television. His writing has been published in the *New York Times*, the *New Yorker, Zoetrope*, and *the Paris Review*, and his books have been published in more than forty languages. His latest book, *The Seven Good Years*, was chosen by the *Guardian* as one of the best biographies and memoirs of 2015. Etgar Keret is the winner of the 2016 Charles Bronfman Prize.

ALI LIEBEGOTT is the author of *The Beautifully Worthless, The IHOP Papers*, and *Cha-Ching!* She currently writes for the TV show *Transparent* and lives in Los Angeles.

GREGORIO MAGINI created the collaborative writing method SIC-Scrittura Industriale Collettiva, employed in the production of *In territorio nemico* (minimum fax, 2013), a historical novel that involved the work of 115 authors. His next novel, *Joystick*, is a solo work due out in 2018. Many of his short stories have been published in prominent Italian literary reviews and blogs, including *minima&moralia*, *Il primo amore*, *Mostro*.

KIT MAUDE is a translator based in Buenos Aires. His translations have been featured in *Granta*, *the Short Story Project*, *the Literary Review*, and *Samovar*.

MIA MCKENZIE is the author of *The Summer We Got Free*, which won the 2013 Lambda Literary Award for LGBT Debut Fiction. She's also the creator of *BGD*, a popular media website centering queer and trans people of color. Her work has appeared in *the Kenyon Review*, *Ebony*, and *the Guardian*, among other cool places.

NATHANIEL MINTON's fiction has appeared in previous issues of McSweeney's, as well as in *ZYZZYVA*, *Dustup*, *Hawk & Handsaw*, *Five Chapters,* and elsewhere.

HADLEY MOORE's short stories, novel excerpts, and nonfiction have appeared or are forthcoming in *Newsweek*, *Witness*, *Day One*, the *Alaska Quarterly Review*, the revived *December*, *Indiana Review*, *Anomaly* (formerly *Drunken Boat*), *Quarter After Eight*, *Confrontation*, *the Drum*, *Ascent*, *Midwestern Gothic*, *Redux*, *Knee-Jerk*, and other publications. She is at work on a novel and a collection of stories, and is an alumna of the MFA Program for Writers at Warren Wilson College.

XAVIER NAVARRO AQUINO's fiction has appeared in *Guernica*,

the *Literary Review*, and *Day One*.
He has received scholarships
from the Bread Loaf Writers'
Conference and travel grants to
Ghana, Spain, and Morocco from
the University of Puerto Rico,
Río Piedras, where he earned
an MA in English Caribbean
Studies. Born and raised in
Puerto Rico, he is currently a
PhD candidate in English at the
University of Nebraska Lincoln,
where he finished work on his
first novel and story collection.

NIELA ORR is a writer from
Philadelphia. She is a columnist
for the *Baffler* and a contributing
editor of the *Organist* podcast.
A graduate of the CalArts
MFA Writing program, she
has published work in the *New
York Times Book Review*, *Elle*, the
Believer, and *BuzzFeed*.

ARMIN OZDIC was born September 14, 1989, in Sarajevo. He
graduated from the Secondary
School of Applied Arts, after
which he attended the Academy
of Fine Arts. He has worked for
a large number of indie publishers, and is currently working for
the French publisher Soleil. He
won the Nikola Mitrovic Kokan
Award for the Balkan's best
young cartoonists at the seventeenth Balkans Festival of Young
Comics Creators in Leskovac in
2015. He lives in Sarajevo.

SONDRA SILVERSTON is a native
New Yorker who has been living
in Israel since 1970. Among
her published translations are
works by Israeli authors Amos
Oz (her translation of *Between
Friends* won the 2013 National
Jewish Book Award for fiction),
Eshkol Nevo (her translation of
Homesick was on the Independent
Translation Prize long list in
2009), Ayelet Gundar-Goshen
(her translation of *Waking Lions*
won the 2017 Jewish Quarterly
Wingate Literary Prize), Savyon
Liebrecht, Alona Frankel, and, of
course, Etgar Keret.

ARMONIA SOMERS (1914–1994)
was one of the most important Uruguayan writers of the

twentieth century and a leading figure in international education studies. Her work is often compared to that of Clarice Lispector and Silvina Ocampo. Her first novel to appear in English, *The Naked Woman*, will be published by the Feminist Press in the fall of 2018.

NADJA SPIEGELMAN is the web editor of the *Paris Review* and the author of *I'm Supposed to Protect You From All This*. She is also coeditor of *Resist!*, a free feminist publication of comics and graphics and the author of several graphic novels for children, including *Lost in NYC: A Subway Adventure*. She lives in Brooklyn and loves Coney Island.

JOSÉ VADI is a writer based in Oakland, California. He is the recipient of the San Francisco Foundation's Shenson Performing Arts Fellowship, and his poems and essays have most recently appeared in *the Capilano Review, HOLD: A Journal, Catapult*, and

the *LA Review of Books*. (josevadi. com; @vadiparty)

CLAIRE VAYE WATKINS is the author of *Gold Fame Citrus* and *Battleborn*, winner of the Story Prize, the International Dylan Thomas Prize, the New York Public Library's Young Lions Fiction Award, the Rosenthal Family Foundation Award from the American Academy of Arts and Letters, and a Silver Pen Award from the Nevada Writers Hall of Fame. A Guggenheim Fellow and an assistant professor at the University of Michigan, Claire is also the codirector, with Derek Palacio, of the Mojave School, a free creative-writing workshop for teenagers in rural Nevada.

RJ VOGT is currently a legal news reporter in Los Angeles. His previous jobs have included stints as a radio DJ, a songwriter, and a dishwasher. He graduated from the University of Tennessee in 2015 with a degree in literary journalism, and his job in Myanmar was initially made possible by Princeton in Asia.

ERNIE WANG resides in Las Vegas. He received his MFA in fiction from the University of Nevada, Las Vegas.

LATOYA WATKIN'S work has appeared or is forthcoming in *West Branch*, *Kweli Journal*, *Passages North*, *Pushcart Prize anthology*, and elsewhere. She has received fellowships and scholarships from the MacDowell Colony, the Bread Loaf Writers' Conference, Hedgebrook, and Kimbilio Fiction. LaToya writes and teaches in a suburb of Dallas, Texas.

LAWRENCE WESCHLER, a longtime contributor, is in addition the author of *Everything That Rises: A Book of Convergences* (McSweeneys, 2007). More can be found at www.lawrenceweschler.com.

JEFFREY WILSON is the author of graphic novels. His current comic book is based on an interview with MIT professor Noam Chomsky and will be released by Seven Stories Press in early 2018. His academic and popular writing focuses on the intersection of foreclosures and health in Detroit. Currently, he is writing a comic book recounting the deeply personal stories of everyday Detroiters standing up and fighting housing displacement.

ELENA XAUSA is an Italian illustrator based in Milan. She grew up in the hills near Venice, constantly drawing for her family, friends, and pets. This has become her job, and her illustrations and visual ideas are spreading across the world. www.elenaxausa.com

McSWEENEY'S WOULD LIKE TO
THANK THE FOLLOWING DONORS FOR
THEIR BOUNDLESS GENEROSITY.
YOU MAKE OUR WORK POSSIBLE.

A. Dupuis · A. Elizabeth Graves · A. Haggerty · A. Lee · A. Reiter · Aaron · Aaron Cripps · Aaron Davidson · Aaron Flowers · Aaron Mcmillan @ Ericrosenbizzle · 826 Fan · A.A. · Aaron Quint · Aaron Rabiroff · Aaron Richard Marx · Aaron Sedivy · Aaron Stewart · Aaron Vacin · Aaron Wishart · Abbey · Abigail Droge · Abigail Keel · Abigail Kroch · Adam Alley · Adam Angley · Adam Baer · Adam Batty · Adam Blanchard · Adam Cady · Adam Colman · Adam Esbensen · Adam Hirsch · Adam J. Kurtz · Adam Keker · Adam Kempa · Adam Mueller · Adam O'Riordan · Adam Shaffer · Adam Wager · Adam Weiss · Adam Zaner · Addison Eaton · Adeline Teoh · Aditi Rao · Adriana Difranco · Adrienne Adams · Adrienne Kolb · Adrienne Spain Chu · Adscriptum.nl · Agatha Trundle · Aida Daay · Aiden Enns · Aimee · Aimee Kalnoskas · Akiko K · Alaina Roche · Alan Federman · Alan Keefer · Alana Lewis · Alana Stubbs · Alanna Watson · Alessia Rotondo · Alex · Alex Andre · Alex Atkinson · Alex Daly · Alex Field · Alex Grecian · Alex Haynes · Alex Khripin · Alex Motzenbecker · Alex Power · Alexa Dooseman · Alexa Huyck · Alexa Pogue · Alexander Birkhold · Alexander Carney · Alexander F. Myers · Alexandra Cousy · Alexandra Kordoski · Alexandra Phillips · Alfie · Alfredo Agostini · Ali Procopio · Ali Sternburg · Alice Armstrong · Alice Christman · Alice Curtis Cline · Alice Freilinger · Alice Gardner Kelsh · Alice Mccormick · Alice Quinn · Alicia Kolbus · Alicia Mullen · Alijah · Alina Shlyapochnik · Alisa Bonsignore · Alisa Morgan · Alison Benowitz · Alison Huffman · Alison Lester · Alison Michael · Alison Thayer · Alissa Elliott · Alissa Sheldon · Alistair Bright · Alisun Armstrong · Allan Weinrib · Allen Eckhouse · Allen Rein · Allie Carey · Allison · Allison Arieff · Allison B. Bransfield · Allison Downing · Ally Kornfeld · Allyson Fielder · Altaire Productions · Alvin Tsao · Alyson Levy · Amalia Durham · Amanda & Keagan · Amanda Bullock · Amanda Canales · Amanda Duling · Amanda Durbin · Amanda Niu · Amanda Roer Duling · Amanda Uhle · Amanda Wallwin · Amandeep Jutla · Amazing

Grace! · Amber · Amber Bittiger · Amber D. Kempthorn · Amber Murray · Amro Gebreel · Amy · Amy Blair · Amy Brownstein · Amy Henschen · Amy Lampert Pfau · Amy Macauley · Amy Marcus · Amy Ponsetti · Amy Rosenthal · Amy Shields · Amy Wallace · Amy Ware · Amy Welch · Amy Wolfner · Ana Cr · Ananda V.h. · Andi Biren · Andi Winnette · Andra Kiscaden · Andre Kuzniarek · André Mora · Andrea Biren · Andrea D'tonio · Andrea Dahl · Andrea Lunsford · Andrea Pilati · Andrea Sammarco · Andrew Bailey · Andrew Bannon · Andrew Benner · Andrew Blossom · Andrew Cohn · Andrew Crooks · Andrew Durbin · Andrew Eichenfield · Andrew Eisenman · Andrew Glaser · Andrew Glencross · Andrew Gurnett · Andrew Hirshman · Andrew Holets · Andrew Jensen · Andrew Kaufteil · Andrew M. Jackson · Andrew Macbride · Andrew Mason · Andrew Mclaughlin · Andrew Mcleod · Andrew Miles · Andrew Noonan · Andrew Patton · Andrew Perito · Andrew Rose · Andrew Rosen · Andrew Sachs · Andrew Stargel · Andrew Steele · Andrew Stratis · Andrew Watson · Andrew Yakas · Andrew Alan Ferguson · Andy Banks · Andy Barnes · Andy Dobson · Andy Que · Andy Steckling · Andy Steele · Andy Waer · Andy Yaco-Mink · Angel Logue · Angela Hunter · Angela Johnson · Angela Johnson · Angela Lau · Angela Petrella · Angela Saunders · Angelo Delsante · Angelo Pizzo · Angie · Angie Boysen · Angie Holan · Angie Newgren · Anisse Gross · Anja R. · Ann Giardina Magee · Ann Gillespie · Ann Gillespie · Ann McDonald · Ann McKenzie · Ann Morrone · Ann Sieber · Ann Stuart King · Anna Bond · Anna Calasanti · Anna Luebbert · Anna March · Anna Stroup · Anna Wiener · Anna-Marie Silvester · Annalisa Post · Anne Connell · Anne Fougeron · Anne Gaynor · Anne Germanacos · Anne Holland · Anne Lebaron · Anne Petersen · Anne Shelton · Anne Tonolli Cook · Anne Wheeler · Annemarie Gray · Annette Toutonghi · Annick Mcintosh · Annie Ganem · Annie Logue · Annie Lynsen · Annie Neild · Annie Porter · Annie Ross · Annika Shore · Anonymous × 9 · Antares M · Anthology LLC · Anthony "Tony" Schmiedeler · Anthony Clavelli · Anthony Devito · Anthony Effinger · Anthony Ha · Anthony Marks · Anthony Myint · Anthony St George · Anthony Teoh · Anthony Thompson · April Fry Ruen · April Ruen · Arianna Reiche · Ariel Hartman · Ariel Zambelich · Arielle Brousse · Arlene Buhl · Armadillo & Dicker · Arthur Hurley · Arthur Strauss · Arturo Elenes · Ash Huang · Asha Bhatia · Ashima Bawa · Ashley · Ashley Aguirre · Ashley Kalagian Blunt · Ashley

Otto · Ashraf Hasham · Atsuro Riley · Audrey · Audrey Butcher · Audrey Fennell · Audrey Yang · Augusta Palmer · Christopher Robin · Ayni · Azro Cady · Balz Meierhans · Barbara Barnes · Barbara David · Barbara Demarest · Barbara Kirby · Barbara Passino · Barry Traub · Basil Guinane · Beau Bailey · Becca · Becky · Beckyjo Bean · Beejieweejie · Bekah Grim · Beki Pope · Ben Ames · Ben Blum · Ben Crowley · Ben Gibbs · Ben Goldmam · Ben Hughes · Ben Larrison · Ben Matthews · Ben Pfeiffer · Ben Zotto · Benjamin Elkind · Benjamin Han · Benjamin Jahn · Benjamin Liss · Benjamin Novak · Benjamin Peskoe · Benjamin Petrosky · Benjamin Russell · Benjamin Small · Benjamin Southworth · Bernadette Segura · Bernard Yu · Berry Bowen · Bertis Downs · Beth Ayer · Beth Chlapek · Beth Daugherty · Beth Duncan · Beth Mcduffee · Betsy Ely · Betsy Henry Pringle · Betsy Henschel · Betsy Levitas · Betsy Pattullo · Betty Jane Jacobs · Betty Joyce Nash · Bill Bonwitt · Bill Crosbie · Bill Frazier · Bill Hughes · Bill Manheim · Bill Owens · Bill Rising · Bill Spitzig · Bill Weir · Billy Moon · Billy Taylor · Billy Tombs · Bindi Kaufman · Birch Norton · Birchy Norton · Blair Roberts · Blake Coglianese · Blaz · Blythe Alpern · Bob · Bob Blanco · Bob Den Hartog · Bob Sherron · Bob Slevc · Bob Wilson · Bonnie Garmus · Bookman · Boris Glazunov · Boris Mindzak · Boris Vassilev · Bosco Hernandez · Bourbonsmartypants · Brad Feld · Brad Kik · Brad Marcoux · Brad Phifer · Bradley Clarke · Bradley Flynt · Bradley Harkrader · Bradley Mcmahon · Brandon Amico · Brandon Bussolini · Brandon Chalk · Brandon Flammang · Brandon Forsyth · Brandon Wynn · Brenda A Vogan · Brendan Dowling · Brendan James Moore · Brendan Mcguigan · Brenna Field · Brent Emery · Brett Anders · Brett Goldblatt · Brett Klopp · Brett Silton · Brett Yasko · Brian Agler · Brian Bailey · Brian Bowen · Brian Cassidy · Brian Chess · Brian Cobb · Brian Cullen · Brian Dice · Brian Dillon · Brian Eck · Brian Gallay · Brian Godsey · Brian Green · Brian Grygiel · Brian Guthrie · Brian Hiatt · Brian James Rubinton · Brian Knott · Brian M Rosen · Brian Meacham · Brian Pfeffer · Brian Pluta · Brian Turner · Brian Z Danin · Brianna Kratz · Brianna Suzelle · Bridget · Brinda Gupta · Brittany · Brittany Carroll Jones · Brittany Medeiros · Brnnr · Bronwyn Glubb · Brooke Haskell · Brooke Lewis · Brooke Prince · Brownstone BBQ · Bruce G Gordon · Bruce Gordon · Bruce Greeley · Bruce King · Bryan Alexander · Bryan Curtis · Bryan Waterman · Bryce Gorman · Bryn Durgin · Brynn Elizabeth Kingsley · Bsj · Buffalo

Architectural Machine · Buffy · Buttocks · C Broderick · C. Odal · C.d. Hermelin · C.j.winter · C.m. Tomlin · Caedlighe Paolucci · Caitlin · Caitlin Fischer · Caitlin L. Baker · Caitlin Van Dusen · Caitlin Webb · Callie Ryan · Calvin Crosby · Camaro Powers · Cameron David · Candice Chiew · Capelesst · Cara Beale · Cara J Giaimo · Cara Mchugh · Cari Hauck · Carisa Miller · Carl Grant · Carl H. Hendrickson Jr · Carl Jacobsen · Carl Salbacka · Carl Voss · Carleton Smith · Carley Phillips · Carlos Parreno · Carly · Carmel Boerner · Carol Anne Tack · Carol Davis · Carole Sargent · Caroline · Caroline Carney · Caroline Moakley · Caroline Pugh · Carolyn Anthony · Caryn Lenhoff · Cassie Ettinger · Catastrophoea · Cate Trujillo · Caterina Fake · Cath Keenan · Cath Le Couteur · Catharine Bell · Catherine · Catherine Chen · Catherine Coan · Catherine Flores Marsh · Catherine Hagin · Catherine Jayne · Catherine Keenan · Catherine Leclair · Catherine Shuster · Catherine Smith · Cathi Falconwing · Cathryn Lyman · Cathy Nieng · Catie Myers-Wood · Cb Murphy · Cece · Cecile Forman · Cecilia Holmes · Cecilia M Holmes · Cecilia Mills · Cedric Howe · Celbridge Rob · Celeste Adamson · Celeste Hotaling-Lyons · Celeste Roberts-Lewis · Cesar Contreras · Chad Gibbs · Chad Gibbs · Chairs And Tables · Char Kuperstein · Charibdys · Charis Poon · Charlene Ortuno · Charles · Charles Bertsch · Charles D Myers · Charles Dee Mitchell · Charles Irby · Charles Lamar Phillips · Charles Pence · Charles Spaht, Jr. · Charley Brammer · Charlie B Spaht · Charlie Garnett · Charlie Hoers · Charlotte · Charlotte Locke · Charlotte Moore · Cheesybeard666 · Chef Ben Bebenroth · Chelsea Bingham · Cheng Leong · Chenoa Pettrup · Cherisse Datu · Cheryl · Cheryl Flack · Chester Jakubowicz · Chris · Chris Baird · Chris Brinkworth · Chris Bulock · Chris Clancy · Chris Cobb · Chris Duffy · Chris Foley · Chris Hogan · Chris Kleinknecht · Chris Maddox · Chris Martins · Chris Niewiarowski · Chris Ohlson · Chris Preston · Chris Remo · Chris Roberts · Chris Roe · Chris Saeli · Chris Sandoval · Chris Schmidt · Chris Warack · Chrissy Simonte Boylan · Christen Herland · Christi Chidester · Christian Gheorghe · Christian Lovecchio · Christian Rudder · Christian S. · Christian Smith · Christina Dickinson · Christina Erickson · Christina Grachek · Christina Macsweeney · Christina Schmigel · Christine Allan · Christine Chen · Christine Delorenzo · Christine Evans · Christine Langill · Christine Luketic · Christine Lyons · Christine Ogata · Christine Rehm · Christine Ross · Christine Ryan · Christine Tilton · Christine Vallejo · Christopher

Benz · Christopher Carver · Christopher Fauske · Christopher Fox · Christopher Greenwald · Christopher Harnden · Christopher Hinger · Christopher Knaus · Christopher Madden · Christopher Maynard · Christopher Mclachlan · Christopher Naccari · Christopher Sarnowski · Christopher Soriano · Christopher Stearly · Christopher Strelioff · Christopher Todd · Christopher W Ulbrich · Christopher Wright · Christy Brown · Christy Fletcher · Christy Rishoi · Chrysta Cherrie · Cindi Hickman · Cindi Rowell · Cindy Foley · Cindy Lamar · Cirocco · City Tap House · Claire Burleson · Claire Swinford · Claire Tan · Clare Hyam · Clare Louise Jones · Clare Wallin · Claudia · Claudia Milne · Claudia Mueller · Claudia Stein · Cleri Coula · Cleri Coula · Clint Popetz · Clive Thompson · Cloe Shasha · Cmg · Cns · Cody Hudson · Cody Peterson · Cody Williams · Colby Aymar · Colby Ray · Colin · Colin Nissan · Colin Urbina · Colin Winnette · Colleen Bright · Collin Brazie · Colton Powell · Connor Kalista · Conor Delahunty · Corey & Meghan Musolff · Corinne Caputo · Corinne Marrinan Tripp · Cortney Kammerer · Cory Gutman · Cory Hershberger · Cory Hershberger · Courtney A. Aubrecht · Courtney Hopkins · Courtney Nguyen · Craig Clark · Craig New · Craig Short · Cris Pedregal Martin · Crystal · Curt Sobolewski · Curtis Edmonds · Curtis Rising · Curtis Sutton · Cyd Peroni · Cydney Stewart · Cynthia Baute · Cynthia Foley · Cynthia Yang · D · D Cooper · D Miller · D. Whiteman · D.a. Pratt · Daan Windhorst · Dale Sawa · Damfrat · Damian Bradfield · Damien James · Damon Copeland · Damon-Eugene Rich · Dan Ashton · Dan Carroll · Dan Colburn · Dan Grant · Dan Haugen · Dan May · Dan Mckinley · Dan Money · Dan Pasternack · Dan Pritts · Dan Rollman · Dan Schreiber · Dan Spealman · Dan Stein · Dan Winkler · Dana K · Dana Skwirut · Dana Werdmuller · Dani D · Daniel · Daniel A. Hoyt · Daniel Bahls · Daniel Beauchamp · Daniel Berger · Daniel Dejan · Daniel Edwards · Daniel Erwin · Daniel Feldman · Daniel Grossman · Daniel Grou · Daniel Guilak · Daniel Hoyt · Daniel Khalastchi · Daniel Levin Becker · Daniel Morgan · Daniel Ness · Daniel Ridges · Daniel Tovrov · Daniel Wilbur · Danielle Bailey · Danielle Gallen · Danielle Granatt · Danielle Jacklin · Danielle Kucera · Danielle Lavaque-Manty · Danika Esden-Tempski · Danny Richelson · Danny Shapiro · Danyl Garnett · Darby Dixon Iii · Darcie Thomas · Dargaud-Fons · Darko Orsic · Darlene Zandanel · Darrell Hancock · Darren Higgins · Daryl Dragon · Dash Shaw · Dave · Dave Baptist · Dave Curry ·

Dave David · Dave Forman · Dave Haas · Dave Lucey · Dave Madden · Dave Polus · Davi Ferreira · David · David · David + Kami · David Andrews · David Baker · David Bradley · David Brett Kinitsky · David Brown · David Burns · David Charlton · David Chatenay · David Cornwell · David Desmond · David Dietrich · David E Baker · David Eckles · David F. Gallagher · David Frankel · David Galef · David Givens · David Givens · David Goldstein · David Guerrero · David Hodge · David J. Whelan · David James · David K · David Karpa · David Kneebone · David Knopp · David Kurz · David L Gobeli · David Leftwich · David Lerner · David Levy · David M · David Macy-Beckwith · David Mccarty · David Nilsen And Melinda Guerra · David Peter · David Pollock · David R Lamarre · David Rodwin · David Sam · David Sanger · David Sievers · David Springbett · David Strait · David Sundin · David Thompson · David Wolske · David Wright · David Zaffrann · David Zarzycki · D.b. Ramer · De_hart · Dean · Dean O'donnell · Deane Taylor · Deb Olin Unferth · Debbie Baldwin · Debbie Berne · Debbie Millman · Debby Weinstein · Deborah Conrad · Deborah Urban · Deborah Wallis · Debra Bok · Demeny Pollitt · Dena Verhoff · Denae Dietlein · Denise Sarvis · Denise Witherspoon · Dennis Caraher · Dennis Gallagher · Dennis Marfurt · Derek Van Westrum · Designers & Books · Devon Henderson · Diana Behl · Diana Cohn · Diana Funk · Diana M. · Diana Tomchick · Diane Arisman · Diane B Kresal · Diane Fitzsimmons · Diane Holdgate · Diane Lederman · Diane M. Fedak · Diane S. · Diane Wang · Dianne Weinthal · Dianne Wood · Dillon Morris · Dinika Amaral · Dirk Heniges · Dom Baker · Dominic Lepper · Dominic Luxford · Dominica Phetteplace · Don Smith · Donald Deye · Donald Schaffner · Donald Solem · Donald Woutat · Donna Copeland-Fuller · Donna Fogarty · Doreen Kaminski · Doro · Dory Culver · Doug · Doug Dorst · Doug Green · Doug Mayo-Wells · Doug Messel · Doug Michel · Doug Moe · Doug Schoemer · Doug Taub · Doug Wolff · Doug Wykstra · Douglas Andersen · Douglas Candano · Douglas Hirsch · Douglas Kearney · Douglas Mcgray · Dov Lebowitz-Nowak · Dr. Demento · Dr. Hornet · Dr. Meredith Blitzmeyer · Drew Atkins · Drew Baldwin · Drew Sussman · Duane Murray · Duane Murray · Dustin Mark · Eap · Ed Freedman · Ed Krakovsky · Ed Riley · Ed Rodley · Ed Sweeney · Edie Jarolim · Edinblack · Edward · Edward Crabbe · Edward Lim · Edwina Trentham · Eileen Consedine · Eileen M Mccullough · Eileen Madden · Eitan Kensky · El Chin

· Elaine Froneberger · Elana Spivack · Elda Guidinetti · Eleanor Cooney · Eleanor Horner · Elia Wise · Elinor Wahl · Elisa · Elisa Harkness · Elisabeth Carroll · Elisabeth Hammerberg · Elisabeth Seng · Elise Persico · Elizabeth Alkire · Elizabeth Allspaw · Elizabeth Averett · Elizabeth Carmichael-Davis · Elizabeth Chang · Elizabeth Craft · Elizabeth Dalay · Elizabeth Davies · Elizabeth Engle · Elizabeth Gemmill · Elizabeth Gray · Elizabeth Green · Elizabeth Hom · Elizabeth Hykes · Elizabeth Keim · Elizabeth Macklin · Elizabeth Miller · Elizabeth Pfeffer · Elizabeth Ray · Elizabeth Redick · Elizabeth Rovito · Elizabeth Siggins · Elizabeth Smith · Elizabeth Taylor · Elizabeth Weber · Elizwill · Ella Haselswerdt · Ellen Goldblatt · Ellen Line · Ellen Tubbaji · Ellia Bisker · Ellia Bisker · Ellie Flock · Ellie Turzynski · Ellyn Farrelly · Ellyn Toscano · Eloy Gomez · Elsa Figueroa · Elske Krikhaar · Elyse Rettig · Ema Solarova · Emilce Cordeiro · Emily Bliquez · Emily Bryant · Emily Cardenas · Emily Carroll · Emily Diamond · Emily Donohoo · Emily Friedlander · Emily Goode · Emily Harris · Emily Kaiser Thelin · Emily Lynch · Emily M. · Emily Morian-Lozano · Emily Olmstead-Rumsey · Emily Raisch · Emily Schleiger · Emily Schuck · Emily Wallis Hughes · Emma Axelson · Emma Axelson · Emma D. Dryden, Drydenbks Llc · Emma Roosevelt · Enrico Casarosa · Epilogue · Eric · Eric · Eric · Eric Botts · Eric Brink · Eric Brink · Eric Donato · Eric Farwell · Eric Harker · Eric Heiman · Eric Hsu · Eric Johnson · Eric Kuczynski · Eric Larsh · Eric Mauer · Eric Meyers · Eric Muhlheim · Eric Perkins · Eric Potter · Eric Prestemon · Eric Randall · Eric Ricker · Eric Ries · Eric Schulmiller · Eric Segerstrom · Eric Tell · Eric W · Erica Behr · Erica Lively · Erica Nardello · Erica Nist-Lund · Erica Portnoy · Erica Seiler · Erick · Erick Gordon · Erik Henriksen · Erik Pedersen · Erin · Erin Ambrozic · Erin Badillo · Erin Barnes · Erin Corrigan · Erin Eakle · Erin Mcgrath · Erin Senge · Ernesto Gloria · Erwin Wall · Esme Weijun Wang · Ethan Nosowsky · Ethan Rogers · Euan Monaghan · Eva Funderburgh Hollis · Eva Thompson · Evan Brooks · Evan Orsak · Evan Regner · Evan Rosler · Evan Williams · Eve Bower · Evelyn Tunnell · Everett Shock · Evil Supply Co. · Evonne Okafor · Experiencing Life To The Fullest-Da Wolf · Eylem Ezgi Ozaslan · Ezra Karsk · F.p. De L. · Faisel Siddiqui · Fanny Luor · Farnaz Fatemi · Fawn · Felicia · Femme Fan1946 · Fengypants · Fern Culhane · Fernanda Dutra · Fiona Hamersley · Fiona Hartmann · Flash Sheridan · Fotios Zemenides · Frederic Jaume · Fran Gensberg · Frances Lopez · Frances Tuite

· Frances Tuite · Francesca Moore · Francis Desiderio · Frank Drummond · Frank Lortscher · Frank Riley · Frank Ruffing · Frank Turek · Franklin · Franklin Friedman · Freddi Bruschke · Freddy Powys · Frederick De Naples · Frederick Fedewa · Free Expressions Seminars And Literary Services · Frin Atticus Doust · Fualana Detail · Full Gamut Consulting · Gabe Gutierrez · Gabe Mcgowan · Gabriel Pumple · Gabriel Vogt · Gabriela Melchior · Gala Grant · Galen Livingston · Garth Reese · Gary Almeter · Gary Almeter · Gary Beckerman · Gary Chun · Gary Gilbert · Gary Rudoren · Gary Rudoren · Gavin Beatty · Gaye Hill · Gayle Brandeis · Gayle Dosher · Gayle Engel · Genevieve Kelly · Geoff "Not-So-Mysterious-Benefactor" Brown · Geoff D. · Geoff Smith · George Hodosh Associates · George Mcconochie · George Mitolidis · George Veugeler · George Washington Hastings · Georgia · German (Panda) Borbolla · Gerrit Thompson · Gertrude And Alice Editions · Gibby Stratton · Gieson Cacho · Gina · Gina B. · Gina Smith · Ginny · Girija Brilliant · Gisela Sehnert · Gitgo Productions · Glorianne Scott · Gopakumar Sethuraman · Gordon Mcalpine · Grace Levin · Graeme Deuchars · Graham Bell · Greg Grallo · Greg Johnson · Greg Lavine · Greg Lloyd · Greg Prince · Greg Steinberg · Greg Storey · Greg Versch · Greg Vines · Greg Weber · Greg Wheeler · Greg Williams · Gregory Affsa · Gregory Hagan · Gregory Stern · Gregory Sullivan · Griffin Richardson · Guillaume Morissette · Gunnar Paulsen · Guy Albertelli · Gwen Goodkin · Haden Lawyer · Haiy Le · Hal Tepfer · Haley Cullingham · Haley Williams · Hank Scorpio · Hannah Mcginty · Hannah Meyer · Hannah O'regan · Hannah Rothman · Hannah Settle · Hannelore · Hans Balmes · Hans Ericson · Hans Lillegard · Hans Zippert · Hans-Juergen Balmes · Harold Check · Harris Levinson · Harry Deering · Harry J. Mersmann · Harry Mersmann · Harry White · Haruna Iwase · Hassan Fahs · Hassanchop · Hathaway Green · Heather Bause · Heather Boyd · Heather Braxton · Heather Flanagan · Heather Forrester · Heather Guillen · Heckle Her · Hedwig Van Driel · Heidi Baumgartner · Heidi Meurer · Heidi Raatz · Helen Chang · Helen Kim · Helen Linda · Helen Tibboel · Helena · Hemant Anant Jain · Hilary · Hilary Leichter · Hilary Rand · Hilary Sasso-Schleh · Hilary Van Dusen · Hillary Lannan · Holly · Holly Iossa · Holly Kennedy · Houston Needs A Swimming Hole! · Howard Katz · Howeverbal · Hugh Geenen · Hypothetical Development Organization · Ian · Ian Benjamin · Ian Casselberry · Ian Chung · Ian Delaney · Ian Foe · Ian

Frederick-Rothwell · Ian Glazer · Ian Harrison · Ian Joyce · Ian Prichard · Ian Shadwell · Ilana Gordon · Iliana Helfenstein · Ingrid Kvalvik Sørensen · Ioana Popa · Irene Arntz · Irene Hahn · Isabel A · Isabel Pinner · Isabella · J.F. Gibbs · J.G. Hancock · J. Wilson · J.A. López · J.B. Van Wely · J.J. Larrea · J.L. Schmidt · Jack Amick · Jack Dodd · Jack Stokes · Jack Thorpe · Jackie Jones · Jackie Mccarthy · Jackie Yang · Jaclyne D Recchiuti · Jacob Davis · Jacob Haller · Jacob Lacivita · Jacob Leland · Jacob Zionts · Jacqueline Utkin · Jacquelyn Moorad And Carolyn Hsu · Jade Higashi · Jaime Young · Jaimen Sfetko · Jake · Jake Bailey · Jamal Saleh · James Adamson · James And Rasika Boice · James Brown · James Chesky · James Crowley, Jr · James E Wolcott · James English · James Manion · James Merk · James Mnookin · James Moore · James Newton · James O'brien · James Osborne · James Park · James Roger · James Roger · James Ross-Edwards · James Trimble · James Vest · James Woods (Not The Actor) · Jamie Alexander · Jamie Campbell · Jamie Campbell · Jamie Tanner · Jamie Zeppa · Jamon Yerger · Jan Greene · Jan Yeaman · Jane Clarke · Jane Darroch Riley · Jane Gibbins · Jane Jonas · Jane Kirchhofer · Jane Knoche · Jane Nevins · Jane Whitley · Jane Wilson · Janet Beckerman · Janet Beeler · Janet Fendrych · Janet Gorth · Janet M. Fendrych · Janet Marie Paquette · Janice & Cooper · Janice Dunn · Janice Goldblatt · Janie Locker · Jared Quist · Jared R Delo · Jared Silvia · Jaron Kent-Dobias · Jaron Moore · Jarry Lee · Jason · Jason Bradshaw · Jason Chen · Jason File · Jason Gittler · Jason Hannigan · Jason Kirkham · Jason Kunesh · Jason Levin · Jason Martin · Jason Martin · Jason Riley · Jason Rodriguez · Jason S · Jason Seifert · Jason Sobolewski · Jason Sussberg · Jasper Smit · Jasun Mark · Jay · Jay Dellacona · Jay Price · Jay Schutawie · Jay Traeger · Jayveedub · Jbflanz · Jd Ferries-Rowe · Jean Carney · Jean Haughwout · Jean Prasher · Jean Sinzdak · Jean T Barbey · Jeanette Shine · Jeanine Fritz · Jeanne Weber · Jeanne Wilkinson · Jeannette · Jeannie Vanasco · Jeanvieve Warner · Jed Alger · Jedidiah Smith · Jeff · Jeff · Jeff Albers · Jeff Anderson · Jeff Caltabiano · Jeff Campoli · Jeff Chacon · Jeff Dickerson · Jeff G. Peters · Jeff Garcia · Jeff Greenstein · Jeff H White · Jeff Hampl · Jeff Hayward · Jeff Hilnbrand · Jeff Hitt · Jeff Jacobs · Jeff Klein · Jeff Klein · Jeff Magness · Jeff Neely · Jeff Omiecinski · Jeff Peters · Jeff Stiers · Jeff Stuhmer · Jeff Trull · Jeff Vitkun · Jeff Ward · Jeffrey Brothers · Jeffrey Brothers · Jeffrey Brown · Jeffrey Garcia · Jeffrey Meyer · Jeffrey Parnaby · Jeffrey Posternak · Jeffrey Snyder

· Jen Alam · Jen Burns · Jen Butts · Jen Donovan · Jen Jurgens · Jen Lofquist · Jenn De La Vega · Jenni B. Baker · Jenni Baker · Jennie Lynn Rudder · Jennifer · Jennifer Aheran · Jennifer Anthony · Jennifer Cole · Jennifer Cruikshank · Jennifer Dait · Jennifer Day · Jennifer Dopazo · Jennifer Grabmeier · Jennifer Howard Westerman · Jennifer Kabat · Jennifer Kain Kilgore · Jennifer Laughran · Jennifer Marie Lin · Jennifer Mcclenon · Jennifer Mccullough · Jennifer Mcfadden · Jennifer Ratcliffe · Jennifer Richardson · Jennifer Rowland · Jennifer Ruby Privateer · Jennifer Westerman · Jennifer White · Jennifer Wolfe · Jenny Cattier · Jenny Lee · Jenny Stein · Jenzo Duque · Jeremiah · Jeremiah Follett · Jeremy Cohen · Jeremy Ellsworth · Jeremy Fried · Jeremy Peppas · Jeremy Radcliffe · Jeremy Rishel · Jeremy Smith · Jeremy Smith · Jeremy Van Cleve · Jeremy Walker · Jeremy Wang-Iverson · Jeremy Welsh · Jeremy Wortsman · Jerry & Val Gibbons · Jerry Englehart, Jr · Jerry Krakoff · Jerry Pura · Jess Chace · Jess Fitz · Jess Higgins · Jess Kemp · Jess L. · Jess Mcmorrow · Jess Voigt · Jesse Brickel · Jesse Hemingway · Jessi Fierro · Jessica · Jessica · Jessica Allan Schmidt · Jessica Bacho · Jessica Bifulk · Jessica Eleri Jones · Jessica Fiske · Jessica Ghersi · Jessica Hampton · Jessica Martinez · Jessica Mcfadden · Jessica Mcmillen · Jessica Mcmorrow · Jessica Partch · Jessica Poulin · Jessica Shook · Jessica Spence · Jessica Stocks · Jessica Suarez · Jessica Vanginhoven · Jessica Yu · Jessie Gaynor · Jessie Johnson · Jessie Lynn Robertson · Jessie Stockwell · Jett Watson · Jezzka Chen · Jijin John · Jill · Jill Cooke · Jill Ho · Jill Katz · Jillian Mclaughlin · Jillian Mcmahon · Jim And Loretta · Jim Haven · Jim Kosmicki · Jim Lang · Jim Mccambridge · Jim Mcelroy · Jim Mckay · Jim Moore · Jim Redner · Jim Stallard · Jim Taone · Jimmy Orpheus · Jincy Kornhauser · Jjamms Hoffman · Jo Ellen Watson · Joachim Futtrup · Joan Basile · Joan Greco · Joann Holliday · Joann Schultz · Joao Leal Medeiros Hakme · Joddy Marchesoni · Joe Callahan · Joe Dempsey · Joe Kukella · Joe Kurien · Joe Romano · Joe Stuever · Joe Williams · Joel Bentley · Joel Kreizman · Joel Lang · Joel Santiago · Joey & Berit Coleman · Joey Hayles · Johanna Pauciulo · Johanna, Finja, & Charlie Degl · John & Minda Zambenini · John Artrock77 · John Baker · John Bannister · John Bearce · John Borden · John Bowyer · John Cahill · John Cary · John Charin · John Debacher · John Ebey · John Gialanella · John Hawkins · John Hawkins · John Hill · John Justice · John Karabaic · John Keith · John Kornet · John Lang · John Mcmurtry · John

Muller · John Onoda · John P Monks · John P Monks · John P Stephens · John Pancini · John Plunkett · John Poje · John Pole · John Prendergast · John Repko · John Ricketts · John Sarik · John Semley · John Terning · John Tollefsen · John Tompkins · John W Wilkins · John Walbank · John-Fletcher Halyburton · Johnston Murray · Jokastrength · Jon Englund · Jon Folkers · Jon Senge · Jon Stair · Jonas Edgeworth · Jonathan Brandel · Jonathan Deutsche · Jonathan Dykema · Jonathan Fretheim · Jonathan Jackson · Jonathan L York · Jonathan Meyers · Jonathan Van Schoick · Jonathan Wenger · Jordan Bass · Jordan Bell · Jordan Campo · Jordan Campo · Jordan Hauser · Jordan Katz · Jordan Kurland · Jordan Landsman · Jordana Beh · Jorge · Joseph · Joseph Buscarino · Joseph Edmundson · Joseph Fink · Joseph Marshall · Joseph Miebach · Joseph Pred · Josh "The J-Man" Kjenner · Josh Houchin · Josh Mason · Josh Rappoport · Josh Tilton · Joshua Arnett · Joshua D. Meehl · Joshua Farris · Joshua Harris · Joshua Lewis · Joslyn Krismer · Jowi Taylor · Joy · Joyce · Joyce Hennessee · Jozua Malherbe · J.P. Coghlan · Jeremy Radcliffe · Jt Chapel · Juan Mapu · Jude Buck · Judi L Mahaney · Judith · Judy B · Judy O'karma · Judy Schatz · Julena Campbell · Julia · Julia · Julia Bank · Julia Buck · Julia Fought · Julia Henderson · Julia Kardon · Julia Kardon · Julia Kinsman · Julia Kochi · Julia Meinwald · Julia Pohl-Miranda · Julia Slavin · Julia Smillie · Julia Streit · Julia Strohm · Julia Strukely · Julian Gibbs · Julian Orenstein · Juliana Capaldi · Julianne Rhodes · Julie · Julie Fajgenbaum · Julie Felix · Julie S · Julie Schmidt · Julie Stampfle · Julie Vick · Julie Wood · Jumpsaround · June Speakman · Justin Barisich · Justin Foley · Justin Guinn · Justin Katz · Justin Owen Smith Stockard · Justin R. Lawson · Justin Rochell · Justin Wilcox · Justin A. · Justo Robles · K. Edward Callaghan · Kaat · Kai Van Horn · Kaitlyn Trigger · Kali Sakai · Kane E. Giblin · Kara Richardson · Kara Soppelsa · Kara Ukolowicz · Kara White · Karan Rinaldo · Karen · Karen Enno · Karen Gansky · Karen Gray · Karen Hoffman · Karen Holden · Karen K. · Karen Stilber · Karen Unland · Karin Gargaro · Karin J. · Karin Ryding · Karl Gunderson · Karl Petersen · Karla H. · Karla Hilliard · Karolina Waclawiak Derosa · Karrie Kimbrell · Kaspar Hauser · Kat Lombard-Cook · Kat Marshello · Kate · Kate Aishton · Kate Berry · Kate Brittain · Kate Bush · Kate Fritz · Kate Kapych · Kate Ory · Kate Semmler · Kate W. · Kate Webster · Kath Bartman · Katharine Culpepper · Katherine · Katherine Buki · Katherine Harris · Katherine

Love · Katherine Minarik · Katherine Sherron · Katherine Tweedel · Katherine Weybright · Katherine Williams · Kathleen · Kathleen Brownell · Kathleen Fargnoli · Kathleen O. · Kathleen O'gorman · Kathleen Ossip · Kathleen Seltzer · Kathleen Stetsko · Kathryn Anderson · Kathryn Bumbaugh · Kathryn Flowers · Kathryn Holmes · Kathryn Kelley · Kathryn King · Kathryn Lester · Kathryn Page Birmingham · Kathryn Price · Kathy Harding · Kati Simmons Knowland · Katie · Katie · Katie Chabolla · Katie Dodd · Katie Jewett · Katie Lewis · Katie Linden · Katie Love · Katie Mcguire · Katie Y · Katie Young · Katielicious · Katmcgo · Katrina · Katrina Dodson · Katrina Grigo-Mcmahon · Katrina Woznicki · Katryce Kay · Katy Carey · Katy Orr · Katy Shelor Harvey · Katya Kazbek · Kayla M. Anderson · Kaylie Simon · Keiko Ichiye · Keith Cotton · Keith Crofford · Keith Flaherty · Keith Morgan · Keith Van Norman · Kellie · Kellie Holmstrom · Kelly · Kelly Browne · Kelly Conaboy · Kelly Conroe · Kelly Cornacchia · Kelly Doran · Kelly Heckman · Kelly K · Kelly Marie · Kelly Miller-Schreiner · Kelly Wheat · Kelsay Neely · Kelsey Hunter · Kelsey Rexroat · Kelsey Thomson · Kelsie O'dea · Kemp Peterson · Ken Flott · Ken Krehbiel · Ken Racicot · Kendel Shore · Kendra · Kendra Stanton Lee · Kenneth Cameron · Kerri Schlottman · Kerry Evans · Kev Kev Meister · Kevin And Kim Watt · Kevin Anderson · Kevin Arnold · Kevin Ashton · Kevin Camel · Kevin Cole · Kevin Cosgrove · Kevin Davis · Kevin Eichorst · Kevin Felix · Kevin Freidberg · Kevin Gleason · Kevin Hunt · Kevin Johnson · Kevin Keck · Kevin Lauderdale · Kevin Mccullough · Kevin Mcginn · Kevin Mcginn · Kevin Mcmorrow · Kevin O'donnell · Kevin Spicer · Kevin Vognar · Kevin Wynn · Kevin Zimmerman · Khalid Kurji · Kickstarter · Killer Lopez-Hall · Kim · Kim Baker · Kim Ku · Kim Sanders · Kim Wishart · Kimberley Mullins · Kimberley Rose · Kimberly Grey · Kimberly Hamm · Kimberly Harrington · Kimberly Nichols · Kimberly Occhipinti · Kimberly Rose · Kira Starzynski · Kirsten Zerger · Kitkat · Kitz Rickert · Kj Nichols · Knarles Bowles · Knut N. · Kom Siksamat · Kori K. · Kris Majury · Kris S. · Krista Knott · Kristan Hoffman · Kristan Mcmahon · Kristen Ann Tymeson · Kristen Brooks · Kristen Easley · Kristen Miller · Kristen Reed · Kristen Reed · Kristen T Easley · Kristen Westbrook · Kristi Vandenbosch · Kristin M. Morris · Kristin Mullen · Kristin Nielsen · Kristin Pazulski · Kristin R Shrode · Kristina Dahl · Kristina Harper · Kristina Rizga · Kristine Donly · Kristine Donly

· Kristy Kulp · Kristyn Dunn · Krisztina Bunzl · Krystal Hart · Kuang-Yi Liu · Kunihiro Ishiguro · Kurt Brown · Kurtis Kolt · Kyle Dickinson · Kyle Garvey · Kyle Jacob Bruck · Kyle Lucia Wu · Kyle Prestenback · Kyle Raum · Kylee Panduro · Kyra Rogers · L.n. · Landy Manderson · Lang Thompson · Langston Antosek · Lani Yamamoto · Lara Kierlin · Lara Struttman · Larisa Shambaugh · Larry Doyle · Larry Farhner · Launa Rich · Laura · Laura · Laura Bauer · Laura Bennett · Laura Bostillo · Laura Buffington · Laura Celmins · Laura Dapito · Laura Farris · Laura Hadden · Laura Howard · Laura Nisi · Laura Owens · Laura Schmiedicke · Laura Scott · Laura Stevenson · Laura Thomas · Laura Vigander · Laura Weiderhaft · Laura Williams · Laurel · Laurel C · Laurel Chun · Laurel Fedder · Laurel Flynn · Laurel Hall · Lauren Andrews · Lauren Groff · Lauren Isaacson · Lauren O'neal · Lauren Peugh · Lauren Powers · Lauren Rose · Lauretta Hyde · Laurie Bollman-Little · Laurie Ember · Laurie L Young · Laurie Major · Laurie May · Laurie Young · Lawrence Bridges · Lawrence Porricelli · Layla Al-Bedawi · Leah · Leah Browning · Leah Dieterich · Leah Mallen · Leah Murray · Leah Swetnam · Leanne Stremcha · Lee · Lee Ann Albury · Lee Brumbaugh · Lee Harrison · Lee Roe · Lee Smith · Lee Syben · Lee Trentadue · Leigh Vorhies · Leila Khosrovi · Lene Sauvik · Lenore Jones · Lenore Rowntree · Leonard · Leone Lucky · Les Edwards · Lesley A. Martin · Leslie · Leslie Bhutani · Leslie Cannon · Leslie Kotzas · Leslie Maslow · Leslie McGorman · Leslie Mclinskey · Leslie Woodhouse · Lester Su · Lewis Ward · Lex Leifheit · Lian Fournier · Lila Fontes · Lila Lahood · Lillian Rachel Taft · Lily Mehl · Linda Cook · Linda Given · Linda Ocasio · Linda Ostrom · Linda Parker Gates · Linda Schroeder · Linda Skitka · Linda Troop · Linda Weston · Lindsay Hollett · Lindsay Mcconnon · Lindsay Morton · Lindsey · Lindsey Darrah · Lindsey Eubank · Lindsey Shepard · Lindsey Spaulding · Linn Elliott · Linne Ha · Lisa Berrones · Lisa Brown · Lisa Ellis · Lisa Janowski Goode · Lisa M. Geller · Lisa Pearson · Lisa Ryan · Lisa Thaler · Lisa Vlkovic · Lisa Winter · Living Life To The Fullest · Liz Benson · Liz Crain · Liz Flint-Somerville · Liz Nord · Liz Weber · Liza Behles · Liza Harrell-Edge · Lloyd Snowden · Logan Campbell · Logan Hasson · Logan Wright · Lois Denmark · Lora Kelley · Loredana Spadola · Loren Lieberthal · Lorenzo Cherubini · Lori · Lori Blackmon · Lori Cheatle · Lori Dunn · Lori Felton · Lori Fontanes · Lori Hymowitz · Lorie Kloda · Lorin Oberweger · Lorna Craig · Lorna Forbes · Lorraine Dong · Lotus Child · Lou Cove · Louis

Loewenstein · Louis Mastorakos · Louis Silverman · Louisa · Louise Marston · Louise Mccune · Louise Williams · Luca Maurer · Lucas Foster · Lucas Hawthorne · Lukas Drake · Luke · Luke Benfey · Luke Burger · Luuly Tran · Lyn Walker · Lynn Farmer · M Robertson · M. Koss · Madeleine Watts · Madeline Jacobson · Mae Rice · Maggie Rotter · Maggie Stroup · Magnanimus · Maia Pank Mertz · Mainon Schwartz · Maitri Sojourner · Majelle · Major Solutions · Manca G. Renko · Mancinist · Mandy Alysse Goldberg · Mandy Brown · Mandy Kinne · Manion · Mara Novak · Mara Zepeda · Marc Atkinson · Marc Beck · Marc Lawrence-Apfelbaum · Marcella Forni · Marcello · Marcia Hofmann · Marco Buscaglia · Marco Kaye · Marcus Cade · Marcus Liddle · Margaret Bykowski · Margaret Cook · Margaret Grounds · Margaret Harvey · Margaret Kelly · Margaret Landis · Margaret Lusko · Margaret Newman · Margaret Peters · Margaret Prescott · Margaret Wachtler · Margo Taylor · Margot Atwell · Mari Moreshead · Maria · Maria · Maria Alicata · Maria Cunningham · Maria Faith Garcia · Maria Sotnikova · Maria Verloo · Mariah Adcox · Mariah Blackard · Mariah Blob Drakoulis · Marian Blythe · Marianne · Marianne Germond · Marie Dever · Marie Harvat · Marie Hohner · Marie Knight · Marie Marfia · Marie Meyer · Marielle Smith · Marina Meijer · Marinna Castilleja · Mario Lopez · Maris Antolin · Maris Kreizman · Mark · Mark · Mark · Mark Aronoff · Mark Beringer · Mark Bold · Mark Brody · Mark Dezalia · Mark Dober · Mark Dudlik · Mark Durso · Mark Fisher · Mark Fritzenschaft · Mark Gallucci · Mark Giordono · Mark Helfrich · Mark Himmelsbach · Mark Kates · Mark Levine · Mark Macleod · Mark Mandel · Mark Movic · Mark Novak · Mark Ramdular · Mark Reitblatt · Mark Riechers · Mark Ryan · Mark Southcott · Mark Van Name · Mark Weatherup, Jr. · Mark Wilkerson · Markus Wegscheider · Marlin Dohlman · Marlo Amelia Buzzell · Marna Blanchard · Marrion K · Marsha Nunley · Marsha Soffer · Marshall Farr · Marshall Hayes · Martha · Martha Benco · Martha Linn · Martha Pulleyn · Martin Berzell · Martin Cielens · Martin Gelin · Martina Radwan · Martina Schuerpf · Martina Testa · Marty Anderson · Mary · Mary Atikian · Mary Beth Hoerner · Mary Byram · Mary Christa Jaramillo-Bolin · Mary Dumont · Mary Durbin · Mary E I Jones · Mary Elizabeth Huber · Mary F Kaltreider · Mary Gioia · Mary Krywaruczenko · Mary Larson · Mary Lukanuski · Mary Mann · Mary Mannison · Mary Melville · Mary Nieves · Mary O'Keefe Bradley · Mary Williams · Mary Z Fuka · Mary-Kim Arnold · Marya

Figueroa · Marybeth Gallinger · Maryelizabeth Van Etten · Mason Harper · Mateo Sewillo · Mathias Hansson · Matt · Matt · Matt Adkins · Matt Alston · Matt Bouchard · Matt Conner · Matt Davis · Matt Digirolamo · Matt Fehrenbacher · Matt Gay · Matt Greiner · Matt Kelchner · Matt O'brien · Matt Slaybaugh · Matt Slotkin · Matt Werner · Matthew · Matthew Clark · Matthew Edwards · Matthew Grant · Matthew Honeybeard Henry · Matthew Latkiewicz · Matthew Ludvino · Matthew Morgan · Matthew Morin · Matthew Mullenweg · Matthew Rhoden · Matthew Robert Lang · Matthew Sachs · Matthew Smazik · Matthew Storer · Matthew Swatton · Matthew Wild · Matthew Wood · Mattie Armstrong · Maureen · Maureen Mcbeth · Maureen Van Dyck · Maureen Van Dyck · Max Elman · Maxime · Maximilian Virkus · Maxine Davies · May Ang · May-Ling Gonzales · Maya Baratz · Maya Munoz · Mayka Mei · Mayka Mei · Mayra Urbano · Mbhsing · Mc Macaulay · Mckenzie Chinn · Meagan Choi · Mebaim · Meg Ferguson · Meg Palmer · Meg Varley Keller · Megakestirsch · Megan · Megan · Megan Dowdle · Megan Marin · Megan Murphy · Megan Orsini · Megan Reigner-Chapman · Megha Bangalore · Meghan Arnold · Meghan Smith · Meghan Walker · Meghann Farnsworth · Megin Hicks · Meimaimaggio · Melanie Paulina · Melanie Wang · Melia · Melia Jacquot · Melissa · Melissa Boilon · Melissa Locker · Melissa Stefanini · Melissa Weinstein · Melissa Yes · Mellena Bridges · Melynda Nuss · Meredith Case · Meredith Davies · Meredith Payne · Meredith Resnick · Mette-Marie Katz · M. Garvais · Mi Ann Bennett · Micaela Mcglone · Michael Angarone · Michael Ashbridge · Michael Avella · Michael Barnstijn · Michael Bebout · Michael Birk · Michael Boyce · Michael Denning · Michael Donahue · Michael Eidlin · Michael Gavino · Michael Gillis · Michael Gioia · Michael Glaser · Michael Greene · Michael Hall · Michael Harner · Michael Ireton · Michael Kidwell · Michael Laporta · Michael Legge · Michael Lent · Michael Marsicano · Michael Marx · Michael Mazur · Michael Moore · Michael Moorhouse · Michael Moszczynski · Michael O'connell · Michael Olson · Michael Patrick Cutillo · Michael Sciortino · Michael Sean Lesueur · Michael Thompson · Michaela Drapes · Michaelle · Micheál Keane · Michel Ge · Michelangelo Cianciosi · Michele · Michele Bove · Michele Fleischli · Michele Hansen · Michele Howard · Michelle · Michelle · Michelle · Michelle Akin · Michelle Badash · Michelle Castillo · Michelle Clement · Michelle Cotugno · Michelle Curtis · Michelle Floyd · Michelle

Matel · Michelle Nadeau · Mickey Bayard · Micquelle Corry · Miguel Duran · Mik · Mike · Mike Benner · Mike Etheridge · Mike Golay · Mike Lee · Mike Levine · Mike Mcvicar · Mike Munsell · Mike Smith · Mike Thompson · Mike Zuckerman · Mikel Wilkins · Miles Ranisavljevic · Milind Kaduskar · Mimi Evans · Misha Renclair · Missy Manning · Mitch Major · Mitchell Hart · Mo Lai · Moise Lacy · Moishe Lettvin · Mollie Brooks · Molly · Molly · Molly Charnes · Molly Grpss · Molly Guinn Bradley · Molly Mcardle · Molly Mcsweeney · Molly Murphy · Molly Ohainle · Molly Taylor · Mona Awad · Monica Beals · Monica Fogg · Monica Tomaszewski · Mono.kultur · Morningstar Stevenson · Moshe Weitzman · Moss · Muckdart · Mudlarque · Mudville · Murray Gm · Murray Steele · Mygreensweater.com · Myron Chadowitz · Myrsini · Mythmakers · Nadia Ibrashi · Nadine Anderson · Nai-Wen Hu · Nakiesha · Nakiesha Koss · Nalden · Nancy C. Mae · Nancy Folsom · Nancy Friedman · Nancy Goldberg · Nancy Hebben · Nancy Jamieson · Nancy Jeng · Nancy Keiter · Nancy Riess · Nancy Rosenberg · Nancy Rudolph · Nancy Smith · Naomi Alderman · Naomi Firestone-Teeter · Naomi Pinn · Nara Bopp! · Nat Missildine · Natalie · Natalie · Natalie · Natalie Gruppuso · Natalie Hamilton · Natalie Strawbridge · Natalie Ung · Natalie Villamil · Natasha Boas · Nate Arnold · Nate Corddry · Nate Merchant · Nathan Chadwick · Nathan Pyritz · Nathan Rostron · Nathaniel Weiss · Navjoyt Ladher · Neal Cornett · Neal Pollack · Ned Rote · Neda Afsarmanesh · Neil · Neil Blanck · Neil Rigler · Neil Shah · Nelly Ben Hayoun · Nesher G. Asner · Newtux · Nic Barajas · Nicholas Almanza · Nicholas Bergin · Nicholas Herbert · Nicholas Maggs · Nicholas O'neil · Nicholas Van Boddie Willis · Nicholas Walker · Nicholson Baker · Nick · Nick Brown · Nick C. · Nick Cooke · Nick Fraenkel · Nick Kibodeaux · Nick Miller · Nick Peacock · Nick Plante · Nicky Montalvo · Nicolas Llano Linares · Nicole Avril · Nicole Carlson · Nicole Elitch · Nicole Flattery · Nicole Howard Quiles · Nicole Mandel · Nicole Pasulka · Nicole Rafidi · Nicole Ryan · Nicole Yeo · Nicoletta · Nicoletta Beyer · Nicolette Blum · Nigel Dookhoo · Nigel Taylor · Nigel Warren · Nighthawk · Niina Pollari · Nikil · Nikki H · Nikki Thayer · Nil Hafizi · Nils Normann · Nina Drakalovic · Nion Mcevoy · Nirav · Nitsuh Abebe · No · Noah Miller · Noah Slo · Noelle Greene · None · Nora Caplan-Bricker · Nora L · O. Dwyer · Ofpc Llc · Ola Torstensson · Oleg · Oliver Emanuel · Oliver Grainger · Oliver Kroll ·

Oliver Meehan · Oliver Mooney · Omar Lee · Owl · P. E. Zalinski · P.M. · Pamela Marcus · Pamela Pugh · Pamela Rooney · Papermantis · Parashar Bhise · Paris Ward · Parker Coddington · Pascal Babare · Pascalle Burton · Pat Jenatsch · Pat Wheaton · Patience Haggin · Patricia Baas · Patricia Bindert · Patricia Iorg · Patricia Miller · Patricia Parker · Patrick · Patrick Cates · Patrick Cox · Patrick Dennis · Patrick Ducey · Patrick M. Freebern · Patrick Maier · Patrick O'driscoll · Patrick Rafferty · Patrick Schilling · Paul · Paul · Paul Bielec · Paul Bloom · Paul Boxer · Paul Braidford · Paul Cancellieri · Paul Curtin · Paul Debraski · Paul Degeorge · Paul Durant · Paul Dutnall · Paul Eckburg · Paul Ferraro · Paul Ghysbrecht · Paul Kohlbrenner · Paul Lasch · Paul Littleton · Paul Mikesell · Mike Sell · Paul Moore · Paul Nadeau · Paul Rosenberg · Paul Studebaker · Paul Upham · Paul Van Zwieten · Paula Palyga · Pauls Toutonghi · Pax · Payton Cuddy · Pedro Poitevin · Peggy Stenger · Penny Blubaugh · Penny Dedel · Peri Pugh · Perii & John Owen · Pete Mulvihill · Pete Smith · Petel · Peter · Peter Blake · Peter Bogert · Peter Bradley · Peter Brian Barry · Peter Fitzgerald · Peter Gadol · Peter Gerhardt · Peter Hoddie · Peter Hogan · Peter Maguire · Peter Mcnally · Peter Meehan · Peter Paul · Peter Platt · Peter Quinn Fuller · Peter Rednour · Peter Roper · Peter Woodyard · Phil Dokas · Phil Fresh · Philip Kor · Philip Kors · Philip Maguire · Philip Platt · Philip Scranton · Philip Wood · Philip Zimmermann · Philippa Moxon · Phillip Henderson · Phillip Johnston · Phyllis Tankel · Pia Widlund · Pierre L'allier · Pierre L'allier · Poilleux · Prisca Riggle · Priscilla Riggle · Priya Sampath · Prmes · Pro · Quim Gil · Quinn · Quinn Formel · R. Mansolino · Rachael Klein · Rachel All · Rachel Bartlett · Rachel Beal · Rachel Brody · Rachel Didomizio · Rachel Droessler · Rachel Fershleiser · Rachel Newcombe · Rachel Pass · Rachel R. Rdriguez · Rachel Sluder · Rachel Smith · Rachel Unger · Rachele Gilman · Radovan Grezo · Rami Levin · Rana · Randall Imai · Randolph Baker · Ravi And Kaela Chandrasekaran · Ray Adams · Raymond Desjarlais · Raymond Khalastchi · Raymond Zhou · Raysha Gallinetti · Rbeedee · Rea Bennett · Reality Connection · Rebecca · Rebecca · Rebecca Bame · Rebecca Calvo · Rebecca Ha · Rebecca Harlow · Rebecca M · Rebecca Martin · Rebecca Rubenstein · Rebecca Scalio · Rebecca Scalio · Rebecca Schneider · Rebecca Schneider · Rebecca Serbin · Rebecca Wilberforce · Reean · Reed Johnson · Reese · Reese Kwon · Reid Allison · Reina Castellanos · Renée Reizman · Renton

Wright · Rich Hjulstrom · Rich Scott · Richard Busofsky · Richard Byrne · Richard Cripe · Richard Light · Richard Marks · Richard May · Richard Meadow · Richard Nisa · Richard Parks · Richard Rutter · Richard Sakai · Richard Sakai · Richard Stanislaw · Richard Stroud · Richard Tallmadge · Richard Winter · Rick Cox · Rick Lo · Rick Redick · Rick T. Morrison · Rick Webb · Riley · Riley · Rivkah K Sass · Rk Strout · Rkt88edmo · Rob Atwood · Rob Callender · Rob Colenso · Rob Knight · Rob Mishev · Rob Neill · Rob Wilock · Robby Sumner · Robert Amerman · Robert Archambault · Robert Biskin · Robert Brandin · Robert Brown Glad · Robert Denby · Robert Dickau · Robert Doherty · Robert Drew · Robert E Anderson · Robert Fenerty · Robert George · Robert Hilton · Robert Jacklosky · Robert Macke · Robert Okeefe · Robert Rees · Robert St. Claire · Robert Wilder · Robin Nicholas · Robin Olivier · Robin Ryan · Robin Smith Peck · Roboboxspeaks · Rob W · Rochelle Lanster · Ron Calixto · Ron Charles · Ron Sanders · Ron Wortz · Ronald Neef · Ronnie Scott · Rory Harper · Rosalie Ham · Rosanna Yau · Rose · Rosie Cima · Ross Goodwin · Rosy Capron · Rotem Shintel · Roy Mcmillan · Roy Mcmillan · Ruari Elkington · Russ Maloney · Ruth Franklin · Ruth Madievsky · Ruth Wyer · Ryan + Lucy · Ryan A. Millager · Ryan Abbott · Ryan Bailey · Ryan Barton · Ryan Curran · Ryan Hetherington · Ryan Molony · Ryan Pitts · Ryan Stenson · Rye Sour · S.P. Garrett · S. Tayengco · S. Grinell · Saelee Oh · Safwat Saleem · Sage Dahlen · Sairus Patel · Sal Macleod · Sally · Sally Brooke · Sally Jane Weed · Sally Macleod · Salpets · Sam · Sam Barrett · Sam Brightman · Sam Hockley-Smith · Sam Skrivan · Sam Sudar · Sam Sweeney · Sam Wright · Sam Zucchi · Sam Zuckert · Samantha · Samantha Armintrout · Samantha Bloom · Samantha Grillo · Samantha Hunt · Samantha Krug · Samantha Netzley · Samantha Schoech · Samia Haddad · Samir Shah · Samuel Cole · Samuel Douglas Miller · Samuel Preston · Sandra Delehanty · Sandra Edwards · Sandra Spicher · Sandy Cooley · Sandy Guthrie · Sandy Stewart · Sanford Nathan · Sara Arvidsson · Sara Corbett · Sara K. Runnels · Sara M · Sara Mouser · Sara Rowghani · Sara Satten · Sarah · Sarah · Sarah · Sarah · Sarah Aibel · Sarah Bacon · Sarah Bownds · Sarah Brewer · Sarah Burnes · Sarah Carter · Sarah E Klein · Sarah Elizabeth Ridley · Sarah Frazier · Sarah Getchell · Sarah Hotze · Sarah Hutchins · Sarah Johnson · Sarah Lavere · Sarah Lincoln · Sarah Litwin-Schmid · Sarah Lukachko · Sarah Maguire · Sarah Mundy · Sarah Rosenshine · Sarah Scire

· Sarah Stanlick Kimball · Sarah Tiedeman Gallagher · Sarah Towle · Sarah Walker · Sarah Weissman · Sarita Rainey · Sasqwatch Watch Company · Savannah Adams · Savannah Cooper-Ramsey · Scooter Alpert · Scott A. Harris · Scott Bateman · Scott Callon · Scott Dagenfield · Scott Elingburg · Scott Farrar · Scott Ferron · Scott Malagold · Scott Mcgibbon · Scott Olling · Scott Paxton · Scott Rinicker · Scott Shoger · Scott Snibbe · Scott Stanfield · Scott Stelter · Scott Stelter · Scott Suthren · Scott Thurman · Scott Underwood · Scott Wahl · Scott Williams · Sean · Sean Baker · Sean Beatty Oaktown Ss · Sean Boyle · Sean Carr · Sean Harrahy · Sean Jensen-Grey · Sean Kelly · Sean Langmuir · Sean Mcindoe · Sebastian Campos · Sebastianfidler · Sebastien J Park · Segundo Nallatan Jr · Serjio · Seth Casana · Seth D. Michaels · Seth Fowler · Seth Reiss · Shane P. Mullen · Shane Pedersen · Shane Tilton · Shane Ward · Shannon Christine · Shannon David · Shannon Dunbar · Shannon Kelly · Shari D Rochen · Shari Rochen · Shari Simpson · Sharon Lunny · Shaun Bossio · Shaun Pryszlak · Shauna Sutherland · Shaunda Tichgelaar · Shawn Calvert · Shawn Calvert · Shawn Hall · Shawn Lee · Shawn Liu · Shawn Lucas · Sheenagh Geoghegan · Sheila Mennis · Shelby Black · Shelby Kling · Shelley Vinyard · Shelleyboodles Gornall · Shelleysd · Shelly Catterson · Sheri Kenly · Sheri Parsons · Sheri Sternberg · Sheridan Fox · Sherry Suisman · Shevaun Lewis · Shield Bonnichsen · Shih-Lene Jee · Shira Geller · Shira Milikowsky · Shoshana Paige · Simon · Simon Bird · Simon Groth · Simon Harper · Simon Hawkesworth · Simon Kuhn · Simon Nurse · Simon Petherick · Simon Pinkerton · Simon Smundak · Siobhan Dolan · Sisyphus · Smilner · Smivey · Solange Vandermoer · Solenoid · Somedaylee · Somrod Creative · Sona Avakian · Songeehn Choi · Sophie Malone · Sophine · Soraya Okuda · Spencer Coates · Spencer Nelson · Spencer Tweedy · Ssk · Stacey Pounsberry · Stacy Murison · Stacy Ryan · Stacy Saul · Stan Smith · Stanley Levine · Stef Craps · Stefanie Pareja Reyna · Steph Hammell · Steph Widmer · Stephan Heilmayr · Stephanie · Stephanie · Stephanie Anne Canlas · Stephanie Arman · Stephanie Goode · Stephanie Mankins · Stephanie Morgan · Stephanie Murg · Stephanie Wagner · Stephanie Wan · Stephanie Wu · Stephen Angelette · Stephen Beaupre · Stephen Benzel · Stephen Berger · Stephen Bronstein · Stephen Bryce Wood Jr · Stephen Fuller · Stephen Hahn · Stephen Hairsine · Stephen Kay · Stephen Littell · Stephen Mallory · Stephen Murray · Stephen Northup · Stephen Paul · Stephen Schifrin ·

Stephen Shih · Stephen Shocket · Stephen Smith · Stephen Tabler · Stephen Williams · Steve · Steve Beaven · Steve Berkovits · Steve Caires · Steve Clancy · Steve Conover · Steve Jackson · Steve Kern · Steve Kindrick · Steve Lewis · Steve Maher · Steve Marian · Steve Mockus · Steve Payonzeck · Steve Rivo · Steve Smith · Steve Sweet · Steve Thornbury · Steve Tsuchiyama · Steve W. Jones · Steven Canning · Steven Danielson · Steven Elias · Steven Friedman · Steven Friedman · Steven Hemingray · Steven Hudosh · Steven Jay Athanas · Steven Kindrick · Steven Lowry · Steven Marten · Steven Morley · Steven Powell · Stewart Davis · Stuart Macdonald · Stuart O'connor · Stuart Rosen · Sue Diehl · Sue Naegle · Sue S · Susan · Susan Auty · Susan Barrabee · Susan C. · Susan Clements · Susan Cooke · Susan Cormier · Susan D. · Susan Davis · Susan Eichrodt · Susan Fitzgerald · Susan Hobbs · Susan Hopkirk · Susan Ito · Susan King · Susan Loube · Susan Miller · Susan Morrissey · Susan Mosseri-Marlio · Susan Schorn · Susan Spradlin · Susan Strohm · Susan Yuk · Susanna · Susanne Durkin · Susanne Durkin-Schindler · Susheila Khera · Suzanna Zeitler · Suzanne Scott · Suzanne Scott · Suzanne Spencer · Suzanne Wilder · Suzi Albertson · Suzie Baunsgard · Syafii · Sydney Blackett · Sydney Morrow · Sydney Sattell · Sylvia Tran · Sylvie L. · Syncione Bresgal · Szienceman · T Cooper · T S Plutchak · T. L. Howl · T.m. Ryan · Tabitha Hayes · Tamar Shafrir · Tamara Zver · Tami Loeffler · Tami Wilson · Tangerine0516 · Tanya F · Taryn Albizzati · Taylor Baldwin · Taylor F. · Taylor Kearns · Taylor Pavlik · Taylor Smith · Taylor Stephens · Tdemarchi · Ted Jillson · Tedder · Teresa Hedin · Teresa Sweat · Terna · Terrence Hayes · Terri Arnold · Terri Coles · Terri Leker · Terry Morris · Terry Wit · Tershia D'elgin · Tess Kornfield · Tess Marstaller · Tess Swithinbank · Tessa Holkesvik · Thanh Tran · The Creature · The Duke Of Follen Street · The Haikooligan · The Lance Arthur · The Nyc Cooper Clan · The Shebooks Team · The Tomato Head, Inc · The Typewriter Revolution · Thedammtruth.com · Thempauls · Theo Ploeg · Theresa · Theresa C Kratschmer · Thientam Nguyen · Thierry / On The Road To Honesty · Thomas Barron · Thomas Belote · Thomas Demarchi · Thomas Green · Thomas Kiraly · Thomas La Farge · Thomas Moore · Thomas Moore · Thomas Pluck · Thomas W. Conway · Thomas Weverka · Thousand · Tieg Zaharia · Tiff Chau · Tiffany · Tiffany Cardoza · Tiffany Holly Lyon · Tiffany Peon · Tiffany Tseng · Tim Gaffney · Tim Keogh · Tim Larrison · Tim Lash · Tim Perell · Tim Ruszel @ Ruszel Design Company · Timothy Blackett

· Timothy Clark · Timothy Johnstone · Timothy Mey · Timothy N. Towslee · Timothy Paulson · Tina Burns · Tina F. · Tinderbox Editions · Tirza Ben-Porat · Tobias Carroll · Tobin Moss · Tod Story · Todd · Todd · Todd Abbott · Todd Barnard · Todd Bever · Todd Fell · Tom Fitzgerald · Tom Garbarino · Tom Gonzales · Tom Head, Ph.d. · Tom Hood · Tom J Clarke · Tom Joiner · Tom Keekley · Tom Marks · Tom Skoda · Tom Steele · Tom W. Davis Iii · Tomasz Werner · Tony Puccinelli · Tony Solomun · Tori Bond · Tracey A Halliday · Traci Ikegami · Tracy Cambron · Tracy Middlebrook · Travis Burton · Travis Gasser · Trevor Burnham · Trey Kuchinsky · Tricia Copeland · Tricia Psarreas · Triscuit Vallejo · Trisha Bunce · Trisha Weir · Tristan Telson · Troy Goertz · Troy Napier · Tttt · Tucker Christine · Turner Partain · Turtlepants · Tyler Cazes · Tyler Cazes · Tyler Cushing · Tyler Munson · Tyler Robertson · Tyler Smith · Uccf · Uncle Doug · Under Construction Dvd.com · Uttam Kumbhat Jain · V Hollingsworth · V. · V. Stoltz · Vaia Vaena · Val Emmich · Valerie Gprman · Valerie Seijas · Valerie Sonnenthal · Valerie Woolard · Vanasa Bowden · Vanessa Allen · Vanessa Kirker · Vaughn Shields · Veena · Vera Hough · Vernon · Veronica V-V · Victor Jih · Victor Kumar · Victoria Bartelt · Victoria Davies · Victoria Evert · Victoria Marinelli · VII · Vika · Viken · Viktor Balogh · Vinay · Vincent Hsieh · Vinson Cunningham · Virginia E Mead · Virginia Killfoile · Vitor Neves · Vivian Wagner · W.C. Beck · Waipo5kathryn Blue · Wayfarer · Wayne Gwillim · Wendi Aarons · Wendy Ju · Wendy Koster · Wendy Molyneux · Wendy O'neil · Wes Wes · Whitney Isenhower · Whitney Pape · Wiebke Schuster · Will Brodie · Will Cavendish · Will Johnson · Will Mellencamp Leubsdorf · Will Ramsey · Will Skelton · Willa Köerner · Willh · William · William · William Amend · William Donahoe · William Farley · William Hatt · William Kirchner · William Mascioli · William Noonan · William Ross · William Smith · William Van Zandt · William Woolf · Willliam Merrill · Winnie Dreier · Winston Finlayson · Wire Science · Www.smltalk.com · Wythe Marschall · Xiangyun Lim · Yahaya Baruwa · Yang Dai · Yani Robinson · Yeekai Lim · Yew-Leong Wong · Yodiez · Yosef · Yoshihiro Kanematsu · Yotta Sigma · Yuen-Wei Chew · Yukiko Takeuchi · Yvette Dezalia · Yvonne Mains · Yvonne W · Zabeth Russell · Zach · Zach Blair · Zach Lascell · Zach Lipton · Zachary Amundson · Zachary Beamer · Zachary Doss · Zack Daniels · Zack Peercy · Zain Khalid · Zainab Juma · Zalfer · Zanne Cameron · Zoe Laird

THE BEST OF
M^cSWEENEY'S
INTERNET TENDENCY

INCLUDING:

IT'S DECORATIVE GOURD SEASON,
MOTHERFUCKERS.

ON THE IMPLAUSIBILITY OF THE DEATH
STAR'S TRASH COMPACTOR.

I REGRET TO INFORM YOU THAT
MY WEDDING TO CAPTAIN VON TRAPP
HAS BEEN CANCELED.

HAMLET (FACEBOOK NEWSFEED EDITION).

I'M COMIC SANS, ASSHOLE.

IN WHICH I FIX MY GIRLFRIEND'S
GRANDPARENTS' WI-FI AND AM HAILED
AS A CONQUERING HERO.

AND MORE OF THE BEST OF FIFTEEN YEARS
OF THE WEBSITE.

Edited by CHRIS MONKS *and* JOHN WARNER

THE BEST OF M^cSWEENEY'S
INTERNET TENDENCY
edited by Chris Monks and John Warner

"{The Best of McSweeney's Internet Tendency} *is just like
those chocolates that hotels put on pillows, if the chocolate were
laced with acid.*" —*Michael Agger, the* New Yorker

THE BEST OF McSWEENEY'S
edited by Dave Eggers and Jordan Bass

"The first bona fide literary movement in decades." —*Slate*

"An inimitable retrospective on modern storytelling."
—Publishers Weekly

FLOWERS OF ANTI-MARTYRDOM
by Dorian Geisler

"Flowers of Anti-Martyrdom... *is exactly the book you need
to read right now... a mix of cautionary wit, a dash of profound
sadness, and a heavy dose of quiet empathy.*" —Dorothea Lasky

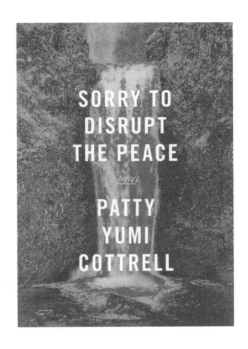

SORRY TO DISRUPT THE PEACE
by Patty Yumi Cottrell

*"Her voice is unflinching, unforgettable, and animated
with a restless sense of humor."* —Catherine Lacey

ALSO AVAILABLE FROM McSWEENEY'S
store.mcsweeneys.net

FICTION

ART & COMICS

ALL THIS AND MORE AT

store.mcsweeneys.net

Founded in 1998, McSweeney's is an independent publisher based in San Francisco. McSweeney's exists to champion ambitious and inspired new writing, and to challenge conventional expectations about where it's found, how it looks, and who participates. We're here to discover things we love, help them find their most resplendent form, and place them into the hands of empathic, engaged readers.

THERE ARE SEVERAL WAYS TO SUPPORT MCSWEENEY'S:

Support us on Patreon
visit *www.patreon.com/ mcsweeneysinternettendency*

Volunteering & Internships
email *interns-sf@mcsweeneys.net*

Subscriptions & Store Site
visit *store.mcsweeneys.net*

Books &
Quarterly Sponsorship
email *kristina@mcsweeneys.net*

To learn more, please visit *www.mcsweeneys.net/donate* or contact Director Kristina Kearns at kristina@mcsweeneys.net or call 415.642.5609.

All donations are tax-deductible through our fiscal sponsorship with SOMArts, a nonprofit organization that collaborates with diverse artists and organizations to engage the power of the arts to provoke just and fair inclusion, cultural respect, and civic participation.